"*Gender for the Warfare State* helps us to think afresh about how we can use literature, including women soldiers' own writings, to shed light on and pose new questions about the dynamic relationships between militarism, the liberal state, wars, women's soldiering, and gender ideologies."
          Cynthia Enloe, author of *Globalization and Militarism: Feminists Make the Link 2e* (Rowman & Littlefield, 2016)

"*Gender for the Warfare State* offers provocative insights along a trustworthy road map that lead us all the way back to the earliest intersection of female warrior and literature. In doing so, Goodman provides fresh analysis on both twenty-first century warfare and female subjectivity in combat."
          Tracy Crow, author of *On Point: A Guide to Writing the Military Story* (Potomac Books, 2015)

GENDER FOR THE WARFARE STATE

Gender for the Warfare State is the first scholarly investigation into the written works of U.S. women combat veterans in twenty-first century wars. Most recent studies quantify military participation, showing how many women participate in armed services and what their experiences are in a traditionally "male institution." Many of these treatments regard women as victims solely of enemy fire, even as they are also often victims of their own military apparatus and of their own involvement in global aggression. By applying literary analysis to a sociological question, *Gender for the Warfare State* views women's experiences through story and literary traditions that carry meaning into present practices. Goodman shows that women in combat are not just entering and being victimized in "male institutions," but are also actively changing the story of gender and thus the structure of power that is constructed through gender. Moreover, this book unveils a new narrative of *care* that affects economic relations more broadly and the contemporary politics of the liberal social contract.

Women's participation in combat is not just a U.S. event but global and therefore has a deeper historical range than current sociological accounts imply. The book compares the political contexts of women's entry into war now with their prior, twentieth-century contributions to wars in other cultural settings and then uses this comparison to show a variety of meanings at play in the gender of war.

Robin Truth Goodman is Professor of English and Director of the Literature Program at Florida State University. Her recent books include *Literature and the Development of Feminist Theory* (ed., Cambridge University Press, 2015) and *Gender Work: Feminism After Neoliberalism* (Palgrave Macmillan, 2013).

CRITICAL INTERVENTIONS

Politics, Culture, and the Promise of Democracy

Edited by Henry A. Giroux, Susan Searls Giroux, and
Kenneth J. Saltman

Twilight of the Social: Resurgent Publics in the Age of Disposability
By Henry A. Giroux (2011)

Youth in Revolt: Reclaiming a Democratic Future
By Henry A. Giroux (2012)

The Failure of Corporate School Reform
By Kenneth J. Saltman (2012)

Toward a New Common School Movement
By Noah De Lissovoy, Alexander J. Means, and Kenneth J. Saltman (2015)

The Great Inequality
By Michael D. Yates (2016)

**Elsewhere in America: The Crisis of Belonging in Contemporary
Culture**
By David Trend (2016)

**Scripted Bodies: Corporate Power, Smart Technology, and the
Undoing of Public Education**
By Kenneth J. Saltman (2016)

Gender for the Warfare State: Literature of Women in Combat
By Robin Truth Goodman (2017)

GENDER FOR THE WARFARE STATE

Literature of Women in Combat

Robin Truth Goodman

NEW YORK AND LONDON

First published 2017
by Routledge
711 Third Avenue, New York, NY 10017

and by Routledge
2 Park Square, Milton Park, Abingdon, Oxon, OX14 4RN

Routledge is an imprint of the Taylor & Francis Group, an informa business

© 2017 Taylor & Francis

Chapter 3, "A Critique of Violence in the Age of Mechanical Drone Warfare," © *symplokē*. Reprinted with permission.

The right of Robin Truth Goodman to be identified as author of this work has been asserted by her in accordance with sections 77 and 78 of the Copyright, Designs and Patents Act 1988.

All rights reserved. No part of this book may be reprinted or reproduced or utilised in any form or by any electronic, mechanical, or other means, now known or hereafter invented, including photocopying and recording, or in any information storage or retrieval system, without permission in writing from the publishers.

Trademark notice: Product or corporate names may be trademarks or registered trademarks, and are used only for identification and explanation without intent to infringe.

Library of Congress Cataloging in Publication Data
A catalog record for this book has been requested

ISBN: 978-1-138-67528-5 (hbk)
ISBN: 978-1-138-67529-2 (pbk)
ISBN: 978-1-315-56078-6 (ebk)

Typeset in Bembo
by Apex CoVantage, LLC

CONTENTS

	Acknowledgments	*viii*
	Introduction	1
1	Women in the War Story: What Work Does Gender Do?	16
2	From Decolonization to Body Bombs: Tragedy, Feminist Political Theory, and the Female Militant	60
3	A Critique of Violence: In the Age of Mechanical Drone Warfare	96
4	Killers and Spies: The Postcolonial Legacy in Real Estate	121
5	The Woman, the Worker, the Warrior, and the Writer: The Military Nation and the Making of Female Neoliberal Subjectivity	140
	Conclusion	165
	Works Cited	*171*
	Index	*185*

ACKNOWLEDGMENTS

I am truly indebted to Kenneth J. Saltman, who saw this book through from its very inception. He offered hours of encouragement as well as editorial assistance. In addition, as scholars know, ideas often come to fruition through intense debate and argument, and Ken has been what Hannah Arendt would call my inner interlocutor, sitting inside my head and demanding the world to be better, playing Nil to my Will. In addition, I thank the other series editors, Henry A. Giroux, an inspiration always, and Susan Searls Giroux, and the editor at Routledge, Dean Birkenkamp. I wish to thank others who have offered advice, help, and encouragement over the course of this writing: Anne Coldiron, Tracy Crow, Jeffrey Dileo, David Downing, Cynthia Enloe, Barry J. Faulk, Isabel Careloa Gil, Peggy Kamuf, Irene Padavic, Masood Raja, and Elizabeth Spiller. The Office of Research at Florida State University has supported part of this project through their grant program.

INTRODUCTION

On 6 December 2015, the *New York Times* published an article called "Penis Transplants Being Planned to Help Wounded Troops." In it, reporter Denise Grady gives us uplifting news. Medical science has developed a way to replace penises lost in battle. Despite risks of cancer, organ rejection, infection, and bleeding, surgeons can sew onto live men the penises of dead men, repairing the damage and eventually restoring full utility. This is good news, indeed, as the article estimates that from 2001 to 2003 alone, "1,367 men in military service suffered wounds to their genitals." Everybody agrees, writes Grady, including the caring, long-suffering wives of veterans with infected, mutilated, or impaired penises, that injuries to that organ "eroded their husbands' sense of manhood and identity." Three serious men with eyeglasses and surgical blues, surrounded by shelves full of test tubes, pill packages, and x-rays, reassure us in a photograph at the article's head that science has at last triumphed over man's deepest fears: that men in battle could be turned into women. We can assume the wives will be happy now, rewarded for their solicitude. The new penises would come replete with urinary function, sensation, erectile function, and maybe, too, fertility. In a flash, then, military science has ended the castration complex and psychoanalytic trauma, adding another layer of dirt over Freud's grave.

This book re-assesses the relationship between gender and violence as contemporary wars refashion it. A standard reading (like the one in the *New York Times* article mentioned above) may insist that men make war while women make peace. Yet, this seems a particularly twentieth-century viewpoint. Think of a novel like William Thackeray's (1847) *Vanity Fair,* where men make war reluctantly while women make, well, trouble. Contrast this with Virginia Woolf in *Three Guineas* (1938): "As it is a fact that she cannot understand what instinct compels him, what glory, what interest, what manly satisfaction fighting provides for him . . ., as

2 Introduction

fighting thus is a sex characteristic which she cannot share, the counterpart some claim of the maternal instinct which he cannot share, so is it an instinct which she cannot judge" (107). Women should go so far as to stop making munitions, cease nursing, and express a complete indifference to fighting men, she says, in order to stop war. The construction has been controversial in feminist debate where, for some, the separation of women from violence relegated women to stereotypical passivity and agentlessness, particularly in relation to citizenship.[1] As Jasbir Puar has shown, the insistence, even in feminist circles, that women are outside of violence rather than perpetrators of it voids out, in contemporary discourses, how "women are not only the recipients of violence, but are actually connected to and benefit from forms of violence in myriad ways" (90), including in furthering racist and imperialist agendas.

In the late twentieth century, the attitude linking feminism to pacifism changed. Even while some feminists persist in claiming that women's empowerment augurs the end of war, other feminists started believing that women were necessary for war. Women's absence from direct participation in war was underscored as a problem for democracy. Denaturalized, women's exclusion was conceptually linked to other exclusions, like exclusions from politics and the workforce. Instead of a critique like Woolf's, where gender differences are mediated through different and separate types of interest, focus, nature, biology, and psychology, you see calls for equality, where women should be permitted to assume the same privileges and activities as men, regardless of differences. During World War I, "women," exalts Sandra Gilbert, "seemed to become, as if by some uncanny swing of history's pendulum, ever more powerful. As nurses, as mistresses, as munitions workers, bus drivers, or soldiers in the land army, even as wives and mothers, these formerly subservient creatures began to loom malevolently larger" (200). Even if military life for women is far from rosy, its "communal delight seems real enough," (1987: 11) opines Jean Bethke Elshtain. If war is the largest expression of action in common with others that modern life has to offer, guaranteeing exaltations and pleasures that only life in common can grant, then should not, Elshtain asks, women be involved?

Women, as equals to men, were not to be thought predisposed constitutionally to remain outside of mobilization as they were for Woolf. The question became a matter of inclusion, whether or not war opened possibilities for women's entry into work and public life. Even critics who concluded that women's military service would not serve women's interests based their arguments on the fact that women left the workforce after armistice, so that the "benefits" to women as workers were only temporary, as though sustained employment in industry would have made war better for women: "Some [women] were glad," affirm Margaret Higonnet and Patrice Higonnet, critically, "to give up work on the night shift in heavy industry and return to more protected work in the tertiary sector" (40) or the home. Industries, they assume, are what industries are, and workers with different fixed identities might pass in and out of them without changing either their identities or the spaces that they enter. To be inside of them is thus beneficial because it means accommodation, adaptation, and acceptance into the world at large, even if the industry was in the business of making killer machines. The debate over whether women should participate in military service serves as a synecdoche within a much broader debate about women's access to public life, without a consideration of why war itself might be a unique and worthy object of critique (as Woolf realized) or whether we agree to the terms of this form of public life.

On the flip side, other social critics have avowed that, instead of women's exclusion from war being unfair and discriminatory for women, war is what suffers from not incorporating distinctively women's spheres of feeling and relatedness. By considering how women have written themselves into the war story, Miriam Cooke alleges for example, both men and women will realize that "[r]esponsibility [in war] . . . entailed *duties* towards others" (original emphasis; 16). According to one of her sources, the admittance of women—or "mother-soldiers"—into the military "challenges basic beliefs or myths" such as that "[w]ar is manly" (33) and introduces the possibility that "the military might pioneer social reform" (34). Even besides assuming women's traits as essentially nurturing and maternal, the possible conclusion of such an analysis—that war would be a better war if it were a nicer war—falls short of any appraising of what war intends, what are its means, and what kind of "*duties* towards others" could be expected in a situation that demanded the killing of others and the usurping of their territory, their state, and their self-determination. What kinds of "nice" or "*duties* towards others" would battle implicate? Is the inclusion of women in a public life defined as violence really a desired type of inclusion or the only parameters to imagine the composition of public life today?

Gender for the Warfare State takes an alternative approach to either of these two. It asks about the shifting gender of the battlefield. Because gender operates in relation to the symbolic, and because the symbolic is socialized historically by those who invoke its categories, when gendered bodies interact within a social context, identities on all sides change. As Judith Butler teaches, the bad fit of socially-sanctioned gender "suggests a radical discontinuity between sexed bodies and culturally constructed genders" (1990: 9) that exposes and challenges the limits of what it means to be gendered in an unfittingly gendered world. Though the heroes of the *New York Times,* restoring penises for their bereft and beleaguered brothers, may see themselves as poised for defending the masculinity threatened in war, the masculinity preserved in the battlefield is currently fractured beyond what such nerve grafting can manage to remedy. Certain services that, in the history of war practices, were placed away from the frontline and often performed by women are now integrated militarily into protected "green" zones in range of the fight, often contracted or privatized. These include laundry service, food provision, transport, supplies, community outreach, communications, development, spiritual counseling, and care. The zone of combat cannot now, if it ever could, be

4 Introduction

equated with types of work assimilated to masculinity or the expected physique of the male body, especially when physical bodies have been made less consequential, replaced by machines that perform war work better and faster with less risk.

Additionally, the space of conflict has altered, encompassing domestic and urban areas where armed searches infiltrate families and their private lives, often under enemy fire, and women sometimes hold vital intelligence and may be the key to essential and tactical alliances. Women must be incorporated in combat because the needs of the battlefield require particular types of service that are typically performed by women. The military's reframing of its mission and shifting functionality means that traditional masculinity is never totally in line with combat operations, despite the surgeons' best efforts, and what counts as combat operations is not fully consistent with lived masculinity. The inclusion of women in battle did not lead to peace and nurturance in the military and did not create better jobs or opportunities for homecoming veterans. Women often find themselves with even more restricted access to care and public supports on return than their male counterparts.

Rather than "women's values" remaining the same as they are transferred from private to public warrior life, gender categories have historically been conflictual, as different classes and interests vie to set their definitions, aiming for such broad socially-organizing categories to answer to particular needs. Combat is no different than other activities in this regard. The invitation of women's presence on the battlefield is a response to both changes in the gendered body *and* changes in the contours, definitions, and attributed tasks of combat. According to Cynthia Enloe, the question of women in combat needs to be accounted for in terms of the way particular institutions of power disperse populations and functionalities, and the question of military recruitment is affected by concerns such as the birthrate, the draft (or its reversal), technologization, the duration of the war, available worker skill sets, employment rates, and industrial demand. Sometimes, for example, if the war lasts for longer than expected, authorities will need to draw on potential that had previously been allocated elsewhere. The reserve army of military personnel, says Enloe, overlaps with the reserve army of labor that Marxism theorizes: instead of gender being seen as a set of natural traits, assumed tasks, or geographical spheres, the military understands gendered bodies to designate populations that are ready, competent, and reliable for war work and can be kept on the margins until such a time that war needs available recruits. At that time, while the military's framing of gender may stay the same, the terms that have limited women's participation in the world of public action are reordered. "In the process," Enloe concludes, "they [military commanders] will have incentives to redefine 'battlefield,' 'front,' and 'combat' so as to tap that female pool with minimal ideological disturbance . . . Changes in terms of debate and actual deployment parallel changes in the structure of the 'battlefield'" (1980: 44). Women can, then, be easily demobilized when, for example, the state is at risk of insufficient future soldiery or of domestic

Introduction **5**

employment pressures, and what counts as gender norms come into conflict with their social role or ideological use. In her ensuing career, Enloe focuses on a wide array of women's activities in and around war, showing how gender in combat is part of a wide gender coding encompassing combat and non-combat roles alike: commercial, diplomatic, conjugal, manufacturing, or other types of support, where gender is used to designate value in certain social activities, and to circumscribe a "sideline" of indirect involvement as a back-up force. Part of what makes this "sideline" possible is the stories people tell about gender.

Gender for the Warfare State looks to literature to ask the question of why it is so surprising, to the U.S. military and culture at large, that women engage in combat? What can we learn from looking at the deeply historical and widely geographical literary treatment of women and war to think about the contemporary relation between women and state or non-state violence? As Miriam Cooke has recognized, stories organize what seems like the chaos of social interactions, making it possible to see an order of experience out of the confusion: "The War Story," she writes, "gives order to wars that are generally experienced as confusion" (15). Citing past wars and their social fallouts, war literature not only makes sense of war's broad effects on bodies, subjectivities, and social codes but also shows, as contrast, the non-conforming patterns that new wars produce, historical changes between the expectations of deployment and the expectations of gender. In the present moment, the relation between women and military violence is tied to broad economic and political transformations, where the military has taken over many welfare-state practices.

As Michael Dillon and Julian Reed have pointed out, liberal theory has envisioned war as instrumentalized for particular political ends or state goals, the balance of power between states needing to be aggressively defended for the perpetuation of perpetual peace. Under this logic, war is inherently limited. However, "[r]estricting war by limiting it to the ends of state politics works only if the political ends, as well as the technical means, of war themselves remain limited. . . . Not only have the political ends of state regularly become unlimited and incalculable, but with its many weapons of mass destruction modern war is now also capable of threatening the very habitability of the planet" (6). In other words, the liberal license of war to keep the peace overturns by necessarily creating the means of increasingly limitless destructibility. As the liberal story of war's limits has become unsustainable, women's position as symbolizing the outside of war through their care-giving function is disappearing.

Within a liberal culture where the state is supposed to care for and protect rights and freedoms, I argue that new female militarized figures are products of a global crisis in care—a marketing of care, a militarization of care, and an administering of care—as the sphere of violence is spreading and intensifying, causing the liberal contract theorized first by Hobbes to unravel. I mean "crisis" in a Marxist sense—as an historical break that is deliberated, planned, promoted, orchestrated,

6 Introduction

and delivered by its beneficiaries, not as a natural or inevitable rupture. As the civil arm of the state backs off in the obligations it has historically held towards its citizens—i.e., education, health care, labor protections, environmental protections, infrastructure—and fulfills its security promise increasingly through outright acts of aggression, women have moved from welfare into warfare. As the current wars expand and proliferate, women will most likely have proportionally increased participation not because of a liberal largesse that has suddenly understood the error of its exclusionary ways but rather because women serve both material and ideological purposes for the military apparatus' continuity.

Literature written by, for, or about veterans of the current engagements clarifies the symbolic and distributive mechanisms of the social setting in which the war must be organized and for which it must make sense. War literature, of course, has always had a place for women, often in moments of war's repose or when injuries needed to be attended. Even so, literature about women in combat offers a significant challenge to these older conventions. As women, embodying the tradition of the home front, move into the war zone, the home front—or civil society— comes increasingly to resemble the war zone, with care's intimacies transformed into work's routines. Women's appearance as fighters in combat zones demands the overcoming of bodies' limitations—including gender, death, pain, weakness, and injuries—in a celebration of new equipment, technologies, and prostheses, and biology is treated as a fetishized commodity (Chapter One).

Conjointly, literature, too, breaks out of its traditional molds. Though war literature has been elevated in the "high" forms of novels, poems, short stories, epics, and plays, other genres have been more prominent, as well, in the telling of women's contemporary war experiences: memoirs, testimonials, journalism, blogs, diaries, soliloquies, travel accounts, epistolaries, radio broadcasts, autobiographies, and ethnographies, often found in commercial/popular, academic, and independent/small presses, or even self-published. Whereas literary scholarship has often studied war literature within national contexts, war is by definition transnational; war literature reflecting on women in combat has far-ranging influences and—like its contents and characters—by straddling borders, exposes their shiftiness. As well, visual culture portrays the woman soldier in ways that produce a narrative structured around gender as vision. In such narratives, the gender of the warrior becomes the story to tell, unstable, the lever of suspense, or the "kernel" around which the plotline turns and for which the image expresses desire (Chapter Three). Whereas, arguably, the tradition of Western literature may have claimed its foundations in the heroes of antiquity—with plots of conquest and physical overcoming that mark temporalities, intrigues, and formal structures—, the combat woman reorganizes the building-blocks: she remixes the relation between public display and private sentiment, between hero and victim, between individualistic survival and social reproduction, between adventure and drudgery, between action and repetition, between violence and care. The very idea of women in combat pushes literature beyond its boundaries by opening a

Introduction **7**

more expansive thematic range, reshaping literary expression as it interacts with the sociology of war.

The adoption of the woman fighter into literary form is not new. She hails from the mythological (Chapters Two and Three). Yet, since the middle part of the twentieth century, she injects administrative and technological reasoning into war work. Her thinking, as Horkheimer and Adorno's administrative form of reason, "objectifies itself to become an automatic, self-activating process; an impersonation of the machine that it produces itself so that ultimately the machine can replace it" (30). Her work, driven by obedience and submission, resembles their descriptions of modern work, where "the recurrent, eternally similar natural processes become the rhythm of labor according to the beat of cudgel and whip which resounds in every barbaric drum and every monotonous ritual" (21). Horkheimer and Adorno's point is that the new modern bureaucracies, by making workers infinitely exchangeable, mechanize work in endless repetition governed by technological rhythms, and my point is that the woman in combat introduces this administrative form into war narratives. She brings to light the replacement of bodies by machines in the work process by showing how technology makes possible the interchangeability of bodily identities in the work of war (Chapters One and Three). In fact, from her first introduction in the second half of the twentieth century (Chapters Three and Four) and increasingly into the neoliberal turn of the 1970s and after (Chapter Five), women's violence became more imaginable as women's war identities were made more proximate to market appropriations, calculations, technology proxies, and abstract circuits of exchange. The woman warrior becomes increasingly relevant and apparent within the increasingly administrative organization of contemporary warfare and its working cultures.

The increasing incorporation of women in armies responds to a need for personnel driven by the end of the draft, the longevity of mobilization, and the needed skills of a contemporary fighting force in an increasingly administered and technology-saturated world. This incorporation, further, is made possible because the avenues to public assistance and democratic access have been divested, leaving citizens floundering. Ideologies invest in feminine bodies certain traits and competencies that the military turns to its advantage as it transfers health and reproduction over to administration and machines (Chapter One). The militarization of women's work bureaucratizes care. In canonical war novels, women have often designated the "home front." The movement of women into the zone of combat changes the conventional narratives of care: instead of woundings and deaths on organic flesh being attended by nurses, wives, and mothers, the military itself now is the main protagonist of care, and the machine defends the body by replacing it. The military combatants who volunteer for service do not expect care from any other sources besides other military personnel and technologies, not from families, educational institutions, health care establishments, welfare, career training, or job availability, and the military often fails in providing the care expected.

8 Introduction

As Pierre Bourdieu has noted, the caring arm of the liberal state has been sacrificed to its punitive arm and policing function—"the owners of capital ... preach the subordination of the national states to the demands of economic freedom ..., the reduction of public and welfare spending ... also and above all the destruction of the collective institutions capable of standing up to the effects of the infernal machine" (100–102). David Harvey agrees that "the typical neoliberal state" will favor "good business or investment climate" over either "the collective rights (and quality of life) of labour or the capacity of the environment to regenerate itself" (70), fueling the need for more enforcement.[2] Neoliberalism diminishes institutions of caring and replaces them with a market in technologized, routinized administrative work, or work by command. While the market freedoms promoted by neoliberalism cause insecurity, the life-protections and political interventions that might offset such excesses are handed over to mechanisms in the business of death. The notable entry of the combatant woman into the center of literary narratives demonstrates that neoliberalism is producing and managing its own self-legitimations through literatures of women in combat.

Comparing twentieth century literatures about women in combat against the U.S.'s engagements in wars currently, *Gender for the Warfare State* traces, in both normative terms and in specific cases, how literary narratives about war now make women's combat identities into the doleful "success" story of market societies' liberalization. It is concerned with how women soldiers embody the diminishment of the liberal state's caring functions as they are militarized and mechanized for the neoliberal state, and the accompanying expansion of violent means over politics (Chapters Two and Three). The technologization of war that accompanies women's combat has changed politics: as technologies produce ideologies of invulnerability on the battlefield, states require less buy-in from citizens. The bond of the liberal state—where citizens are asked to sacrifice for state security, in exchange for recognition and rights—diminishes, and politics becomes less a question of appeal and consensus than a question of effectivity. Perhaps, then, even in the face of posthumanist philosophies that see technological rationalities as infusing social relations at every point, the argument it is necessary to make is an argument for reconsidering an obligation of politics to bodies because they are vulnerable. As Judith Butler explains it, a political vision of cohabitation among the world's inhabitants, of sharing the world with others, must be

> one in which physical need and vulnerability would become matters for mutual recognition and regard. . . . It would seem then that any effort to reconstruct the human after humanism, that is, after humanism's complicity with colonialism, would have to include an understanding of humans as those who may suffer death in advance of the cessation of bodily function, who suffer it at the heart of life itself.
>
> *(2015, Senses: 189–190)*

Culture

The arguments surging in the mainstream press for or against women in combat reference a panoply of media representations that are saturating the airwaves as well as the digital circuits. Though certain media presentations and news reports on the topic profess an utter disbelief that any armed forces would even consider including women in their ranks, at the same time cultural production is obsessed with their presence. Offering to viewing audiences both sexual enticement and versatility of plots and intrigues, such media representations range from TV series like *Caprica*, *Dollhouse*, *The Americans*, and *Homeland* to low-budget films such as Santosh Sivan's *The Terrorist*, countless *anime* and martial arts features, a generous sampling of superhero spectacles, and Hollywood blockbusters such as *Courage Under Fire*, *Mr. and Mrs. Smith*, *Terminator II* and *III*, the *Hunger Games* series, the *Matrix* series (made by Lilly Wachowski, a recently declared transgender woman), *Edge of Tomorrow*, *Ex Machina*, *Star Wars: The Force Awakens*, *Mad Max: Fury Road*, *Suicide Squad* and Academy Award-winning Kathryn Bigelow's *Zero Dark Thirty*. Why, in a culture so saturated with narrative images of women engaged in state and non-state violence, is the concrete possibility of women in combat greeted with so much incredulity, skepticism, and opposition, if not disgust?

The proliferation of representations of women in combat has taken a variety of forms, aligned as it is with a variety of interests. One could remark on a noticeable transition from an earlier version of popular culture's female combatant—such as *G.I. Jane* (1997) or *Private Benjamin* (1980) where female militarization serves as a foil or an aberration to the point of ridicule—to a later version, such as *Battlestar Galactica*, where women's militarized violence defines a new norm, to *Tomb Raider* or *Salt*, where women's violence exemplifies an exception that justifies heroic extralegal action. One might also look to some European renditions, where—as in the Spanish TV series *Entre Tiempo*, the British series *The Bletchley Circle*, and the 2008 French film *Les femmes de l'ombre* by Jean-Paul Salomé—World War II histories are being revised to inform us that women soldiers and spies saved D-Day, leading the Allies to noble victory. David Green's 1990 schlock film *Fire Birds: Wings of the Apache*—with the all-star casting of Nicolas Cage, Tommy Lee Jones, and Sean Young—views like a commercial for the Black Hawk helicopter before any of the Persian Gulf wars, when such new flight technologies promised new securities, policing the border and ending drug use in the United States forever. Despite taking an initial stand against marriage and for independence, the woman combat pilot ends up tying the knot with the male combat hero who rescues her, a feel-good ending offering romantic success in the technological promise as the lovers fly off into the sunset. Telling, in a much grittier and more cynical vein, of a woman FBI agent who inadvertently gets caught up in druglord assassinations and torture alongside CIA, DEA, state police, and a former member of the Medellín drug cartel, Denis Villeneuve's 2015 *Sicario* uses the militarized woman to give

10 Introduction

a moral cover to the ethically and legally questionable activities of a cross-border invasion. The FBI agent Kate, played by Emily Blunt, threatens repeatedly to "walk-out" of the operation because of the disregard for legal regulations, including when unknowingly she is offered up as sexual bait to a major informant who is also a rapist. In the end, however, she signs a non-disclosure agreement confirming that the armed paramilitary was justified in its actions as it was more effective in killing the druglords than either the federal or local police. Granting legitimacy for an attack on another nation's sovereignty that was already apparently in shreds, the woman, though now de-romanticized, still serves to create a moral structure where the effectiveness of the instrument counts for more than the judgment of right or wrong (Chapter Three). In other contexts, the combatant woman calls into play cultural difference and political opposition, in such films, for instance, as Siegel and Green's *Weather Underground*, Edel's *The Baader Meinhof Complex*, Weingartner's *The Edukators*, Bellocchio's *Good Morning, Night*, Schlondorff's *The Legend of Rita*, Pontecorvo's *The Battle of Algiers*, Diab's *678*, Borden's *Born in Flames*, Barbeau-Lavalette's *Inch'Allah*, and Suleiman's nationalist comedy of abstraction, *Divine Intervention*. These films also deploy the female combatant to exhibit that war is deeply enmeshed in the social fabric rather than separated out in exclusive temporal or spatial zones of action.

The idea that women enter military service because of economic hardship is rarely if ever directly considered. A film like the 1981 documentary *Soldier Girls* is rare in this regard, dramatizing the difficulties women face in basic training for combat (even though women supposedly were not allowed in combat at the time, and the film makes a case that women should never be allowed in combat because they would lose what remains of the humanity in their souls and their capacity to love). Though, as Yvonne Tasker argues, the film exhibits "different levels and types of motivation" (238), the focus is on women who fail at drills, fail at endurance, fall behind at running, cannot keep their bunks neat, cannot follow orders, cannot stop crying or exhibiting other signs of emotion even against orders, and are targets of constant grueling punishment. As the ultimate example of failure, when the soldiers are being taught how to respond to a nuclear attack (lie flat on the ground, facing away from the explosion), the trainee does not squeeze her legs together in order "to protect the next generation." As Tasker describes the film, "a survival instructor bites off a chicken's head and hurls the still mobile body towards the recruits. . . . [T]he recruits are assured that, in the event of a nuclear accident or attack, they can simply brush off radioactive dust. . . . The indifference toward the life and health of these recruits speaks volumes of the value placed on their lives" (242). The women privates are so insulted and abused by superiors and drill sergeants that they look forward to leaving the army so they can go back to their drudgery jobs or no jobs at all. *Soldier Girls* reveals an economic depravity that borders on military service, recognizing the "revolving door" between military service for women in combat and other low-level economic sectors; they work while acknowledging the tedium as acceptable because all other sources of care and self-improvement are drying up. *Gender for the Warfare State* places the woman combatant in the context of such contemporary politics, proposing that the gender values engendered in the current wars connect to social relations that define the present.

Ironically, perhaps, much of the popular debate in the U.S. over whether women should be admitted into military combat roles takes place on the level of culture. This might be because the female militant is so prevalent in cultural production to the point where her cultural production overwhelms any other terms and takes precedence over her existence. Such references suggest that real-life examples are unavailable so that the outcome of such an enormous policy shift is undeterminable and barely imaginable, or that the outcome of women's actualization as soldiers is untried, unpredictable, haphazard, and leading towards a future of frenzy and uncertainty. The enormity of the female combatant's cultural presence, however, could also be an acknowledgement that the imagination is engaged with seeing the future as it is already taking shape in the present. In other words, references to culture within policy debates suggest a reading where culture expresses what does not fit with current practices or ideological comfort because it is what happens next. If some fear culture for its prophecies of the future unknown, or even for ruffling against the present, the reaction might be a retrenchment, a calling back of what once seemed safe because you knew what to expect—you could preserve the present into the future by affirming the facts of bodies as repeating over past time and so repeating, still, going forward. If the future is linked to culture, the future can be dismissed as inconsequential, marginal, immaterial, and fake even while such critics still insist that all resources must be employed to route it out.

By referencing culture, such pundits imply that what is present is really the future that we should avoid, a future that would create dystopic upheavals and civilizational ruin. For Kingsley Browne, for example, women should not serve in combat: they are smaller, slower, dumber, and more submissive, and these traits are not cultural and changeable but rather biological, maintained through genes and hormones, as the scientific evidence shows. The military experts who once opposed integration policies but swung to the other side are the handmaidens, says Browne, not of conviction about military needs but rather of popular culture's promotion of "girl power," held hostage by feminists who erroneously believe that women can do anything men can do or that warfare has changed so much that manly muscular strength is not necessary for victory. An example Browne offers of a "Make-Believe World of Sexual Integration" is Paul Verhoeven's 1997 movie *Starship Troopers*. "Will the science fiction of *Starship Troopers* become fact?" asks Browne. "Some people envision such a military for the United States" (5). In particular, Browne focuses on a co-ed shower scene, where infantry personnel stand together naked and wet without any inclination for "seductions of the flesh" (3). Browne concludes that the movie assumes for the future a new "attitude" where "ignoring sex differences renders them

12 Introduction

inconsequential" (4), where sexiness has been shut off, and where a ridiculous belief in equality trumps the truth of the body. Browne insists that bodies reproduce meaning mechanically and compulsively like machines reproduce objects, that is, that gender and sexuality are necessarily outside of politics. For him, men and women together, naked, and wet would be indelibly eroticized if only we would accept inequality as the basis of that physical relationship. Browne asserts that women should be banned from service because of men's uncontrollable, bodily sexism. He expresses frustration at anyone who might believe that ideology were possible or malleable.

Now, quite conspicuously, *Starship Troopers* is a farce. As a pre-9/11 cult film, it ridicules the excesses of militaristic escalation, showing children "doing their part" by stomping on cockroaches, for example. *Starship Troopers* spoofs on the authoritarianism behind endless military expansion. Before women were legally allowed into combat-designated military roles in the U.S., the endlessly reproductive body mocks hysterically, in the film, the endless need to power an endless and preposterous war by including females in the ranks. The global Federation composed of Americans (the main characters come from Buenos Aires but are distinctly American) is forced to retaliate against a planet of bugs that attacks them by firing an asteroid at the great city of Buenos Aires and destroying it. At first, the humans think they can outsmart the bugs because they are, after all, bugs. The humans fight with hyped-up aircraft, nuclear guns, and artillery against mosquito stingers and green beetle spray that douses them in snot-like greenness. Once under siege, however, the humans learn that the bugs are strategizing, and they soon also learn that the bugs are under the control of a giant brain bug. The brain bug acquires human intelligence simply by eating and absorbing the brains of soldiers, not necessarily the average grunts but the ones who are obviously good at math. A slew of war movie clichés ensues, including when the main female officer fighter character crashes her aircraft and gets caught in a den full of evil, giant mosquitoes working for the brain bug who wants to eat the poor victim's brain (she is good at math), and the main male infantry character succeeds in rescuing her but, conveniently, not her boyfriend. In a mockery of the long tradition of films that equate horror with female sexuality,[3] when the brain bug appears on screen, she is quite explicitly a giant vagina bug, that is, a brain vagina: when she is probed by a stick, a "Censored" sign pops up to block partially the image of her orgasmic pleasure. Though the troopers catch the vagina brain bug in a net and bring her to their lab for testing, she is not defeated. Instead, the war goes on. Her vagina brain intelligence has thought into existence an endless reproduction of the warrior bugs (she herself is now good at math too), and the troopers—boys and girls alike—go off heroically to fight another generation of bugs.

Though imagining what might happen to humanity if it is attacked by enemy vagina brain bugs with mosquito platoons might be scary for some, Browne has surely missed the point. Quite clearly ridiculing those who believe, like Browne, that equality will bring about the apocalypse, or that female sexuality and intelligence are threats to humanity as we know it, the film is not engaged in a social experiment but in a critique of perpetual war that demands perpetual reproduction. Not quite getting the joke, Browne worries, in reverse, that the film's promoting of a feminist ideal of physical and intellectual equality for women will dangerously lead to a society that cannot protect itself against oversex, and that such feminism as exhibited in the film has had such a big influence that politicians and joint chiefs alike do not anymore realize how essential the manliness in men's bodies is for combat. Winning the war, says Browne, depends on scientifically-proven attributes of masculinity like "physical strength and endurance, physical aggressiveness, willingness to kill strangers, willingness to expose oneself to physical risk, and some cognitive abilities, such as the three-dimensional spatial ability that is so critical to the 'situational awareness' of fighter pilots" (6–7). There is a "primitive connection" (88) between war and men where war "stimulates some pleasure center deep within the brain" (87) so that war cannot be disassociated from maleness and men's desire, and men want to fight wars because wars make them happy. Browne assumes that war happens when a bunch of muscular male bodies euphorically throw themselves in a physical display of superior strength against another set of male bodies and tear those bodies apart by sheer force. Taken out of the equation are technology investments, strategies, preparation, organization, command, culture, psychology, supplies, and training. Taken out also is the vast range of war's work needs, in response to which the war itself demands differences, even differences in how force is applied, and where gender— combined with its technologies, attributes, and identity codes—is constructed to answer to those needs.

The main problem in Browne's analysis is that he confuses culture with science in order to deny history. Much of his evidence is from reports of Americans in the Vietnam War, or Soviets in World War II, and for him, this tells us everything we need to know. Other evidence comes from recorded conversations of men at war describing events in sexist terms: "A scared little bitch" (99), one Marine calls another Marine, implying the need of masculinity to accomplish acts of valor. Other evidence still is drawn from social science studies that grant eternal truths to data collected at particular moments, as though such conclusions are not inflected with ideological contingencies, debates, and belief systems of those moments. Because studies have shown that women are more empathetic (by what criteria?) and more likely to experience post-traumatic stress disorder (PTSD), "not only are women less likely to kill but also they are likely to pay a heavier psychic price" (105). According to Browne, such effects cannot be caused by social expectations that reward women for empathy, nor might women be more stressed because they are more mistreated in the military, or more isolated, as the literature shows. Instead, such reactions can only be inscribed in the flesh, determined in the body, as though gender has an instrumental rather than a social existence. For Browne, the body's actions are not cultural markers but rather component facts,

14 Introduction

steady and observable now as always, and so *predictable*. The problem with *Starship Troopers* is that it gets the facts wrong; it is not scientific.

Starship Troopers is a warning: rather than telling us the way things are, have been, and always must be, it looks into the chaos of its present in order to urge us to worry about what comes next. Now, three decades later, the woman in combat continues to crack open the future as a story in the present. As what jars against the contemporary war narrative and gives rise to apocalyptic terrors, she reveals what could be: a future taking shape in the present that ought to discomfort us. This glimpse of the future does not inspire panic because girls refuse to behave as girls or because men who can protect us are being denied the opportunity, so we must go back to the way things were if we know what is good for us. Rather, the woman in combat brings with her an alarming change in the culture of care. The inclusion of women in war is sad not because they put civilization at risk or leave our borders without security, but rather because women are called to action for the sake of a growing commitment to military expansion and a transfer of resources away from civil society to feed that commitment. I would even go so far as to say that these wars have become *necessary,* as the neoliberal corporate economy has made unavailable the basic needs, cares, and living wages of citizens *except* when they join up, and even then inadequately.

Literature written by, for, or about women in combat shows us this. These works are often heartbreaking because, even while maybe leaving their children in the care of others or sustaining incapacitating life-altering mental and physical injuries, the women often express a compelling desire to be working for the good of their country or serving others or just trying to get by for themselves and their families, without being able to articulate clearly—or at all—the connection between what they are doing in the field and these caring goals. Indeed, the absence of an articulation of such a connection is telling, as such soldiers risk their security and that of their nation in order to boost the financial securities of those who make more insecurity for others. The answer should not be to enlist more women in the military in the interests of equality but rather to stop these wars in the service of life.

Notes

1 Though the early twentieth century produced a certain equation of feminism with pacifism, feminist critical and literary theory of the Second Wave has always understood violence as vital in the construction of feminist agency, in figures ranging from the phallic mother to the indigenous insurgent, from Kristeva's abject to Fanon's veil, from Sophocles' *Antigone* to Wittig's *les guérillères*, from Beauvoir's existentialist Resistance fighter to El Saadawi's imprisoned sex worker, from Frankenstein's monster to the cyborg.
2 Neoliberalism has many more elements to it than this description implies—cultural, ideological, economic, and political. For example, it reduces all calculation to market calculation, makes markets solve social problems, and eclipses the power of the nation-state in the rise of corporate power.

3 See, for example, Barbara Creed: "My intention is to explore the representation of woman in the horror film and to argue that woman *is* represented as monstrous in a significant number of horror films . . . I will argue that when woman is represented as monstrous it is almost always in relation to her mothering and reproductive functions" but that "woman's monstrousness is linked more directly to questions of sexual desire than to the area of reproduction" (7).

1

WOMEN IN THE WAR STORY

What Work Does Gender Do?

On 24 January 2013, then U.S. Secretary of Defense Leon Panetta, with the unanimous consent of the Joint Chiefs of Staff and with rare bipartisan Congressional support, announced the end of the military's exclusion of women in combat. Under Panetta's plan, each branch of the military would assess what would be entailed for implementing these changes and for specifying the reasons for exceptions even as 237,000 new positions would open to women. The policy was to be fully implemented in 2016. On the eve of full implementation, Panetta's successor, Secretary of Defense Ashton Carter, expanded the policy's reach, opening all combat roles to women without exception.[1]

The restriction on women in combat had meant that women were not allowed to take jobs classified as artillery specialist, infantry, special operations, or tank crew. Since 1948, women have been banned by the Women's Armed Services Integration Act from serving on Navy ship-board or in any aircraft on a combat mission. These restrictive regulations had put a limit on military women's careers and leadership advancement. The work of women has traditionally defined the area outside the war, a visual marker for identifying civil society and cultures of protection. However, the changing formation of the frontline in the wars of the past two decades has meant that women's service and auxiliary roles can no longer be claimed as outside of combat. As, for example, medics are called upon to assist in the aftermath of IED (improvised explosive devices) explosions during convoy transports, women's military work has found itself under barrage and in the direct line, often without proper training or equipment. "I gunned. I drove. I ran as a truck commander. And underneath it all, I was a medic," confessed one army specialist, who won a Bronze Star for valor, to L. Alvarez of *The New York Times*. "I was attached as a turret gunner to a military police unit that specialized in convoy security, during a period of high risk for IED attacks," reports

Mariette Kalinowski. "I operated all of the weapons systems used by that unit, and was expected to perform at the same level as a man. I did." As infantry units were tasked with house searches and scouting out fighters in urban neighborhoods, checkpoints, and domestic sites, women soldiers—named "Lionesses"—were needed to pat down and guard local women and children, often finding themselves in the midst of firefights at close range.[2]

As Elisabeth Bumiller and Thom Shanker claim in *The New York Times,* Panetta's "groundbreaking decision overturns a 1994 Pentagon rule that restricts women from artillery, armor, infantry and other such combat roles, even though in reality women have frequently found themselves in combat in Iraq and Afghanistan, where more than 20,000 have served. As of last year, more than 800 women had been wounded in the two wars and more than 130 had died." Jessica Lynch's high-profile kidnapping by Iraqi militants in An Nasiriyah and subsequent rescue by the Marines during the 2003 forward offensive made the stakes even more urgent: Lynch had been trained in an Army supply role as a truck driver and landed in a hostile zone because of an accidental wrong turn, when her vehicle crashed. Proponents maintain that Panetta's move only made official a change that had already taken place in work on the ground. In other words, Panetta's policy did not alter anything much except for allowing women to rise into the pay and rank categories that men doing similar work already achieve. Yet, it caused quite a media stir.

The arguments either for or against the participation of women in combat often can be said to include assumptions about what work women do, and those assumptions are based on an unconscious sense of how work, in general, is structured in the neoliberal present. I do not mean to say the obvious here, that civilian work often performed by women in the twentieth century—such as manufacturing of ammunitions, of transportation, and of other supplies—advances the war effort, as Angela Woollacott points out.[3] Rather, with Yvonne Tasker, I want to highlight "that to a large extent a place appears for military women as and when their labor is required. In our current historical context of open-ended war and ongoing military interventions, that labor has been integral to American assertions of military authority" (15). I explore here how what I may call neoliberal economic relations—the diminishment of institutions of caring and their replacement by a technologized, routinized work structure, or work by command—have entered our normative expectations of work through the representational politics of women in combat.

War literature has traditionally produced narratives around the space of women's work, linking such women's work to civil space.[4] Sam Sacks in *Harper's* argues that contemporary war fiction "shows how traditional the veteran's narrative remains. There are more than 200,000 women on active duty in the military, but the female experience of warfare has been barely broached." Sacks' criticism of the contemporary war-writing scene is that its products are novels developed within elite creative writing programs in U.S. universities, and as such, their perspective

18 Women in the War Story

tends to depoliticize the war, portraying it through an intensely individualized and closed-in subjectivity based in therapeutic culture. Yet, women's contemporary war writing does exist, it exists in multiple literary forms, and its subjectivities are positioned politically. Modern war invented the figure of the soldier-poet as very educated men in World War I trenches sent home poems to their families, but it also inspired the literary nurse—e.g., Vera Brittain's *Testament of Youth,* Irene Rathbone's *We That Were Young,* Mary Borden's *The Forbidden Zone,* Helen Zenna Smith's *Not So Quiet . . .,* Enid Bagnold's *A Diary Without Dates,* among the most famous—, where women, waxing romantic about their duty to the nation and "doing their part," restored that nation's health, mourned its losses, and took up the reins of its intellectual and cultural life.

A book like Vera Brittain's memoir—*Testament of Youth,* adapted into a 2015 film by James Kent—connects a woman's wartime work as a nurse to her post-war work as a suffragette and as an international pacifist lecturing for the League of Nations. "Surely," contemplates Brittain, "since the finest flowers of English manhood had been plucked from a whole generation, women were needed as never before to maintain the national standard of literature, of art, of music, of politics, of teaching, of medicine?" (610).[5] The extension of Brittain's wartime experience to 1925 creates a sense of war's effects spreading beyond armistice, not just halting when and where civil society stakes a separate claim in women's work. Santanu Das writes very compellingly about World War I as a watershed in cultures of care, traced through these nursing memoirs. In Das' reading, the nurse feels exalted for being invited to play a role in history (such women "would be identified as the first generation of 'feminists'" (186)) but then is made helpless, guilty, and horrified when confronting such extremes of suffering and injury with very little knowledge of how to heal. "[I]n a world where morphine and anaesthesia were forever in short supply, the 'real' enemy was not death but pain, a 'monster bedfellow' which . . . often rendered the nurse 'helpless'" (204). Second, according to Das, such war memoirs are incredibly detailed in describing the physical contours of the place of pain. Women's modern subjectivities, according to Das, would be constructed in the hiatus between the broken body and its traumatic witness as they are marked by anxieties in the face of a painful, paralyzing gash in the male body. The feeling of exaltation in participating in history in a kind of intimacy with the male body might have been confused with prohibited sexual desires, and the writing was concerned in specifying this distinction. What is so provocative in this analysis for my project here is the way Das reads modern women's subjectivity as constructed very intimately around a type of care that is already fractured, incapacitated, and challenged at its inception: "If moments of actual physical contact help the nurses to stake their legitimate claim on history and establish a common ground with the soldiers, the recollection of the traumatic moments also serves as faultlines within the text, marking points of ideological rupture" (203). War nurse narratives in Brittain's model make clear that women's war stories politicize care by connecting big history with subjectivity formations and psychological drama around the concept of care.

The transformation of women's work into the direct work of violence in the current wars demands that narrative conventions defining peaceful civil space as women's work are reconsidered. This chapter looks at the "women in combat" question as it appears in contemporary literary texts.[6] It argues that the literary narrative is necessary for the framing of this question of "women in combat" because of literature's relation to working time, and how a reconceptualization of time underlies the meanings that surface in the identity of the fighting woman. As war narratives traditionally tend to move back and forth between the civil sphere and the line of battle, literature acknowledges that the atrocities of war in the twentieth century and beyond have become too momentous to be categorized within these conventional concepts that organize social space and time. In the context discussed here, the "woman in combat" text reveals that the time of care is now absorbed within the working time of the soldier. The chapter goes on to show: 1) the transformation of the protective, caring function of the civil sphere in the "woman in combat" literary text; 2) the bureaucratization of work that takes on what is left of this protective function; and 3) the dehumanization of the worker resulting from the change of care-work into the mechanized operation of the technologized war process.

Throughout the world, women have participated in both state and non-state violence, and not only as helpless victims, though much war coverage—including documentary films like Kirby Dick's 2012 film *Invisible War* and Meg McLagan and Daria Sommers' 2008 film *Lioness*—would have us see them as such, like children: "innocent civilians" and casualty counts. According to the U.S. Army's own statistics, women have been serving since 1775 and currently make up 15.7 percent of those in active service (most statistics count 14 percent in the military as a whole).[7] Women were first inducted into the army in 1901, when it organized the Army Nurse Corps, and into the navy in 1908, though only in auxiliary roles until the end of World War II. Though in the early 1960s, women constituted less than the 2 percent legal maximum in military service, in 1967 the quota was removed in Public Law 90–130, leading to a very slow and gradual increase. More than 40,000 served in Operation Desert Storm in the early 1990s, even while restrictions on women's participation in direct combat remained. According to feminist sociologist Nancy Goldman, there are three reasons that the military projected a growth in women's military participation: 1) a change in U.S. culture under the influence of feminism and the increase in women's skilled work and professionalism more generally; 2) the movement, after Vietnam, to an all-volunteer force— not only did the military search for personnel in marginal sectors, e.g., black and rural areas, including women, but also women were more likely to be called into service sectors and low-status professions, of which the military comprised one, and women have always been volunteers in the military, even under the draft; and 3) the character of military work changed towards more administration (892) as "in all of the services women were employed mainly as clerks, secretaries, and in routine types of communications" (901). The designation of "non-combatant"

20 Women in the War Story

has allowed the military to categorize certain areas and operations under women's command as outside of direct armed conflict. Through such designations, the military distributes types of equipment, security, wages, and personnel, so that non-combat positions receive less defensive supplies and more independent contractor and privatized civilian hires.[8] The participation of women in the U.S. military must be seen as part of a broader effort to use the gendering of work in order to regulate labor markets under cover of ethical objectives like equality.[9]

What is really surprising is the surprise, discomfort, suspicion, and frequent disgust that much U.S. coverage displays about women's encounters as agents in battle. Women in the armed services, Brian Mitchell, for example, suggests in his dire warning prophecy *Women in the Military: Flirting With Disaster*, are a security breach and the harbingers of civilization's demise: "[T]he presence of women is damaging our armed forces . . .; a rash of . . . celebrated cases have exposed the dangerous effects of sex-based integration and affirmative action on standards, safety, training, and discipline" (xv). For Mitchell, the creeping new admittance of women into military service results from an insidious plot on the part of female civilian leaders in government, starting with Eleanor Roosevelt, who promoted their agenda of equality against the historical record, which proved women's inadequacies in such roles. Mitchell insists on warning the dupes of evil Eleanor and her ideologue female followers that, whereas the evidence shows women are not needed and not useful in the military, the outcome of their inclusion has been catastrophic: a softening of discipline, a censoring of vulgarities in drilling, an upgrade of accommodations from dirty barracks to dormitories, and a lowering of physical performance expectations.

The media coverage of Panetta's plan suggests that involving women in combat is a cultural innovation in a military organization, a liberal victory, and that such a reorganization demands not only logistical modifications, changes (or improvements) in accommodations, and an updating of training protocols, but also, more importantly, a psychological shift in both military and civilian culture. On the one hand, new consumer commodities and entertainment reflect an acceptance that gender has already been militarized: "Toy makers have begun marketing a more aggressive line of playthings and weaponry for girls—inspired by a succession of female warrior heroes like Katniss, the Black Widow of 'The Avengers,' Merida of 'Brave' and now, Tris of the book and new movie 'Divergent'—even as the industry still clings to every shade of pink," note Hilary Stout and Elizabeth Harris in *The New York Times*. "The result is a selection of toys that . . . challenges antiquated notions." Popular film and TV promote an uncanny number of militarized women, from the sexy but militant Cylons of *Battlestar Galactica* to the psychotic CIA-operative Carrie Mathison in *Homeland* sniffing out terrorists with her global surveillance systems and bi-polar security instincts.

Even so, on the other hand, Panetta's lifting of the ban evoked shock, fear, and backlash from those who read doomsday in such a radical new world: "[M]ilitary news sites like *Army Times* and *Marine Corps Times* lit up with comments, some ranging from laughably sexist to reprehensible," *The New York Times* mentions in its editorial on Panetta's decision, "Women in the Battlefield," "'They shouldn't be bused in from the field every 3 days for a shower while the guys stay out for 45 days,' said one commenter. 'The castration of the U.S. Army continues,' said another. 'God help us all.'" Yes, such pronouncements worry, women's obsession with clean-smelling hair and freshly painted nails will loosen the guard, allowing the barbarians to bust through the gates guarding all we value most, God and penis, and nothing will be able to stop them. Great claims of apocalypse are supported by evidence of the pettiest sort. What accounts for the distinction between, on the one hand, a policy debate where it is assumed to have been impossible, until now (but possibly even now), to imagine women in combat and, on the other, a popular culture that seems almost at the point of not imagining anything else?

The total consensus between the Pentagon, the Defense Department, and both parties in Congress on this issue should make anyone terrified, even if the level of rhetoric on both sides were not chilling, with either its triumphalism over girls with guns or its apocalyptic and hateful mania over the risks of equality in the service of violence. Though I clearly do not agree that women's combat status threatens military strength because it requires the censoring of aggressive swearing and rape epithets during drills, neither do I believe that women's inclusion in the military is an expansion of democracy or part of a construction of a civil society more open to difference and diversity in its institutions, of which the military is one. Major Katelyn van Dam, Marine attack helicopter pilot and combat veteran, is irresponsible to declare, as she does on NPR's *The Diane Rehms Show,* that "Combat is the great equalizer," when historically only death has been granted that role. I contest those "proponents of equal access" who, according to Miriam Cooke, see military service as "a central tenet of citizenship in a democracy" (30) that is "no longer so different from civilian life" (33)—it still seems important to make distinctions between war and other practices, even when war seems ubiquitous and pervasive, and I do not believe that participation in wars should be the measure of democratic citizenship. Nor do I abide by Lucinda Joy Peach's proposition that the recognition of women's capacities to use state-sanctioned forms of violence in effective or appropriable ways "would likely have several beneficial consequences, including creating opportunities for more women to occupy more positions of authority and leadership, both within and outside the military" (68). Nor do I buy Tom Digby's assessment that the inclusion of women in combat "degenders" war and might inaugurate "a profound shift regarding gender that is complementary to the diminution of the importance of warrior masculinity" (186). On the contrary: the expansion of war is the expansion of the military personality. And I would not, either, embrace Mia Bloom's assessment that, for a woman, military conflict—in this case, in the name of *jihad*—is where she "can express her own convictions and [be] a personal platform calling for . . . resistance" (205). The evidence does not suggest that women's participation in combat has led to the end of sexism, an end to femininity's expressions of passivity, an end

22 Women in the War Story

to women's exclusions in the echelons of power, an end to masculine aggression towards women or other men, or a surge in feminism.

Criticizing feminist beliefs in the moral superiority of women, Barbara Ehrenreich encourages us to revise a feminism that assumed women's inclusion in combat would make war more humane and culturally sensitive. "A certain kind of feminist naiveté," she writes, "died in Abu Ghraib. It saw men as the perpetual perpetrators, women as the perpetual victims, and male sexual violence against women as the root of all injustice" (2). This view of women, which perpetuates an image of feminine passivity that even Freud criticized, never could—despite Ehrenreich's claims to the contrary—fit comfortably within a feminist theory that sought for agency in a world saturated in social inequalities, public disenfranchisement, and technologies of control and command.

I am more sympathetic to Francine D'Amico's view that "women's increasing presence in the military does not change the institution's fundamentally gendered structure, which at its core is coercive, hierarchical, and patriarchal" (122). The military has not been the bastion of feminist organization or even feminist identification: "Women recruited into the military," shows Nancy Goldman, "or who are planning to enter, reveal that they are not attached to the militant women's liberation movement" (902). In fact, "[s]electing the military as a place of employment goes hand in hand with a rejection or indifference to the militant women's liberation movement" (902). Cynthia Enloe in *Maneuvers* agrees that "Women who serve . . . usually do not see themselves as bound together by their shared womanhood" (xii) and in earlier work advanced the idea that "[u]se of women in militaries has rarely been the product of an assertive women's movement" (1980: 51). She goes on, "Being hunted down by a helicopter gunship in a dry riverbed does not usually constitute liberation from patriarchy. Nor is gaining enough public trust so that one is aiming airborne machine guns at desperate figures darting from bush to bush along the riverbed the typical goal of feminist political activism" (1980: 51). Gayatri Spivak puts it well when she says that "expanding the war endlessly will not necessarily produce multiple-issue gender justice in the subaltern sphere. The most visible consequences, the exacerbation of state terrorism in Israel, Malaysia, India, and elsewhere, have nothing to do with gender justice at all" (2004: 84). With Zillah Eisenstein, I believe that "there is nothing more undemocratic than war, so it is highly unlikely that women's presence can mean anything good" (27), and with Angela Davis, I agree that "feminism does not say that we want to fight for the equal right of women to participate in the military, for the equal right of women to torture, or for their equal right to be killed in combat" (21).

I might look, for example, at Gayle Tzemach Lemmon's novel-like report, *Ashley's War*, to show how seemingly feminist tropes and positions can be distorted when forced to take a side on this issue, or how arguments for democratic inclusion, as Eisenstein and Davis warn, can support the most radical exclusion. *Ashley's War* is a heroic tale of a group of dedicated, ambitious, "beautiful" women who answer the call of the Navy Rangers to train for special-ops missions in Afghanistan as the first team in a pilot program. The purpose is to show that women can meet military standards, that their bodies are not a handicap. Neither Ashley nor any of her teammates mention what they understand as the reasons for the invasion or whether they agree with them. There are no politics, only obedience to trainers and commanders, and effort spent in meeting equal standards in performance goals. The women display their valor and courage in a series of training rituals and physical proofs: "But then came the PT text. Scott had seen their scores going in . . . He set the distance for the first running test at two miles, and within moments of completing her run one of the CSTs [Cultural Support Team] was in his face. 'Sergeant, this course isn't two miles,' she threw at him. 'I know what my two mile run time is. It is not twelve twenty-five, it is twelve thirty'" (123–124). Tragically, Ashley is killed in a bomb explosion while pursuing a Taliban arms manufacturer in Kandahar. The last sixty pages of the book, after Ashley's death, treat her death as a success, evidence that women are equal on the frontline, and her fellow lieutenants double down their commitment: "They were all soldiers, and death was part of their business. Ashley hadn't wanted any special treatment in life, and she certainly wouldn't have wanted it in death" (242). Ashley lied to her parents about serving in combat, and when they learn that she had volunteered for combat, lied to them about it, and died, they feel proud and honored that their daughter died equally on the battlefield. The combat argument reduces the liberal feminist ideal to equality in physical traits, stamina, and death, a martyrdom commemorating the capacity of the body-mechanism for work. Equality proves the worker completely expendable and replaceable. The attribute of womanness to the worker reduces her to the pure instrumental physicality of her body, what Simone de Beauvoir would call her "immanence" (xxxv).[10]

My goal here is not to rehearse familiar arguments, celebratory approval, or nightmare scenarios on one side or the other. To take a position "for" or "against" women in combat is unanswerable, much like taking a position "for" or "against" homosexual marriage, as Judith Butler has pointed out. Butler worries that turning to the state for an acknowledgement, recognition, and acceptance of difference compels a project of normalization which necessarily delegitimates inconsistencies and outliers while promoting some versions of reality over others. "[C]ritical reflection," Butler concludes, "which is surely part of any seriously normative political philosophy and practice, demands that we ask why and how this has become the question, the question that defines what will and will not qualify as meaningful political discourse here" (2004: 107). What is being camouflaged, so to speak, by such a demand to take a side in this debate, and what options get erased as outside of the possibility of meaning and legibility that this demand frames and legitimates? We might scratch our heads before an inquiry, in this case, into which position might allow a refusal of violence as the dominant shape of the democratic moment? Which side opens a perspective besides this or that method of accepting perpetual and expansive war, and whose interests get served in posing

24 Women in the War Story

this as the entire scope of political viability today? Why would we want *more* people included in *this* war? And how did women in war come to be the promise of the democratic future, or of its demise?

Literature in Combat

In the perspective of the twenty-first century, the extension of the war story has meant that war provides the framing for economic crises that become, as narrative, psychological dramas. Indeed, at the beginning of the twenty-first century, one might talk about an identity, a case history, a life story of the combatant in a similar way to what Foucault identifies as the life cycle of homosexuality at the end of the nineteenth. I want to look to literature to see what may account for the symbolic crises elicited in women's call to violence.[11] Traditionally, war stories have been bound up with reflections on mortality, on the status of the body as marking the time of life and subject to its vulnerabilities. These reflections have been deeply gendered, with men expending the time of life and women restoring it through reproductive labor. The current tendency of war literature, however, changes the time of the war narrative from reflecting the time of life to absorbing the time of work, rife with work's routines, flowcharts, banalities, repetitions, and everyday mechanical assembling and re-assembling. The war scene itself is the place of reproduction.

Even as some believe that women in combat are an unprecedented and unexpected scourge, literature began to consider the symbolic fallout of women in modern armed conflicts as early as the 1905 performance at the Royal Court Theater of George Bernard Shaw's *Major Barbara*, and then again with the 1924 opening of *Saint Joan* in New York. More recently, often in defense or rejection of positions in the public discussion about women in combat in the context of the wars in Iraq and Afghanistan, there have been a slew of literary contributions, from novels such as Helen Benedict's *Sand Queen*, Carver Greene's[12] *An Unlawful Order*, Julia Spencer-Fleming's *One Was a Soldier*, and Cara Hoffman's *Be Safe I Love You*; to short story and poetry collections like *Powder*; to memoirs such as Tracy Crow's *Eyes Right: Confessions from a Woman Marine*, Jane Blair's *Hesitation Kills*, Lynda Van Devanter's *Home Before Morning: The Story of an Army Nurse in Vietnam*, Rhonda Cornum's *She Went to War* about her experiences as an Army doctor captured and held as a prisoner of war in the first Gulf War, Jess Goodell's chronicle of the Marines' Mortuary Affairs unit, *Shade it Black: Death and After in Iraq*, Michelle Zaremba's *Wheels on Fire: My Year of Driving . . . and Surviving . . . in Iraq*, Janis Karpinski's *One Woman's Army: The Commanding General of Abu Ghraib Tells Her Story*, Kayla Williams' *Love My Rifle More than You: Young and Female in the U.S. Army* and *Plenty of Time When We Get Home: Love and Recovery in the Aftermath of War*, about dealing with her husband's post-traumatic stress disorder (PTSD) after deployment; to plays such as George Brant's *Grounded*, about a female air pilot whose job changes to drone control in Nevada (performed off-Broadway, directed by Julie Taymor, starring Anne Hathaway); Shirley Lauro's *A Piece of My Heart*, an experimental play about nurses in Vietnam; and Judith Thompson's *Palace of the End* with its interior monologue reconstructions of Lyndie England and Nehrjas Al Saffarh (a Communist Party member tortured by Saddam Hussein's secret police); to a form of ethnography/journalism splattered with fictional license exemplified in a book like the acclaimed *Soldier Girls* by Helen Thorpe and Gayle Tzemach Lemmon's much publicized *Ashley's War: The Untold Story of a Team of Women Soldiers on the Special Ops Battlefield*, among others. Some of these works display establishment endorsements or ideological perspectives, like a foreword by Major Tammy Duckworth (Director of the Illinois Department of Veterans' Affairs) for Kirsten Holmstedt's *Band of Sisters*, its sequel *The Girls Come Marching Home: Stories of Women Warriors Returning from the War in Iraq* with its research assistance from the Pentagon, Leon Panetta's blurb in Tanya Biank's *Undaunted*—"women had to be given a fair shot to serve in combat. In fact, they were already in combat"—, or, in contrast, the first pages of Helen Benedict's *The Lonely Soldier*, where she talks about an anti-war protest with women soldiers speaking out against the insufficiencies of equipment, sexual assaults, and other mistreatments. Indeed, as Anna Krylova has demonstrated in the context of Soviet women combatants in World War II, "the very notions of womanhood and soldierhood [do] not stand in self-evident intuitive disagreement with each other" (13).[13]

Literature, it may be said, has a long history of involvement in war, possibly dating back to its "beginnings," where war can be considered as literature's condition of possibility (i.e., *The Iliad*). In fact, war literature has its own economies of meaning. What I mean by that is that when a novel constructs its own scene of war experience, it refers as much to other literary texts as to literature's outside; it circulates, judges, borrows from, and exchanges with other literary texts, specifically ones about war. The current "surge" of literary interest indicates that taking a position in relation to the question of women in combat lends itself to literary form—in other words, that literature's history helps to build a context in which such a question can reside. The inclusion of women combatants in war literature mixes up war's structural forms with civil society's narratives, to the extent that normal economic relations resemble a war zone. This has large implications for what we expect as civil society's functions.

In a liberal society, the civil sector is meant to be the space where human need is tended to for the sake of living, that is, a zone—often identified through the work of women—where the human body is recognized as vulnerable and so requiring care and protection; in opposition, war is imagined through the continuity of health, strength, and vitality in the service of violence, the physical body resisting the onslaught of time or the infliction of injury for the sake of action. In the twenty-first century, advances in technology have allowed the organic human body to seem to transcend the life cycle, need, the wearing of time, and the susceptibility to injury. Women's bodies at war must then appear differently from

26 Women in the War Story

their historical image on the edge of the war narrative.[14] The women's combat narrative rewrites liberalism's versions of the time of life and the time of care in relation to state violence by recoding its tale about gender. Specifically, this chapter shows, the women in combat narratives rely on a denial of gender—a statement about why gender does not matter in the business of war, why it no longer needs to be considered in relation to care—in the name of the body's abilities to overcome adversity, threat, and dissipation through technological enhancement. This claim of the body's merger with technology offsets expectations of work based on improving the human condition through effort, by reconceiving the protective function of civil society as technological management rather than as a response to human need.

Literature indicates that, as much as war is an event, it is also a narrative—it produces relationships between identity, history, and time. Specifically, inserting a woman into a war narrative serves to expand the narrative out of the traditional time-and-space frame containing war—the "field"—so that the time of war exceeds the time of battle, the time of action, and even the time of deployment. The shift in the conventions of telling time in the war narrative is significant, because wartime traditionally has been measured in terms of the soldier's corporeal presence in the action, or rather, his time of life as a fighting force. The lengthening frame of story time in the war story occurs through forms of repetition that characterize the experience of time in war and model work on the outside. The narrative boundary between war and its afterwards, or between war's build-up and war itself, becomes less discernible. Instead of civil society marking the end or the border of war, it appears no different, another phase of the fight. Whereas, for example, in *Fighting France, From Dunkerque to Belfort*, Edith Wharton travels into the war zone in the wake of the battle, observing from a distance its frightfully beautiful remains—"When I looked out my window this morning I saw only the endless stretch of brown sand against the grey roll of the Northern Ocean and, on a crest of the dunes, the figure of a solitary sentinel" (no page number)—, a figure like Riverbend in the two-part blog *Baghdad Burning* describes civil society itself as inside the war, and the war as defined through a set of work stoppages, equipment breakdowns, and domestic outages: "The electricity has been terrible lately—it comes in fits and starts. The moment it goes off, we start running around the house unplugging things and flicking off the power switches" (162). War temporalities repeat as administrated civilian relationships, mundane activities, and everyday transactions, and the war work itself can be seen as modeling other work, like mirrors upon mirrors, an endless repetition of the same.

In the traditional war narrative, the zone of injury, on the one hand, and, on the other, the zone of securities, protections, and care were separated by a barrier of violence: the frontline. In the women's combat narrative, injury prevails within civilian relationships. In *Band of Sisters,* for example, a U.S. Navy nurse, Lieutenant Estella Salinas, for example, is known as one of "the healers of the guardians of peace" (269). Salinas' commitment to helping the troops distinguishes her from the Iraqi mother and father who refuse to accompany their injured child being medevaced to a hospital base, or the Iraqi grandmother and aunt who sit at a distance from a boy who has been shot at a checkpoint. While criticizing the Iraqis for such disaffected parenting, about herself Salinas remarks, "How could a woman who prided herself on providing a stable environment for her children agree to go to war?" (268). Perhaps hypocritically, Salinas considers her own departure from her children, in contrast to the Iraqis' (which was evidence of bad parenting, even though they did not "choose" war), as a "job equalizer" (270): women should leave their children because men do, so that the family, any "good" family by definition, has a tear at its very center. Not only does Salinas "treat these patients [American service members] as if they were a family member" (271), painting an image of the family as bound through injury, but also her own family is constituted through sacrifice and abrasion.

The war story might be called a *genre*, and, as such, its contemporary features can be compared to other samplings of the genre in other periods and settings. Since one of the features differentiating these war stories from the canonical ones is the recognition of women in combat, the mutations of the narrative can be said to constitute, at least in part, an emergent narrative about gender.[15] I am interested here, as well, in how the home front takes on war's narrative features. Challenges to habits of representation spill out over the barriers of war's harried twentieth century front in order to upset our conventional narratives about the sociality that the war inhabits. In particular, the repetition of the war story's conventions within civil society's narratives reveals new economic relations under neoliberal governance as constructed with features, forms, tropes, codes, and lineages of contemporary war cultures.

The literature of women in combat works at the point of breakage between war as a specific system of representation and everything else. The traditional war narrative sees the time of the war as unique and set apart, the time of adventure or the event: special and different, ebullient, ecstatic, momentous, as I describe below, linked to the male body in living action. In narratives of combat women, the representation of war occurs outside of war as much as inside of it, and often there is no difference. As the woman's war narrative understands the war as a continuation of everyday practice instead of as a time of exception, civil society's deprivations and alienations echo the effects of war work. "At least from Michelle's vantage point," Helen Thorpe expounds in *Soldier Girls,* "war consisted of being stuck every night on a former Soviet base where the biggest issue was boredom" (189). War is a prolonged reflection of the regularities and recurrences of the everyday time on the home front, extending without limit. "What would happen after we occupied the country?" reflects Jane Blair on the eve of the Iraq invasion, "Would Walmart and McDonald's miraculously appear?" (98). The co-extension of civil society's narrative of care with war's story of violence lays bare the repetitive and administrative time of civil society as war, structured as a schedule of controlled and repeatable, commercializable, alienable tasks rather than through a model of

28 Women in the War Story

progress, that is, rather than as a break, an exception, a redirection, or an escape from the controls of mechanized or routinized time,[16] a transformation of the world. War no longer seems like an adventure—a forward-propelled destruction of its past—but, rather, like a job.

Conventions of Care

Whereas the civil sector in the liberal state is seen to be responsible for the flourishing of functions of care, women's combat narratives slide civil society's functions into the military apparatus, making the military itself what the civil sector is supposed to be. As the only remaining source of public or political agency, violence is normalized, as Zygmunt Bauman shows, in response to "a *structural* problem, related directly to the passing of control over crucial economic factors from the representative institutions of government to the free play of market forces" (19), creating insecurity. In the absence of a functional civil sector with institutions promoting security and care and representing citizens, military institutions are tasked with taking on that role. When, for example, Michelle Zaremba questions one of her companions about deploying after giving birth, she responds, "in order to better her life for her son, she needed to stay in so she could receive the educational benefits" (104). The debates about women in combat reinforce general trends in economic restructuring, corporate dominance, and insecurity, where civil society's function of care has broken down, and civil society itself needs, instead, to be commanded by corporate regulative controls, work routinization, labor discipline, bureaucratic repetitions, and violence. These women's combat narratives extend beyond the framing devices used in earlier works, where the war is depicted as a series of battle scenes and actions. In contrast, in the lead-up to the war, the would-be woman combatant confronts multiple situations, for the most part, of absences or failures of care: in the face of a type of brutal economic blockade caused by unemployment, undereducation, deprivation, and the like, those in parenting roles fail to protect and provide, and, in parallel, the state via the military fails to come through on its promises to substitute in for the parents by providing the missing care. The women's combat narrative foregrounds the narrative of the broken democratic, care-giving promise of the welfare state that Bauman scrutinizes.

The combat woman narrative makes civil society's insecurities recognizable, even eventful. The canonical image of women in war stems from the dutiful Penelope in *The Odyssey* who faithfully awaits her husband's return. If the home in liberal society is meant to be a refuge from the hostilities of public interaction and exchange, the woman combatant shows that this space of care and this world of hostility reside in the same body. They do not, as in *All Quiet on the Western Front,* for example, sit at different ends of a train journey, separated by meadows and farmyards and waving children on station platforms. In George Brant's one-actor soliloquy play *Grounded,* rather, the pilot is peering into a screen inside the desert hills of Nevada, following a lead terrorist who is driving in an Iraqi desert, and she sees that "A girl runs out of the house, Runs out toward the car, A little girl is running . . . It's not his daughter it's mine" (66–67). The temporal and spatial hiatus collapses; the woman's promise of care and the soldier's engagement with violence combine so that the narrative is repeatedly pushing against two phases of the social contract. The war narrative ceases to progress towards an ending outside of war but rather spirals back inside so that the outside is revealed as inside all along. The woman combatant's narrative promises care and simultaneously breaks that promise. Instead of building towards some resolution or end of conflict, history repeats as moments of care's failure.[17]

Traditionally, features of care are pushed out to the edges of the conventional war narrative: "But we are swept forward again," Remarque details the experience in the trenches in *All Quiet on the Western Front*, "powerless, madly savage and raging; we will kill, for they are still our mortal enemies, their rifles and bombs are aimed against us, and if we don't destroy them, they will destroy us" (115). "Taken from their women," writes Enid Bagnold in *A Diary Without Dates*, ". . . as monks or boys or even sheep are housed, they do not want, perhaps, to be reminded of an existence to which they cannot return; until a limb is off, or the war ends" (123). The temporal framing of the women combatant's war narrative challenges the spatial expectations that would place women outside of the war scene where social wounds can be healed, as an "after" or an "elsewhere" to war.

The conventional war narrative tells the story of war by starting with the war already *in media res,* with men already in action—"Sometimes in the dark we heard the troops marching under the window and guns going past pulled by motor-tractors" (5), Hemingway begins *A Farewell to Arms*, after describing the landscape, or "We shot dogs," opens Phil Klay's award-winning collection *Redeployment*. "I hear O'Leary go, 'Jesus,' and there's a skinny brown dog lapping up blood the same way he'd lap up water from a bowl" (1). "When the Iraqi army of Saddam Hussein invades Kuwait City," boasts Anthony Swofford in *Jarhead*, "I'm in the base gym at noon . . . lifting a few hundred pounds over my chest" (9). Whereas the conventional war narrative limits the occurrences of war to a particular place and time, an exceptional moment that begins and ends, a defined location related to the male body in action, the U.S. combat women's narratives see the war as spread out and the characters as repeatedly confronting war's effects, war's enticements and sentiments, and war's destructiveness beyond what we conventionally recognize as the battle scene.

Narratives about women soldiers open often at home and often include the return home. Such expansion of the space of war infuses civil society with the destructiveness of battle: "Michelle had thrust through a childhood full of neglect, making her both headstrong and vulnerable" (3), Helen Thorpe remarks at the outset of *Soldier Girls*. "When Mickiela was fifteen," recounts Helen Benedict in Chapter One of *The Lonely Soldier,* "her mother was evicted for not paying rent, and the family was out on the street" (15). Such narratives, as well, frequently

30 Women in the War Story

do not end at the close of the battle action, including, also, familial disruption upon return. In *An Unlawful Order,* for example, Captain Chase Anderson, head of public relations, is the victim of the Marines' upper administration that wants to silence her discoveries of corruption: the Marine-81 helicopter is defective, but both political interests and private contractors have a stake in continuing its use. While in her post-deployment in Hawaii, her command chases her down, kidnaps her daughter, abducts her into a deserted wood, and threatens to kill her with a shovel and a pistol. In the combat women's narrative, war's distortion of care spreads throughout the social landscape. These narratives might point to the war as the cause of devastation in the social landscape otherwise attributable to changes in the economy, in the structure of jobs, and in the relationship between the state's public function and the state's citizens.

The combat woman's narrative is a developmental narrative, extending the war into its conventional "outside," where functions of womanly care traditionally set up a barrier to the war story. Enlistment is a choice, connecting war with the civilian field through a calculation where the risks of deployment are measured against the risks of staying home, equalizing the two. "'So there I was,'" explains Eli Paintedcrow in *The Lonely Soldier* about the aftermath of her husband Eddie landing in jail after attacking her, "'living in a one-bedroom, cockroach-infested apartment in San Jose with two kids, on welfare, and I'm thinking, 'What am I going to do?' That's when I decide to join the army'" (24). The list of hardships in the everyday encounters of such would-be enlistees raises the question of whether an all-volunteer army could sustain itself without large cuts in most other parts of the social safety net. Such characters often join the military in order to get such protective life-services as work, education, and social benefits for themselves and their families, and often learn that such benefits are still unavailable or insufficient.[18] In Julia Spencer-Fleming's *One Was a Soldier,* Clare Fergusson returns from war as a preacher unable to tend to her "flock" because of her addiction to drugs; George Stillman returns as a doctor with brain trauma who, having lost short-term memory, cannot serve patients; the veterans' therapist ends the session with the comment "*What a waste*" (original emphasis; 382); the problem of corruption in the military cannot be resolved; and Clare's declaration at the end that "I'm pregnant" (383) seems an insufficient remedy for this community in the process of dissolution. "It's like we're all sick" (167), announces Mary McNabb at a therapy session before committing suicide in her pool. The end of the war and the return of the soldiers do not promise security but rather an extension of the war zone's failures and insecurities.

In *Soldier Girls,* the field of war includes soldiers' social relationships and custodianship roles. Often, the women guards are communicating with home via Internet and cell phones while on the base or in the field, addressing problems of their kids at school or parental sickness. This contrasts with older stories where mail call was such an anticipated break to war's boredom and deprivations. The war itself is connected to failures of parenting resulting from economic downturn, and the civil plane shares scenes of devastation and abandonment that resemble combat. Commenting at the outset on the policy in the armed forces that "women could serve their country but only men should be asked to experience combat" (35), *Soldier Girls* follows and intertwines the life stories of three women characters through multiple deployments in Afghanistan and then in Iraq. Michelle's father had worked for Swanson Electric, but that had closed down, while her mother was a bookkeeper for General Waste, which also shut its doors. Michelle's military service evolves out of the loss of steady income due to deindustrialization in the heartland. Before enlisting, Michelle lived with her mother, who was poor and periodically unemployed, while her father, a truck driver who often landed in jail, lived in a trailer on the opposite side of town. "She wanted to get out of this forgotten place where good jobs evaporated and bad jobs drained the life out of people" (15). The two other main characters, Desma Brooks (who was in and out of foster care as a child and goes into debt paying for the hospital bills from her children's births) and Debbie Helton (who became a grandmother while deployed), were mothers themselves, often unable to provide basic security and care for their own children without their National Guard salaries.

Such breakdowns in mothering and nurturance in home life furnish the military with a ready-set of recruits who might look to the military for a substitute. "Big Brother," announces Emma Sky in *The Unraveling*, for example, "was watching you, taking care of you" (34). As the only remaining institution to promise care, however, the military, as depicted in *Soldier Girls*, practices bad mothering. "Debbie came to play a maternal figure to most of the men in the unit, and to a growing number of women who served alongside them" (28). Before 9/11, Debbie joined the Indiana National Guard's recruitment team and operated the retention unit out of a hot dog wagon, from where she listened to soldiers' complaints, providing "emotional lift" (39). After a time, the hot dog wagon started turning a profit, and rather than returning the money back to the state of Indiana, she gave it to soldiers who had trouble paying their bills. "Debbie adopted them all" (40), concludes Thorpe. As the civil sector is full of debt, depression, untrustworthy relationships, derelict authority, and helplessness, the military promises caring assistance, "tuition benefits as an inducement to enlist" (40), "a viable future" (27), a meaningful (262) and steady job, training, and income. Relationships developed in the army, conclude all three women, "were even more like a family than their 'real' families" (394). Yet, these families, the book shows, are no different.

Like the promises of security premised in civil society's protective role under liberalism, and like the security of parental nurture, the promises of a substitute military form of care are exposed as unfulfilled through the course of this book and others. Michelle, for example, has panic attacks and gets paralyzed in the toilet paper aisle at Target, overwhelmed by the abundance. Desma comes back with unbearable nightmares, loss of focus, and headaches, causing her to drive dangerously, even with her children in the car, and years later is diagnosed with a traumatic brain injury and given a small compensation that does not adequately

32 Women in the War Story

cover the financial losses sustained in her insecure employment. "None of the soldiers," Michelle concludes, "wanted to admit any difficulties, which would only get them tangled up in the army's cumbersome bureaucracy" (237). Just as the women themselves cannot adequately secure the well-being of their children, under the parent army's care they are exploited, exposed to risk, their education cut short, and their financial and emotional crises remain unresolved or worsened. As veteran medic Abbie Pickett confesses to Helen Benedict in *The Lonely Soldier*, "[T]here are women soldiers in Iraq who have been abused as children, who are abused again by their fellow soldiers, who are harassed by their comrades, who are serving with the men who attacked them, and who are enduring mortar and fire attacks, seeing the wounded and dead, fighting in combat, and living in constant fear for their lives. Every one of these experiences is a trigger for PTSD, and many women are enduring them all at once" (210). While the parenting role becomes economically ineffectual, the protective role of the welfare state also degenerates as it gets subsumed into war form. As Army sergeant and medic Michelle Wilmot realizes in *The Girls Come Marching Home,* "She would ask for night-vision goggles for evening convoys. Instead of getting the goggles, she was told to stop doing convoys. So she was supposed to stop helping wounded soldiers? It's a violation of every medic's code to refuse to give care . . . Time after time, Wilmot's requests for much-needed supplies were denied" (198). Later, Wilmot is arrested for trying to help a rape victim on another base.

War is both the cause of economic insecurity and the only projected solution to economic insecurity. A twist on this vision appears in Helen Benedict's novel *Sand Queen*, where the Iraqi home front intersects with the U.S. military base's prison. The frontline where the war zone touches the home territory becomes the setting for the entire novel. At the gate to the prison, the two main characters, Army Specialist Kate Brady and Iraqi medical student Naema, meet. The introduction of a woman in a combat situation is quite explicitly intended to project "the idea that the sight of a female soldier will win hearts and minds" (8), and the relationship between the two women initially opens the possibility of a mutual cross-cultural exchange of care between military and civil space. Ultimately, the U.S. military cannot accommodate this feminine ideal of care. Kate works as a guard and is assigned to the front gate to block the entry of prisoners' family members into the compound. Families of the Iraqi dispossessed line up at the gate to demand information about internees, and the army command worries that violence will break out at the base. Kate tells the Iraqis that the Army will provide a list of names of those held, but such a list never materializes. Naema Jassim is an Iraqi former medical student who speaks English and tries to bargain with Kate: in return for serving as an informal interpreter, she asks Kate to look after her father and her younger brother who had been rounded up in a house search. Kate seems at first to want to abide by her promise to account for Naema's kin but, in the meantime, gets harassed and nearly raped by a superior and then reassigned to a tower guardpost, where the prisoners shower her with verbal abuse, throw waste at her, and expose themselves. Distraught, Kate kicks a prisoner in the head, later to learn that this was Naema's father, and soon afterwards discovers that both her father and brother have died.

This breakdown in military authority parallels the breakdown in Iraqi civil structure. "A father carrying a blood-smeared infant, tears down his careworn face" (219), observes Naema while driving her grandmother to the hospital, where the grandmother will die. "I need water for my wounded grandson" (249), pleads an old man at the hospital, though water is unavailable. "Time becomes one long stream of agonized faces, heartbroken parents, of blood and burns and mutilations" (251), remarks Naema as she herself starts to assist the surgeries of dying children because the hospital is short on staff. As the military fails in its promise to offer security in its own ranks, Kate's promise to provide some security to Naema's family also fails, and Naema's efforts to provide medical assistance do not remedy the breakdown in hospital effectiveness. The army mistreats its promise of care to Kate similarly to the way Kate, as soldier, mismanages Naema's home front security.

With the flood of war-effects into civil life, the conventional methods of securing life and well-being are replaced by violent means. Another example can be found in Cara Hoffman's *Be Safe I Love You,* which recounts the after-effects of Lauren Clay's return from Iraq. Lauren had been abandoned by her mother and brought up in relative deprivation by an incapacitated father and his brother, a Vietnam vet. She joined the military because, in the face of such poverty, "[s]he had people to take care of" (90), she says. In a paranoid reversal of *Catcher in the Rye,* her traumatized response on return is to try to save her younger brother Danny from the same loss of care by kidnapping him, driving out to a deserted Canadian town, and teaching him self-reliance and survivalist skills in frozen isolation until captured in a violent stand-off with police.

The subjectivity of the returning soldier is constituted by broken social relations, institutional crises, and alienation. *Plenty of Time When We Get Home*—a sequel to Kayla Williams' acclaimed memoir about serving as a translator during the Iraq invasion, *Love My Rifle More Than You*—is a book that advocates quite explicitly for reform of veterans' health care and, in particular, for women's supportive services in line with the needs of combat personnel. *Plenty of Time* starts when Williams's friend Brian McGough gets hit by an IED exploding in a bus while returning to base from leave, the shrapnel tearing into his head. The rest of the book relates her constant struggle with his traumatic brain injury as he becomes abusive, even murderous, dysfunctional, and unemployed, unable to concentrate, with terrifying dreams, headaches, and memory loss, while the Veterans' Administration hospital (VA) dishes out the wrong medications and the wrong advice or neglects to pay attention, making it difficult even to get an appointment or diagnosing him inappropriately, resulting in his loss of benefits. As Brian, with Kayla's help, tries to figure his way through an institutional maze, he creates a situation for Williams no different than combat: "He stalked to the closet and grabbed his

34 Women in the War Story

gun from the top shelf . . . Our eyes locked, and he lifted the gun and put the barrel on my forehead . . . When his finger started to tighten, I closed my eyes in anticipation" (125–126). Such scenes repeat, imprecating the war context into the care relationship at home.

For Williams, as for Hoffman, the end of the war and the exit from the field of war mean the extension of the war front into every aspect of civilian life. The war is called upon to heal the economic violence that violates, damages, and disbands the family. The threat originates in civilian life—in the family itself—and continues on in domestic life "after" the war. The woman combatant exposes the contradictions between the promise of care that the liberal state offers in the family, on the one hand, and, on the other, the liberal state's definition of itself as the only legitimate purveyor of violence.

Remaking the World

The end of the caring functions of the liberal state is one aspect of a neoliberal reorganization in work that women's combat narratives help to normalize. The militarization of care assumes an acceptance that expected mechanisms of care are dysfunctional, and the social contract's promise has been misdirected, even discredited. The traditional public institutions that have been the sites to lodge grievances and demands, protests and rights claims within democratic cultures, now appear as failing institutions needing, instead, to implement aggression, discipline, and enforcement in a broken world.

A line of philosophical reasoning suggests that the double function of the liberal state—both violent and nurturing—reflects the contrast between the male body and the female body in the caring role. The man's body holds a residual of natural force that the state needs for defense, but that natural force, once under the custodianship of the state, ought to turn towards productive and cooperative forms of association and work. Hobbes, for example, imagines that man is composed of two bodily motions, one vital (or regular, automatic) and the other animal. The animal or voluntary motion inside men is called Desire and is motivated by appetites. Because there is no internal mechanism to stop this motion, war occurs "during the time men live without common Power to keep them in awe" (13). In forming the state, Man seeks security from the perpetual motions of other men. Man's body is a perpetual war-seeker that only the power of the state to bind men together through common interest and care will tame. The state (often quite insidiously), for Hobbes, breaks animal motion through care and cooperation.

This configuration was evident, as well, in Marx, where the worker takes the form of the Hobbesian instinctual body-in-perpetual-motion that gives itself over to productive cooperation and the security of the apparatus. As Alexandre Kojève points out, what Hobbes calls the Desire or the Appetite to obtain other men's objects becomes, in the master/slave dialectic, a Desire for "*Action* [or fight] that *transforms* the given being" (38) by transforming the object. For Kojève, freedom is defined as the subject's separation from the bodily fact as the subject transforms the material, through work; this separation can only occur by physically risking death in the fight for recognition; work is thus the expression of bodiless, subjective freedom in the violence of material transformation. For both Hobbes and Kojève, the body and its animal violence must be violently overcome in the drive for freedom, but for Hobbes, man surrenders the fight by giving over the body to the state's care, while for Kojève, man returns to the fight for another round. In his critique, Kojève thus notices that the social contract's promise of care is illusory or unsustainable, as care is a repetition of the compulsion to violently transform the world, risking death.

War can be understood, then, as both the clearest display of the social contract's historical moment and a prominent site for the exposure of its contradictions. War provides the conditions for freedom in transforming the world, but it also demands the relinquishing of freedom as a defense against the violent acquisition of others. As a site in the social contract, war also promotes power as a relation to human debility and to the human body in need. War overdetermines this relation and multiplies its expressions. Like war and related to it, language can also be seen to transform the world by substituting terminologies and allusions for physical vulnerabilities. As Elaine Scarry has remarked, "while the central activity of war is injuring and the central goal in war is to out-injure the opponent, the fact of injuring tends to be absent from strategic and political descriptions of war" (12). Scarry elaborates the myriad of linguistic and technical methods used to make the body in war invisible because, she says, physical pain is world-destroying. As the woman warrior threatens to return the body to the fighting arena, flaunting its vulnerabilities, the sense of her flesh must be displaced by prosthesis.

One method for denying the body in war, remarks Scarry, is to use a language that replaces terms of sentience with terms for the weapons that cause the wounding: to use the word "arm," for example, to mean weapon rather than the organic tissue extending between the shoulder and the hand.[19] To have no body is to be able to extend across space, the condition of power: to "have no body . . . is to be the wounder but not oneself woundable, to be the creator or the one who alters but oneself neither creatable nor alterable" (206). War, Scarry continues, is the most rigorous form of work, as it involves interactions with men and material that, as in Kojève, bring about alterations in the world and its systems of meaning that, in turn, alter the body itself (82–83). Even as war destroys the world and work makes the world, what work does, says Scarry, that connects it to war, is to distribute "the power of artifacts to remake sentience" (263). War transforms the world by replacing the care of the body with power.

Women's war narratives compel the soldier to deny the body—to "remake sentience" by substituting technologies for feeling and vulnerability. Comparing Air Force Lieutenant Colonel Polly Montgomery, the first female commander of

36 Women in the War Story

an Air Force combat squadron, to her aircraft the "Herk,"[20] Kirsten Holmstedt writes, for example,

> Montgomery and the Herk are about the same age, work tirelessly, and expect a lot from their crews while giving much in return. And they have similar personalities. However, Montgomery can claim significantly better health than the dilapidated aircraft, which has grown weary over the years.
> (Band of Sisters, *193–194*)

Like the portrait of Dorian Grey, the machine absorbs Montgomery's human side, experiencing the ravages of time to which her once-human body is now immune. The less-than-human woman combat machine dehumanizes the liberal promise and the social relations of work alike. As when those running the war obscure their commitment to out-injuring the enemy underneath a barrage of metaphoric displacements, the denial of the body in the name of equality diminishes the moral resonance of work, ignoring the injuries inflicted on the body by the inequalities inside the work process itself.

The War Novel and the Body at Work

Death, as Steven Miller argues, has historically marked war's limit, so that, as for Hobbes, the traditional modern war narrative often presents the space and time of war and the world as bodily extension. Yet, Miller continues, modernity's death drive has targeted not just life but the conditions that make life possible.[21] Traditional war literature, however, has emphatically insisted that wartime is coextensive with the ability of the male body to exert itself. As elaborated above, the traditional modern war narrative is organized according to the assumed spatial and temporal distance between the war front—the physical strength of the masculine body (its invulnerability) in its moments of action, conflict, adventure, danger, and violence[22]—and the home front—usually dead or alienated time where women and sentiment reside, where the war is over or on hold and the forward, historical movement of the war story is suspended. Think, for example, of arguably the most quintessential of twentieth century war novels, *All Quiet on the Western Front*. The time of the war is defined against Paul's leave, when he takes a train to visit his mother who, he learns, is dying of cancer: "Her hands are white and sickly and frail compared with mine" (159), he observes. "I hear my mother's breathing, and the ticking of the clock" (185). Consider as well Willa Cather's 1923 Pulitzer Prize-winning novel, *One of Ours*. Here, the plains of Nebraska promise Claude alienation and boredom as his wife engages in the temperance movement and sexual abstinence: "Platitudes, littleness, falseness . . . His life was choking him, and he hadn't the courage to break with it. Let her go!" (99). The war, on the other hand, as he runs along the trenches dodging debris and fallen bodies, offers Claude immortality: "Why, that little boy downstairs, with the candlelight in his

Women in the War Story **37**

eyes, when it came to the last cry, as they said, would 'carry on' for ever! Ideals were not archaic things" (188).

As opposed to female bodies, the male physique stands for the possibility of extending time on the frontline, against death and vulnerability. This is not only the case of how it appears in fiction: "Basically, women have turned out to be . . . much less tough and less capable than the leaders of the women's movement claimed they would be," reasons operations specialist and former Army infantry officer Jeff M. Tuten. "The results are clear. Men are substantially larger, heavier, stronger, and faster. Men have greater physical endurance. A larger percentage of their body weight is devoted to muscle and bone mass" (247). "The male/female upper-body strength difference is by now tediously well documented," Stephanie Gutmann criticizes Panetta's decision in *The National Review.* "There is no question that the average woman, . . . especially in our overweight times, will have difficulty, say, carrying a wounded comrade to safety and walking for days dressed in 'battle rattle.'" The male body is pure expenditure of energy: direct and material, spatially oriented, forward-propelled, weighty, blazoned with stamina, and active.[23] "Being an infantryman isn't just about uncomfortable living situations," writes Thomas James Brennan in a *New York Times* blog. "It's kill or be killed, blood, entrails and fear. We are a brotherhood; a collection of ragtag men who hunt and kill the enemy." C. J. Chivers worries in the *New York Times* about how women may fare in the Combat Endurance Test, where every lieutenant-student was forced "to go as fast as he could, never knowing how much energy and food to conserve" ("A Grueling Course for Training Marine Officers"), carrying rifles and packs across a brutal course in the brutal heat. The tradition of war writing has rendered the male body as the body-at-work, pure productive exertion like an industrial factory. "His body could keep up somehow," reflects the main voice in Dalton Trumbo's *Johnny Got His Gun,* "but it was the things inside of him that began to strain and roar. His lungs got so dry that they squeaked with each breath. His heart swelled from pumping so hard" (44).[24]

In fact, the field of battle replicates the features of the active male body: "Sand has invaded my body," Swofford describes his arrival in Iraq in *Jarhead,* "ears and eyes and nose and mouth, ass crack and piss hole" (15). Tim O'Brien's classic Vietnam War "fiction," *The Things They Carried,* starts with a long litany of physical exertion as the band of soldiers tramps through the jungle, hauling equipment, food, and personal effects: "To carry something was to hump it, as when Lieutenant Jimmy Cross humped his love for Martha up the hills and through the swamps" (3). The male body's seepage floods the landscape of conflict in O'Brien's text; the troops come to a field alongside of which a Vietnamese woman is gesturing a warning to them, but they continue to camp in the field and realize that the field is the dumping ground for the village without plumbing: "Just this deep, oozy soup . . . Like sewage or something. Thick and mushy. You couldn't sleep. You couldn't even lie down, not for long, because you'd start to sink under the soup. Real clammy. You could feel the crud coming up inside your boots and pants"

38 Women in the War Story

(139). The male troopers experience war's landscape as the boiling rot of their bodies flooding the frontline. One of the crew, Kiowa, sinks into the stew. The next day the men pull his body out of the waste, and the body itself has melted into the goop: "A piece of his shoulder was missing; the arms and face were cut up with shrapnel. He was covered with bluish green mud" (167). In contrast, O'Brien inserts the theme of the bodiless woman combatant as a romantic parody: one of the troopers arranges for his girlfriend to join them in the jungle, and she runs off with a squad of Green Berets: "No body was ever found," he ruminates upon her becoming-phantom. ". . . She had crossed to the other side" (110).

In the conventions of the war narrative, women, in contrast, suggest injury either in their activities as caregivers or in their own bodies. By showing men's injuries in the face of women's care, works by women describing their own experiences in earlier wars foreground the male body's fitness as what underlies the continuity of time in the war. Women tend to the pain, reviving the warrior's robust physical force. As Mary Borden describes her own "happiness" as a nurse in World War I:

> We conspire against his right to die. We experiment with his bones, his muscles, his sinews, his blood. We dig into the yawning mouths of the wounds. Helpless openings, they let us into the secret places of his body. We plunge deep into his body. We make discoveries within his body. To the shame of the havoc of his limbs we add the insult of our curiosity and the curse of our purpose, the purpose to remake him. We lay odds on his chances of escape, and we combat with Death, his savior.
>
> *(80)*

The intense scrutiny of the male body and the obsession with restoring its activity saturate the war nurse's narrative, even to where a knee joint left in a saucepan on the windowsill might get confused with a *ragoût de mouton* and, as such, nearly eaten. Similarly in Lynda Van Devanter's *Home Before Morning*:

> I could see the morgue and hundreds of bodies strewn haphazardly; the faces of eighteen-year-old kids wracked with pain as they lay dying. There were seventeen-year-old kids who probably hadn't had a chance to make love yet who had lost their penises . . . Or who were paralyzed and would never be able to throw a ball, run along a trail, or even lift a pencil.
>
> *(173)*

Representing care in a protected zone (although less already in *Home Before Morning*'s Vietnam than in Mary Barton's World War I), the woman at war is where the fight breaks down, its outer-edge. The nurse-author, as screen, projects what the male body should be and what the body at the front once was or will be: the active body at work.

Women in the War Story **39**

As a contrast to the pure energy of the working male body that animates the life of war, arguments for restricting women from combat borrow from conventional war narratives the practice of evoking the conventional female body—in its reproductive capacities but also in its sexuality—as a handicap: "There is no question," famously asserted, for example, U.S. General Lewis Hershey, director of the Selective Services from 1941 to 1970, "but that women could do a lot of things in the military services. So could men in wheelchairs" (quoted in Goldman, 895). In conventional war novels, women's sexuality turns into a wound; think, for example, of how, in *A Farewell to Arms,* Catherine, having nursed the narrator back to health, ends up miscarrying during a Caesarian section and then hemorrhages to death, quickly, after a series of desperate but inadequate surgeries: "Down below, under the light, the doctor was sewing up the great long, forcep-spread, thick-edged wound" (325), Hemingway writes, identifying Catherine's defenseless femininity with her surgical wounds. In keeping, in Michael Pitre's novel about the war in Iraq, *Fives and Twenty-Fives,* Sergeant Michelle Gomez (the only female character in the combat group) returns home paralyzed from taking fire in a failed assault, her diminished body visibly exposing the psychic residue of war: "She moans from time to time when she wants her position shifted, and when Denise [her sister] turns her, Michelle's long, black hair falls away to reveal a dent in her forehead where the skull is missing" (361). Women have changed from being attendants of wounds, as they were as nurses, to being themselves the wounds that combat inflicts. Instead of appearing on the edge of combat, envisioning the mended male body into the future, the woman in combat here forms the visualization of men's physical limits in death.

Conventional war narratives show that women's bodies produce vulnerabilities, in part because of their reproductive, sexual, and nurturing functions. Even when women are not riddled with physical shortcomings, disabilities, malfunctions, diseases, wounds, internal bleeding, and missing parts, the female soldier's body is often, as Laura Browder has noted, depicted as a site of sexual excess—"sexually out of control" (6)—treated as a "physical and sexual weakness" (7) or vulnerability, similar to amputation. "Sex is the key to any woman soldier's experiences in the American military" (18), confesses Kayla Williams in *Love My Rifle,* a book concerned with how American male soldiers' unwanted advances on female soldiers causes depression, isolation, and other psychological hardships. "I was tits, a piece of ass, a bitch or a slut or whatever, but never really a *person*" (214), she complains as she describes how group cohesiveness—a hallmark of military preparedness that the military insists women's presence threatens—breaks down in the face of sex. *Eyes Right* tells of a Warrant Officer in the Marines who is accused of "fraternizing" with a superior officer, and her interrogation and possible conviction threatens the career of a military general. Though sexual assault and rape are a real problem in the military, as has been chronicled by Kirby Dick's 2012 documentary *The Invisible War,* for example, its narrative generally forefronts women's sexed bodies, rather than sexism, as a vulnerability or even

40 Women in the War Story

an impairment in the war effort: women, it is understood, are hurt just by being women.

Work and Killing Machines

The combat woman's narrative shows the protective arm of the state absorbed into a scene of violence. Security can no longer hinge on a separation, a contrasted body difference, or a familial comfort in a civil zone. There are no train journeys or waving children between the place of injury and the place of care. Protection is, rather, a direct engagement with machinery. Unlike the security offered with the nurturing female body, technologies of security are not prone to the wearing of time, vulnerabilities to injury, or pain and, instead, can be sustained by replacements and substitutions of mechanical parts. Notice the contrast between, on the one hand, the Vietnam-era classic *Meditations in Green*—which, like *The Things They Carried*, equates the field of war with the field of reference to the active male body—and, on the other, Phil Klay's compilation *Redeployment* along with Kevin Powers' *The Yellow Birds*, both about the second Gulf War. The hallucinogenic quality of *Meditations*, with plants acquiring voice and character while characters are often symbiotically fusing with the plant-life in the jungle, sometimes renders the battle terrain as the outpourings of the insides of the soldier's digestive track, musculature, moisture, or viruses: in an airlift through the fight-zone, "there was the green and there was the blue each in its proper location and, nestling on his lap, inside the plastic map bag, were the warm soggy remains of Griffin's breakfast" (216). Or, on the ground, "He began to itch. But when he scratched he made ugly red furrows down his arms, soft dirty skin rolling up under his nails. Heat steamed from the soil . . . Flesh finally eaten by the plants. Snakes slithering in and out of their skulls . . . Fear smeared with mud the color and texture of human shit. Blood dribbling out of one ear. Claypool pointed to the forest" (157–159). The field of war appears as the circulations internal to the soldier, with the soldier passing through the field as a breath or a swallow would pass through him, absorbing, masticating, regurgitating, excreting, seeping, becoming energy, rotting away.

Alternatively, in *Redeployment* and *The Yellow Birds* (which barely acknowledge the participation of women in the armed services except in a few marginal auxiliary roles), the body is depicted as insufficient to confront the magnitude of the violence on its own, and the idea of technologies are introduced—sometimes in the form of writing or storytelling—to substitute for the body's deficiencies or replace what they lack. The nurse dies under enemy fire and is replaced by the epistolary. In *Redeployment,* women are often the recipients of the narratives that soldiers tell on return; as women, they complete the narrative of war by listening, assembling the fragments, and repairing the broken parts. "War Stories" features Jenks, a burn victim from an IED explosion without hair or ears or use of his legs or sex appeal and with so much scar tissue on his face that he has lost the capacity for facial expressions. Despite (or maybe because of) the narrator's warnings that if he tells his story it will not remain his, Jenks persists in telling it to Sarah, an activist wanting to include it in a play that would teach people about the war. Like technology, storytelling narrative performs as prostheses, functioning as the missing capacities of Jenks' body for the fulfillment of his desire. In "In Vietnam They Had Whores," the role of the woman as enabling what is disabled in the woundable soldier's body is linked quite explicitly to the machine: a whole platoon gets herpes—"half of them were [there] with their dicks oozing" (122)—, and the rest of the company is jealously certain that they have found the one whorehouse in Iraq. When the doctor asks them, however, they respond, "Ain't no whores. We been sharing a pocket pussy" (122). Feminine bodies are other to the male body's meatiness, its woundable mass, its limited time. Whereas, in *Meditations* and *The Things They Carried*, the inescapable, brutal, restrictive, disgusting materiality of the male body foregrounds the vulnerability of that body as the plotline through which the war story must tread; in *Redeployment* as well as in *The Yellow Birds*, the body's vulnerabilities, pain, and limits are made insubstantial as technology (sometimes as written text) supersedes the organic body.

In Kevin Powers' national bestseller and National Book Award finalist, *The Yellow Birds,* the male body-at-war fails as projecting the action that protects civil society's promise of security or transcendence. Instead, it heralds technology's promise as the body's replacement. *The Yellow Birds* tells of John Bartle, who meets Mrs. Ladonna Murphy, the mother of his platoon-mate Murph, on the eve of his deployment. "I promise I'll bring him home to you" (47), he lies. The promise becomes an obsession, a burden, and an oppression as the war progresses. During a patrol in a city, the platoon comes across a body bomb that explodes, leaving "chunks of the body" (127) hung from the low wall of a bridge. From that moment on, Murph begins to fade and disappear with "the actions of someone who was already dead" (159). After witnessing an explosion that kills a woman medic—"the last habitat for gentleness and kindness" (164–165)—, Murph flees. After a protracted search, Bartle and his lieutenant find his tortured corpse. Breaking protocol and risking a jail sentence, they float the body down the river where it joins with a stream of others. Then, Bartle writes a letter to Ladonna Murphy, signed by Murph, to fulfill the promise. The male body here proves to be tenuous, susceptible to carnage and made waste. Whereas the body in action is a vulnerable target, what remains is a promise, technology's defense against death—as writing, a replacement. The promise foreshadows the possibility of a bodiless war. The argument for women in combat is the opening of this possibility.

The argument that women should be able to participate in combat often relies on a denial of the body as gender in favor of the body as technology. As Army Captain Tammy Duckworth writes in the foreword to *Band of Sisters,* "I am not a big fan of being identified as a woman anything. I worked hard not to be different from the other Soldiers for most of my career" (vii-viii), even as she introduces a book specifically about what it is like to be a woman in the armed services. In

42 Women in the War Story

the new wars, technology replaces the body and gender along with it. Highlighting the army's pharmaco-techniques of shutting down feminine biological functions in preparation for battle, Helen Benedict summarizes in her ethnographic report *The Lonely Soldier*, "Women also have to contend with another problematic shot, one that men never get: the Depo-Provera birth control injection" (62). Kirsten Holmstedt's collection of heroic biographies *Band of Sisters* relates stories of women's warrior prowess augmented by technological prostheses that made the deficiencies of the gendered body obsolete: "Beside her was a .50-caliber, automatic, belt-fed, recoil-served, air-cooled, crew-operated machine gun. It was a gun that DeCaprio not only knew how to shoot but loved to shoot. It didn't matter that at sixty-one and a half inches, the .50-cal was as long as DeCaprio was tall" (139). This series of vignettes displays women fitted into jets guiding laser bombs from 17,000 feet above the earth and women's bodies mounted into Black Hawk-like helicopters: "she couldn't reach the pedals. The pedals were adjustable so she slid them all the way forward . . . Her small frame had grown bulkier with the addition of armor and a survival vest" (29). In *Undaunted,* Second Lieutenant Bergan Flannigan, platoon leader, loses her leg in an IED explosion. "She quickly got the hang of driving with her left foot" (299), we learn, and then, leaning on her prosthetic leg, she happily hears from her Captain, "I expect you to command an MP company someday" (300), since her biggest ambition is still to return to the front, no matter how painful and debilitating—and nearly deathly—the injury proved.[25] The wound of the body is overcome not only with technology but also with the indomitable drive of the American spirit and ingenuity. In technology, gender as the body has been surmounted, so the arguments about why women should not be allowed in combat are invalidated. The body has been made invisible along with its physical pain.

The woman's combat narrative proves that war narratives have moved away from their central focus on the physicality of the male body, on its efforts and exertions, its strengths and vulnerabilities. Ironically perhaps, the fleshiness of the male body is not replaced by an assertion of physical presence on the part of the female body and a corresponding awareness of the limitations of the male body's capacities for control and extension. Rather, the female body's differences are rendered as irritating and often amusing obstacles that can be offset by the ubiquitous involvements between humans and machines, the machine in fact transcending at every level the body's susceptibility to need, hurt, and deteriorate. Sentience has been replaced by technology. The argument that gender in war does not exist or matter is not new. What is new here is that the gender of the body does not matter because the body can be replaced by technology. An older version of war's obliteration of gender had to do with how the violence destroyed what was gendered in the body by destroying its life. Mary Borden wrote this about victims of World War I: "There are no men here, so why should I be a woman? There are heads and knees and mangled testicles. There are chests with holes as big as your fist, and pulpy thighs, shapeless; and stumps where legs once were fastened. There are eyes—eyes of sick dogs, sick cats, blind eyes, eyes of delirium; and mouths that cannot articulate; and parts of faces—the nose gone, or the jaw. There are these things, but no men; so how could I be a woman? . . . It is impossible to be a woman here" (43–44). For Borden, organic life is animated in the gender of the body. Now, instead of incipient death destroying gender as life, technology overcomes gender by overcoming death.

The increasing marginalization of the human body in the war narrative can be seen already operative in a book about a woman doctor in the first Gulf War, *She Went to War*. This book explicitly reminds us that the only reason gender matters in the Army is that "Army policy—and army politics—did not allow women in combat" (68) because otherwise "when we're busy doing our jobs, it doesn't matter to anyone if I'm a woman or a man" (68). Army Major Rhonda Cornum gets shot down in a Black Hawk helicopter while on a search-and-rescue mission, accompanying the troops in case the soldier lost behind enemy lines needed medical attention.[26] During the crash, she breaks both of her arms, injures her knee, and is shot in the back of the shoulder, sustaining shrapnel wounds as well as scratches, bruises, a laceration above her eye, and an infected finger. Though as a doctor, Cornum's work was mostly in the service of repairing the broken warrior body and getting it back on the lines like Barton and Devanter, as a prisoner of war, rather, she builds her narrative out of the wreckage of her own body, as its replacement: "It was horribly frustrating," she exclaims, "to not be able to control my own body" (18). Pages and pages are devoted to telling of the physical maneuvers necessary to eat, to wash, to walk, or to sit, or of the complicated details of how Rhonda urinated while in captivity without the use of her arms and with one of her legs dysfunctional. The first time two Iraqi guards help her out of her flight suit: "I could tell these men wanted to help me. They saw the situation as a problem to be solved. . . . They opened their knives and began to pick at the fabric of the sleeves" (53). Another time, she learns to use available tools herself: "By pushing gently with my fingers and rubbing my hips against the wall, I scraped the pants down to my knees" (112). The language of bodily need and dysfunction is quickly overtaken by a calculation about functionality and efficiency and an insertion of metal implements or fixtures that will ease the task that the female body is insufficient for or too damaged to complete. Technology's metaphor, the narrative here performs as the surrogate limb, fulfilling the routine charge that would have been decommissioned by the working limb's absence. This mechanization changes the nature of the work of war from one concretized in muscular power and the human will to modify the surrounding world to one that is automatized, governed by things, and divorced from human input, responding according to the capabilities of an external circuitry, an apparatus powered and authorized from elsewhere. Cornum's report shows the warrior's body as an extension of the machine.

The new field of combat, such reports imply, no longer requires a physical size and strength that would allow one soldier to carry another over a distance,

44 Women in the War Story

complete an obstacle course, or endure while carrying a heavy pack. Bergan Flannigan is flown out in an emergency-response helicopter that is radioed in from the ground after the IED attack on her convoy. The idea implied in these women's combat narratives is that the weaknesses, incapacities, and disabilities of the body can be remedied or absorbed in the machine, and that mechanized labor is therefore the answer to non-productive vulnerabilities, breakdowns in transport or communications, poor intelligence, or other insecurities in the production cycle. According to Manuel De Landa, military technological innovation doubles for historical change, which he calls "turbulence," a kind of self-generating order or self-organizing processes without cause for which he uses the term "machinic phylum": "These include all processes in which a group of previously disconnected elements suddenly reaches a critical point at which they begin to 'cooperate' to form a higher level entity" or "spontaneous 'cooperative behavior'" (6–7). An example would be, say, the invention of the cannon. Before cannons, towns needed tall walls for self-defense, and from the towers on those walls warriors could pour down boiling water or other repellant technologies; when the cannon came into existence, tall walls no longer would provide appropriate protections, and cities needed depth and sprawl rather than height. For De Landa, the cannon becomes a point around which production, social organization, and forms of knowledge are organized, giving new shape to military management, intelligence-gathering, command, control, and communications. The same would be the case for the transistor or the integrated chip; in particular, the chip grants the military methods for the instant feedback of information, avoiding bottlenecks and breakdowns by erasing human input in the process. Nobody, for De Landa, *invents* the cannon; instead, the cannon is the form offered by a group of elements that suddenly come together like a termite colony or a weather pattern, as an organic assembly or a robot. De Landa believes that war comes before production, and that production proceeds like the war, managing its supplies and controls in ways that eventually reach order. Like the women's combat narratives mentioned above, De Landa takes the working body out of its productive or transformative role in history.

The acceptance of women in combat builds on the idea that when they enter combat, they will not have to be women; instead, like De Landa's cannon, they can be parts of a cooperative organization like a "machinic phylum," a motor whose actions are decided elsewhere or not decided at all. "[T]he military has been using computers," De Landa specifies, "to get humans out of the decision-making loop [. . . T]o create a logistic network capable of withstanding the pressures of war, computers and programs must be allowed to make their own decisions, instead of being regulated by a central executive organ" (108). As history's elements assemble in the eruptions of war technologies, De Landa makes history seem increasingly lacking in cause or intent, in decision or responsibility. This effect is similar to the effect when gender disappears into the body of the machine. Portraying the work of her character as collecting the data-bytes of battle movements, Jane Blair in

Women in the War Story **45**

Hesitation Kills is critical of a doctor who claims that women should not serve in combat because they are "too emotional" (80). She responds:

> The imagery analysts were trained to look at extremely fine details—they could literally make out differences in models of vehicles with their extensive training. Their job was to watch the high-resolution video monitor and interpret what we were viewing. The collections analyst's job was to provide an enemy situational update and keep track of enemy movement and changes. He would also copy down SALUTE and SPOT reports on pieces of bright yellow paper.
>
> *(67)*

Devoid of pain or emotion, war is coterminous here with the collecting and sorting of data-bytes that will be organized, ordered, and made sense of by an unseen command center that will turn it into war-narrative, or strategy. The soldiers' bodies are not at risk, nor is the battle scene one of energy expenditure, physical conquest, and overpowering. Instead, friend and enemy alike are reduced to colored marks on a screen,[27] seen from a distance, that can be catalogued in order to produce a total map, an order—an "intelligence picture"—of the enemy's whereabouts and to turn that intelligence into tactics. "Like an elaborate game of Go," remarks Blair, imagining a spontaneous sense of purpose suddenly organizing the tumultuous disarray of electronic impulses, "the blue symbols marked coalition positions or 'friendlies,' and red enemy symbols marked a carefully orchestrated series of actions—together, they marked territory that would continually change as the battle space evolved over time" (85). Flights could then target equipment depots and enemy groups, animals, airplanes, and individuals by aiming at marks on an electronic chart. As officers record artillery distributions and arms networks as little black marks on little yellow post-its or as light paths on a screen, war doubles as a desk job.

As what diminishes the vulnerability or weakness in the female body, technology makes bodies disappear (and gender along with them). Whereas in *The Things They Carried,* the narrator confronts the enemy as a threatening body whose flesh would tear—"the left cheek was peeled back in three ragged strips. The wounds on his neck had not yet clotted, which made him seem animate even in death, the blood still spreading out across his head" (123)—, the enemy in war narratives that defy body-ness is often like a phantom. Shots, blasts, attacks, and explosions come out of seemingly nowhere, a hazy distance, and bombs are placed by the roadside with wires leading into dark holes or open ends. Occasionally, faceless dark shadows run in the distance or flashes of fire drop, without apparent human instigation, from bridges: "The Marines determined that the majority of the firing was coming from one house so they contacted air support. Within minutes, a jet dropped a 500-pound bomb on the house" (*Band of Sisters,* 22). The report does not end with a description of casualties.

46 Women in the War Story

Whereas in *The Things They Carried* and *Meditations in Green,* the war scene is organized around the body's exertions, in *Hesitation Kills* as well as in *Soldier Girls,* war is presented through disembodiment. In concert, whereas in prior war moments, production in ammunitions and supplies factories was removed, like women, to the margins as the war itself shredded structures and distorted meaning in the center, *Hesitation Kills* and *Soldier Girls* do not consider war's role in production or the demands war makes for more objects. Instead, these books envision war as coterminous with mechanical repairs: "She fixed gun trucks that were damaged by IEDs" (*Girls Come Marching Home,* 12). "If the spare aircraft was in the hangar bay," Kirsten Holmstedt describes Petty Officer Third Class Marcia Lillie's work in the Navy, "Lillie would power up the elevator, lower the Viking jet, wait for it to be repaired or for another one to take its place, and see that a functioning plane was ready to go on the flight deck for the scheduled departure" (*Band of Sisters,* 122). War work is the mechanized, controlled reconstruction of broken parts (rather than Borden's or Van Devanter's fixing of organic bodies), restoring the technological order to organized automation. War's assurance of continual maintenance of a familiar, repetitive procession of old commodities makes sense out of its turbulence.

The woman combatant's interactions with machines parody the war nurse's responsibilities towards the human body. Now, the machine is what needs to return to the front. This change means that what was once a project of care in the face of vulnerability is directly translated into a work routine on an ultimately indestructible body of metal. In *Soldier Girls,* the war in Afghanistan looks like a set of repetitive tasks marshaled at ever quicker rates. The soldiers were assigned the duty of repairing old AK-47s and making lists of the serial numbers. The army was concerned with rates of productivity, putting pressure on them to move faster through the process and offering rewards for raising the numbers of rifle repairs and inventory. The women learned to "[b]reathe, eat, and sleep AKs" (166), parts of their biological process, as they replaced old springs with new ones, unclogged the gas tubes, and replaced the missing or broken parts to get them back out in the action. Thoughts about the moral and political effects of quickly putting out more weapons in an already volatile situation[28] are part of the "peripheral vision" that might cause panic and so are stifled (243). Instead, in between work shifts, the soldiers experience boredom: "the biggest challenge she faced was what to do with her time" (190).

Scenes of truck convoys moving at various speeds across the treacheries of Iraq's bombed-out roads, or scenes of figuring out communications pathways, take the place of what in Vietnam novels were scenes of trudging—or in O'Brien's terms "humping"—through the forests. On their second tour in Iraq in *Soldier Girls,* Desma returns as a truck driver, and though traveling in at-risk areas, the work becomes relatively routine: loading heavy equipment daily onto the armored vehicles, repairing and replacing tires and other damaged pieces, adding extra layers of metal, fixing the air conditioner. The narrative edges into an orderly listing of maintenance costs: "Armored security vehicles were expensive—a Humvee cost \$140,000, whereas an ASV cost \$800,000 . . ." (300). When Desma drives onto an IED that explodes, the truck's injuries register pain before human casualties do: "Desma put her thumb into one of them [the deep grooves in the outer hull]. It fit inside the groove all the way up to the meaty part of the joint" (333). "Was he dead?" Desma wonders about her companion in the truck. "No, there he was, picking pieces of her tire assembly out of his gun turret" (332). With her confidence in the smooth and unquestionable, secure and repeatable, operability of her equipment, Desma scolds herself for a driving error, not able to acknowledge the possibility of technological failure, insufficiencies, or the enemy's expert modes of targeting their invaders and breaking apart their convoys by a dexterous concealment of roadside bomb triggers. Meanwhile, Debbie returns in her second deployment to a bureaucratic position, where she had the night shift making Powerpoint slides listing and relisting names of those with access to the base (343).

This workaday obsession with repairing equipment or editing databases can be distinguished from a prior type of war nurse narrative, where quick-fix-it surgery combined with other methods of survival care in order to keep soldiers alive while transporting them to better-equipped facilities for more extensive care. "'Sometimes it's easier,' Carl [the surgeon] said [to the nurse-narrator, Van Devanter], 'if you tell yourself they're not people you're working on, but merely bodies. We're not a hospital, Van. This is a factory'" (97), expounds Lynda Van Devanter in *Home Before Morning*. The point here, though, is not to substitute things for warriors in order to displace the site of injury, as in *Soldier Girls*. *Home Before Morning,* rather, is filled with surgical tales where the warrior's bodies are coming apart and flowing across the floor to the point where the medical professionals' own physical humanity starts to erupt and take over, surrendering, for example, to excessive vomiting, weight loss, exhaustion, and collapse. As the time of the war is structured around both the endurance of the victims' bodies and the stamina of the medical crew, the work of war, unlike in *Soldier Girls,* is not so much about automobile, software, or gun repair but rather about rehumanization: "trying to turn pieces of meat and bone back into human beings" (216). In the new women's combatant narratives like *Soldier Girls*, war work is, rather, standardized in its technological interface. The narrating of human exchanges with machines as war work constitutes what De Landa would understand as disparate, divergent, and chaotic historical elements suddenly and spontaneously coming to a point of order, a "machinic phylum."

Indeed, predictable order, work mechanization, and technological rhythms rather than organic ones are what is at risk. Desma is "ready to go home" (335), but what she and the others might expect as the end of their war story is not death or dismemberment—as the soldiers expected in *The Things They Carried*, *All Quiet on the Western Front*, *The Forbidden Zone*, or *Home Before Morning*, for example— but, instead, unemployment. "I had to go and tell them that, you know," explains Desma, "with the headaches and the anger and the issues I was having after my

48 Women in the War Story

last tour, I was unable to come back to work" (362). *Soldier Girls,* like *Hesitation Kills,* advances through the time of the war as a series of work-details that, in their technological uniformity, blur into each other and easily replace each other, rather than as consecutive episodes of intense danger and heroic feats based in physical prowess, exertion, progress, and transformation of landscapes and worlds. War is treated as a 9-to-5 activity, grudgingly replayed day after day. Alienation rather than fear is the dominant emotion,[29] and sex, drugs, and boredom in the off-hours are more often the response than self-defense, offensive maneuvers, heroism, or glory. *Soldier Girls* locates this type of monotonous enterprise in the "behind the scenes" of the operating base, while *Sand Queen* shows that even in stories taking place in direct enemy confrontation, right on the frontline of a base, women soldiers' work assignments appear as monotonous drudgery not as adventure: "'What a fuckin' dead day,' Kormick finally yells over the noise. 'Yeah, I hate this checkpoint shit,' DJ shouts back. 'No action at all'" (45). The guards stand at the gate all day, every day, with mostly nothing happening, as if they are in the prison rather than working as its guard. "Rows and rows of us robots, standing to attention, hands over our robot hearts, growling and squeaking out our national pride. Rows and rows of bare robot heads . . . We soldiers," Kate later says, "are nothing more than work and killing machines" (274–275). Though there are injuries, deaths, explosions, and attacks in all of these treatments, the banality of work overshadows and often obliterates the thrill and vulnerabilities of the battle, and time is governed by work's endless, daily recurrences, repetitions, and repairs rather than by the expectation of death or injury and the need for care.

The Reproductive Body and the Command Economy

The technologization of the fighting woman's body tells a story of the human, suggesting that the human has been degraded, if not disappeared, as an element around which work processes are organized and decisions made. Stories of women's pain—say, in nursing stories—historically reside at the edge of the war, at the place where the new identity, transformed by participation in a world-destroying moment, begins a new construction in a new world. With women in combat stories, however, the pain intended by war mixes with the pain of giving life that occupies the representational space of the female body, or, as Scarry puts it, world-destroying and world-creating tendencies intermix, forming a tight circle. As with the social contract under liberalism, where moments of care and moments of violence merge in the form of the state, so the pain of giving life converges with the infliction of war's wounds, and the symbolic patterns of identity formation appear as parables of death. Caught between life-giving and death-dealing, women's bodies come to appear as inorganic and non-human, disappearing entirely into the machine, inhabited by death: paralyzed, consciousness-less, impassive, and yielding.

The repercussions of obliterating the warring body in order to reconstruct the body as a working technology have to do not only with a denial of organic

Women in the War Story **49**

processes of death and pain but also with a change in the structure of identity and its relationship to work. As Adriana Cavarero has discerned, whereas the classical scenario of heroic warriors, with their face-to-face, hand-to-hand meetings and strenuous overpowering, assumed a reciprocal relationship between foes, the technologized body of mass destruction implies an asymmetricality as massive violence is levied against the helpless. Cavarero recognizes a state of non-action and non-identity as the human condition in this newly asymmetrical world of technological warfare. For Cavarero, what terrifies us in the face of massacre is not so much fear of death but "the spectacle of disfigurement" (8) where "[t]he body undone (blown apart, torn to pieces) loses its individuality . . . nullifying human beings" (9), where often body parts cannot be sorted out because of the absolute carnage, the total extinction of the human form. This picture of war "transforms the body of the warrior into a peripheral element of its mechanism" (94). This "horror," Cavarero maintains, "has the face of a woman . . . as though horror, just as myth already knew, required the feminine in order to reveal its authentic roots" (14). The entry of women into combat is never, according to Cavarero, a pathway towards equality but rather remains "particularly scandalous" or even "repugnant" (99) because women's roles always bring out the humiliation, degradation, and subordination consigned to a body thought of as giving life, the terrain of identity,[30] now broken and abstracted, no longer individualizable.

Cavarero is mostly concerned here with an ontological question. The question could, however, be equally applied to a changing imaginary of work, where the ascendance of the technological workplace can deny the relevance of the human form. Whereas the laboring body in Kojève, for example, used the tools of labor in its fight for recognition by its mastering adversary, in De Landa, technology guides historical change without the human, discharging the role of the human in ordering the world.

> From the sixteenth century on, drill and discipline were used to turn mercenaries into obedient cogs of the war machine. These military methods were later imported into the civilian world by schools and hospitals. To that extent, tactics, the art of creating machines using men and weapons as components, permanently affected nonmilitary institutions . . . [P]roblems of military procurement and supply shaped the urban environment in the age of siege warfare and continue to shape the world of economics to the present day. Logistics considerations regarding the procurement of manpower are behind the drive to get humans out of the loop.
>
> *(229)*

Controlling physical processes, technology makes the human formless and obsolete, nullified and conceptually void, defenseless before the magnitude and the violence that technology unleashes and demands. Since De Landa's machine landscapes emerge out of chaos, the human condition has no place in his historical view and therefore,

50 Women in the War Story

there is no place for gender. Cavarero, on the other hand, sees women killers as the symbolic form of this annihilation, and the pregnant body or mother as where this shattering takes place. The militarized woman's body—the working machine that ought to produce and reproduce the human form—can be said to be organizing the turbulence of a dehumanized condition in the face of a command economy.

The technologization of the women's combatant body turns upside-down a prior convention where women's bodies provided the sense of life by restoring the human as the answer to war. I might call this the "Mother Courage" effect, where motherhood is the domestic ground for the flourishing of a fighting force, often marshalling an opposition or a possibility of justice that was suppressed by the state or by power. *Peggy Deery,* for example, tells of a woman whose children participate in the Irish Republican drive for independence, her son Paddy dying in prison, her own role being to provide income and housing while also maintaining religious customs even in the face of threats and violence. In her memoir, novelist Gioconda Belli, who fought with the Sandinistas in Nicaragua, likewise equates the violence of the revolutionary struggle with the maternal body: "This slow journey in the truck towards the center of Managua had for me the taste of birth, or the final reward for the pain. My country was being born. I was laughing" (my translation; 326). The testimonial *Poppie Nongena* relates of a woman who is forced by apartheid to live in ever more restrictive housing areas, with ever less available work options until her brother Jakkie, her son Bonsile, and daughters Nomvula and Thandi get arrested: "I have found my way through everything, she thought, but through this I can find no way. Because this has been taken out of my hands, it has been given over into the hands of the children. It is now my children who will carry on" (Joubert, 354).[31] In Nadine Godimer's *My Son's Story,* the narrative focuses the son's attention on the transgressions of the father to conceal that the mother is the one hiding the grenades and the sister Baby, a mother too, is involved with the militias. In Mahasweta Devi's novel *Mother of 1084,* from the distance of her Bengali middle-class home Sujata connects with the political development of her son Brati until he is killed in prison: "He had lost faith in this society ruled by profit-mad business men and leaders blinded by self-interest" (19); she comes to identify with him. And, in a painful reversal of the birthing sequence in the play *Palace of the End*, Nehrjas Al Saffarh, a communist under Saddam Hussein's regime, is tied up and tortured, connected through a cord of sound to her son as he freezes to death on the roof outside for eight consecutive days: "For days and days I lay there, the only thing keeping me breathing, was that I could hear my son coughing on the roof. That gave me such happiness, to hear him cough. I knew he was sick. He probably had even pneumonia, but the coughing meant that he was alive! . . . Every hour was like a day, every day like a year, his cough was stronger and louder and then it began to get weaker" (Thompson, 38). The mother's body is a connection to an alternative world to be constructed, an admission that the present issues, the what-is-to-come of the human. These are only a few examples.

A changing situation of war is reshaping identity formation, even denying that there could be something like the "human" body in the human condition. Technology has captured the reproductive function, and—rather than the massacres that Cavarero notes as turning the body inside-out, destroying its form, and erasing its potential for action—this technological capture of reproduction is what is nullifying the human by undoing the identity of the body. In a Sunday *New York Times* feature, "Reassuring Hands," C. J. Chivers tells of an Afghani woman in labor who was picked up from outside of Kundahar by a U.S. Black Hawk helicopter (usually used for transporting the injured) and flown to a hospital. While Chivers attributes the need for the intervention to the backwater poverty of the province, the woman's birthing body becomes the embattled site between clashing cultural claims. The Afghani woman's full body is veiled, and as the on-board medics are figuring out how to perform a Caesarian section, the Army pilot, Captain Amy Bauer, keeps time: "How much longer?" screams the medic into the cockpit; "Seven minutes," replies Bauer. In the photograph, as the woman's body slopes downward horizontally from the center left to be cut off by the bottom frame, her head is further blocked out by the medic's torso as he monitors the IV. The head that centers the photograph—erect on the vertical—is, instead, that of her husband, surrounded by wires and switches, seeming to be the subject of the action even though he is outside of the action. War technologies are now inside the reproductive process rather than bordered by it.

What is striking in the story is the marginal position of the birthing woman in the depiction of reproduction, as it is overtaken, monitored, and timed by the body of the Black Hawk, its equipment, clocks, and attendants. The article opens with a description of the woman's heart-wrenching pain, but as the woman and her child surprisingly survive, the story fronts a celebration of technological mastery as the goal of the war, "remaking sentience" by "winning" the war against bodies in pain. The triumph is accomplished with the woman, Captain Bauer, at the helm, commanding time. The real difference between the two warring cultures is that Afghani bodies experience pain. Without pain, the U.S. cannot lose the war, the article suggests, and reproduction seems pain's last recourse, its final injury, its dying cry. No longer subject to the pain of reproduction and cultural marginalization, the female captain is at work at the controls from beyond the photographic frame, deciding the victory by—without body—becoming an extension of the timeless machine calculating time.

The war machine projects work as a disembodied control over the activities of bodies in its management of time. In her memoir *Shade It Black* about serving in a Mortuary Affairs unit in the Marines, Jess Goodell's job is to collect and sort human remains for return to the States. With work and technology governing war, marking the identity of the human body becomes the processing of an inventory (37–38), the performing of a work ritual (49), or the enforcing of a regulation (42) rather than the delivery of a child or the granting of a name. Identity is assigned without recourse to the body: "We tried to identify each body," she sketches the

52 Women in the War Story

responsibilities of those in her position, "but that wasn't always easy . . . Initially, we fingerprinted them but did not continue the practice for very long because it became too difficult. There were not always fingers" (38). Here the woman's role is to administer violence by reducing what might once have been bodily pain to a series of calculations, administrative categories, counts, and bureaucratic reports: "We would get the appropriate form and mark the outline of the body with dots or Xs" (38). From beyond the frame, responding to marks on a chart, Goodell, like Captain Bauer, stands beyond human time.

The work of the Marine Corps does not advance according to human decision here but as if obedient to self-operating controls, "parts of a single organism," Goodell continues, "a kind of connectivity" (19). Inside this self-organizing machine, the body has been made obsolete: Goodell displaces what opponents might label as female handicaps[32] onto other physical abnormalities like overweightness or unfitness, submitting that under-performance might be remedied by stricter discipline and command: "If we do not meet regs, we're enrolled in a body composition program" (42). In the face of the massive power of this war machine at work, the human body comes apart helplessly, chopped up into the "vaporized mush" and "liquidy flesh" (109) of the desensitized body. Instead of the feminine body in pain giving life to a human form, Goodell pulls a piece of equipment out of a blasted pile of remains: "At times I found gear in the flesh: . . . I pulled at a line that came up out of the goop, a phone cord with a receiver on the end" (109). As Cavarero anticipates, this loss of identity in the technologized body is "particularly scandalous" when it has the face of a woman: where one expects the giving of life, Goodell is haunted by plastic, metal, wiring, and ghosts. The role that Cavarero grants to the victims of massacres—of exposing the helplessness of the human condition before technologies of mass destruction, the loss of the individual—is here paralleled in the devastated figure of humanity before the overwhelming power of the mechanized work routine and its instruments.

Conclusion

The so-called "War on Terror" unleashed violence across the globe. It was initiated on false pretenses against an enemy that cannot be recognized or defined. It continues to be waged behind a shadow of command and secrecy, impervious to law, with no end in sight. Though justified on the basis of human survival and just living, this war should be acknowledged as creating, instead, threats to security and to life itself. This situation of war rose in conjunction with global economic transformations that shared many of its causes and consequences. The flattening of wages and the consequent surge in worker debt, the transfer of capital from manufacturing to financial speculation, the weakening of democratic national authority in the face of the power of the corporation, the diminishment of the social safety net, the large-scale technologization of capital and the work process, all of these factors contributed to instabilities in the social contract—the historically-developing weakness of the nation-state to deliver its promise of security—that motivated military enlistments.

That such instabilities in the social contract should come to inhabit, even reconstitute, women's bodies should not be a big surprise. After all, women's historical social place—as homemakers and caregivers—situates them as stalwarts of the non-violent half of the state's liberal compromise, its currently dysfunctional caring arm. Cuts in welfare provisions, culminating in the 1996 Welfare Reforms, disproportionally affected women, leaving them in search of alternative resources. As well, their role in prior wars—as nurses, ambulance drivers, suppliers, arms manufacturers, sex workers, letter-writers, administrative staff, cooks, mothers, girlfriends, sisters, and fiancées—made them into standing proof that the military itself could and would become a substitute for what was lost to care.

The politics surrounding Leon Panetta's policy change admitting women into combat compels women to argue that their bodies do not handicap them for military service given the ubiquity of technology in twenty-first century techniques for waging war. The argument forces the image of the technologized women's body as the non-gendered body to resurface continually. The image serves many functions besides simply promoting women's military inclusion, an adjustment that had already occurred anyway on the ground and did not require major logistical maneuvering as its retractors said it would. The narrative of the degendered technologized body of the combat woman also foregrounded an economy less and less responsive to human need. This narrative reveals that the broken promise of the state's protective arm is being replaced, in the name of equality, by the false promise of a dehumanized, mechanized work routine commanded by the impositions of technologized capital. The worker in this view is not connected to the Kojèvian craftsperson, working to transform himself by using his tools to transform the objects of his world in a fight for recognition, but rather to a passive recipient of directives for executing war with no recognition possible. The conceptual collapse of the body into the machine also means an erasure of time from the work equation, for the time of life and the time of care no longer can pose a limit to a war that occurs outside physical corporeal demands (as pensions and healthcare insurance can be erased from the work contract). So, unlike De Landa, I do not believe that the organization of chaos or turbulence into the advent of this new military technology—the technologized body of the combat woman—necessarily happens without intention. The intention is to make war work seem more like civilian work—supposedly, less dangerous, more routine—in order to justify that civilian work should be acceptable as war work, less protected, riskier, more insecure. The loss of the body takes the "human" out of war and its politics. Though the "human" has been treated with skepticism lately and accused as complicit with a universalism that has historically boosted imperialist power, the technological replacement of human sentience invents a post-human that also greases those imperialist wheels.

54 Women in the War Story

An older tradition of war literature that elucidates, with Scarry, that war is about out-injuring the enemy or, with Kojève, that war is about transforming the world through violent physical exertion, insists that war is bracketed in the time of the living body. Just as Marx taught us to understand working bodies as affected by a struggle over working time, war literature reveals warring bodies as engaged in an active political struggle over the control of living time. This understanding sits uncomfortably inside a contemporary technological triumphalism, where wars (like production) are supposedly won by replacing bodies with machines at ever quickening rates, sweeping aside any consideration of human bodies entirely. War narratives bring into focus how the demise of the social contract under neoliberalism has disconnected the body from a discourse on care that needs political reconstitution. Contemporary war literature repoliticizes the body, showing how the vulnerability of the body to injury has faded over time, moved from the center to the margins of the war story, replaced by an image of the body as mechanized as the work process. The ascendance of a culture steeped in celebrations of technology positions the body outside of the political frame. Referencing an older political framework, war literature cannot help but call attention to the body-in-need that demands a political response, a newly constituted "world-creating" through the remaking of sentience.

Notes

1 At the time of this writing, the American public is facing the very real possibility, as well, of a woman, Hillary Clinton, taking on the role of commander-in-chief of the U.S. military.

2 Though the current wars have their own methods and technologies for exposing the falsity in the ideology of the frontline, the frontline has in fact been a fiction for quite some time, and cultural critics have noticed. "[T]he U.S. Army's contradictory attempts to preserve the distinctiveness of the male soldier as combatant during the Second World War," remarks, for example, Yvonne Tasker, "and to treat female soldiers as non-combatants, whatever task each was performing, became increasingly strained" (5). Speaking of World War I, cultural historian Susan Grayzel notes, "While the experience of Frenchwomen under occupation challenged the division between home front and war front, the emergence of air warfare—and the air raid in particular—further blurred these boundaries, such that the crucial divide between combatant and non-combatant began to erode" (13).

3 "For a working-class woman," writes Woollacott of World War I, "munitions work provided a means of patriotic participation . . . Women had entered industry, shifted to munitions jobs, took up charitable works, and joined the paramilitary forces with resolution and energy" (127).

4 Whereas Miriam Cooke remarks on literature's role in turning "the chaos of the civil war into the militarized order of the War Story" (24) or Susan Grayzel proposes that literature exposes "the role of war in determining the meaning of gender and of gender in determining the meaning of war" (3), literature can also play a spectrum of other roles in relation to war: it may call out the disorders, incoherencies, and resistance to meaning in the war experience—as Margot Norris suggests, the "suppression of the historical referent" (34) in the war narrative, or the suggestion that there is something in war that eludes war's narrative.

5 In contemporary war literature, this structure of gender might still appear, but the nurse has been replaced by the civilian diplomat. Emma Sky's war memoir, *The Unraveling*,

Women in the War Story **55**

for example, relates Sky's work, as a British citizen, managing conflict in Kirkuk and then in Baghdad, working directly under the military authority of General Raymond Odierno, even while in the employ of the Coalition Provisional Authority (CPA), established in 2003 under the civilian authority of Joseph Bremer. Sky—"the only female in the room" (46)—starts her Iraqi mission in Kirkuk, where she claims success in mediating antagonistic interests between ethnic and commercial sectors. Sky oversaw the civilian functions that the U.S. military was performing in the absence of an Iraqi civil state, trying to heal the fissures imposed first by Iraqi cultural histories and then by the invasion: "the military," she writes, "had got stuck into trying to improve the lives of the Kirkukis. They were identifying priority projects in the province, tendering out work to local contractors, managing large amounts of money. Tank commanders were working on economic development, paratroopers on governance, civil affairs officers on education" (43). In the second half of the book, both Odierno and Bremer understand the value of having someone who can organize the healing of Iraq much like the nurses administered the healing at an earlier time, and they recruited her to head such efforts in central command. Sky's participation marshals in economic remedies, building markets where, in earlier modern wars, her predecessors bandaged wounds and drained infections.

6   Critics generally classify war literature along familiar lines: by nation, by the particular war, by region, by epoch, or by intention (for example, civil, anti-imperialist, revolutionary). I choose not to make such distinctions here because I want to analyze U.S. women combatants' advent into the literature of war as requiring a distinct set of symbols and narrative considerations that can be identified and distinguished from the conventions of men's appearances in war literature.

7   In his book about the surge in Iraq, *The Good Soldiers,* David Finkle addresses issues of preparedness in this way: "'We got some stupid fuckers,' Kauzlarich [U.S. Army lieutenant colonel who led 800 soldiers in the surge, and the main character] said . . . It was something they had been dealing with since they began forming the battalion. For several years, in order to meet recruiting goals, the army had been accepting an ever-increasing number of recruits who needed some kind of waiver in order to become soldiers . . . Some of the waivers were for medical problems and others were for low scores on aptitude tests, but the greatest percentage were for criminal offenses ranging from misdemeanor drug use to felonies such as burglary, theft, aggravated assault, and even a few cases of involuntary manslaughter. In 2006, . . . 15 percent of the army's recruits were given criminal waivers" (120). The effect on performance was so great that the lieutenant colonel called it a "crack" with a "measurable effect" (119) on the U.S.'s ability to hold the region. Though the rate of women recruits at this juncture would have been the same, Finkle barely notices it.

8   Commenting on the situation at Abu Ghraib before the scandal, Janis Karpinski notes, "The best defense against mortars is offense, but we were not equipped to stop the insurgents before they could strike. That was the job of well-equipped combat units, which should have been provided by the armored division in Baghdad. But none of those units ever showed up at Abu Ghraib for a long enough period of time to be effective" (191). She attributes this under-supply, as well as the growing presence of private contractors, to the designation of Abu Ghraib and other military prisons as under female command and thus "non-combative."

9   As Janis Karpinski reads it, "As the Army restructured itself into a voluntary force after Vietnam, it was attracting plenty of male recruits who wanted education and training that would carry over into civilian life. But the Army also needed warriors, and there were not so many volunteers for that assignment. That's where the women came in. Our policymakers' plan over the next decade was to steadily expand the ranks of women holding jobs in combat support and combat-service support. As more women were given roles as truck drivers, supply officers, intelligence analysts, and the like, more men would find those jobs closed and be forced to join the ranks of the warriors. And

56 Women in the War Story

once you became a professional infantryman, you were much more likely to make the Army your career. There were lots of civilian jobs for truck drivers and electronics technicians trained by the Army—but not so many for combat fighters" (41–42).

10 Man "thinks of his body as a direct and normal connection with the world, which he believes he apprehends objectively, whereas he regards the body of woman as a hindrance, a prison, weighted down by everything peculiar to it" (xxii).

11 Lynda Hart noticed that aggression in women is always connected to deviant identifications: "one ghost in the machine of heterosexual patriarchy is the lesbian who shadows the entrance into representation of women's aggression" (ix). Since femininity has traditionally been bound to passivity, aggression in women is generally placed outside femininity's norms, onto racially, ethnically, or sexually "othered" women. Aggression in females, says Hart, is in fact so outside of expected norms that it can only be framed as criminal. Hart's point helps to elucidate the problem the female combatant poses for representation. The anxiety surrounding her exposes that crisis and threat are already inside any consideration of women and agency, especially violent agency. Freud was more ambivalent about the relationship of femininity and passivity than Hart asserts, attributing this assumed link between femininity and passivity to a social fiction.

12 This is a pseudonym for the same author who wrote *Eyes Right*, Tracy Crow.

13 According to Krylova, 520,000 women served in the regular Soviet Army during World War II, with another 300,000 in combat and home front antiaircraft efforts, "a level of female participation far surpassing that in the British, American, and German armed forces" (3). They made up 70 percent of all Young Communist soldiers between the ages of seventeen and twenty-six on the eve of armistice (3). Leading up to the war, Stalin, starting from the early 1930s, mobilized the population by linking industrialization to militarization, and asserting that both were in preparation of a global workers' revolution that was imminent within the next ten years. Stalin positioned the next generation as the one that would historically prove itself in the coming confrontation with capitalism. As a result, the generation coming-of-age in the 1930s in the Soviet Union witnessed transformations in popular and schooling cultures that encouraged both genders to feel the Soviet project as their responsibility and their challenge. "Party and Komsomol leaders steered away from drawing clear gender lines of inclusion and exclusion around defense campaigns. Nor did they attempt to insert into their public discourse definitive gender divisions of labor in paramilitary training" (48).

14 Modern war literature is tied up with the increasing destruction of the frontline—and its investments in the male physique, the male warrior—as the foundation of war's representation. As cultural historian Susan Grayzel has observed, the making and breaking of the frontline has been a standard feature of war literature throughout the twentieth century. The blurring of boundaries between the war's inside and outside can be seen, according to Grayzel, in the exchange of letters between the war front and the home front, memory, women's involvement in industrial work, arms and ammunition production (done by women workers), prostitution, health care, and technological change: "Zeppelin and airplane raids beyond the battle lines attacked targets miles from the war zone . . . and helped *literally* bring the war home to noncombatants and to women" (45).

15 As Margot Norris elaborates, "war writing is an inevitably intertexted process, obliged to contend with its own tradition of genres and conventions in the spirit of debt, opposition, or subversion even as it is haunted by the betrayals and inadequacies of its predecessors" (24). Norris (among others) links war's literary excess to the increasing inclusion of gender inside the space of war. In other words, the wider range of targets for destructive technologies used since World War I has made evident the impossibility of techniques of representation to catch up with the massive destruction rendered by such technologies (17).

16 As Horkheimer and Adorno explain administrative time: "[M]echanization has such power over a man's leisure and happiness . . . that his experiences are inevitably

Women in the War Story **57**

afterimages of the work process itself . . . What happens at work, in the factory, or in the office can only be escaped from by the approximation to it in one's leisure time" (137).

17 This tendency of the woman's combat narrative to show history as a repetition rather than as a progression is not evidenced in George Bernard Shaw's early twentieth-century plays *Major Barbara* and *Saint Joan*. In the introduction to *Saint Joan,* for example, Shaw writes, "[A]ll evolution in thought and conduct must at first appear as heresy and misconduct. In short, though all society is founded on intolerance, all improvement is founded on tolerance, or the recognition of the fact that the law of evolution is Ibsen's law of change" (34). As a combat soldier dressing in man's clothes, Joan is effective because of her transgression, her break in habit, rather than, as in more contemporary forms, the woman combatant appearing as setting a new norm, becoming the same as what is. Monica A. Zabrouski and Robert P. Kirschmann have analyzed the idea of anomaly that Joan asserts as being representative of Shaw's theory of Creative Evolution, where "humanity bears the onus for evolution" (80), meaning that human creativity and, in particular, technological invention are the cause of progress rather than any sort of biological or bodily hard-wiring.

18 Tim O'Brien breaks with the convention of presenting soldiers as already inside of the war rather than inside of a narrative of process and decision. Though O'Brien's recounting starts with a scene of armed men marching through the Vietnamese jungle, he does return to the moment of decision. The narrator in *The Things They Carried* considers a flight to Canada when he receives his draft notice. The difference here with women-in-war books might be that Tim O'Brien considers his decision as ethical rather than economic. "It was a moral split," he thinks, for example. "I couldn't make up my mind. I feared the war, yes, but I also feared exile. I was afraid of walking away from my own life, my friends and my family, my whole history, everything that mattered to me. I feared losing the respect of my parents . . . I detested . . . blind, thoughtless, automatic acquiescence to it all, . . . simpleminded patriotism, . . . prideful ignorance, . . . how they were sending me off to fight a war they didn't understand and didn't want to understand" (43).

19 As Scarry expounds: "that the 'wounding' language is applied to weapons and arms (that helicopters are injured in the sands of Iran; that the *Sheffield* receives a mortal wound in the waters off the Falkland Islands) would not in isolation be wholly inappropriate since these objects, like libraries and cities, are projections of the human person; but the language is lent to the weapons at precisely the same moment that it is being lifted away from the sentient source of those projections. The language of killing and injuring ceases to be a morally resonant one because the successful shelling of the bodies of thousands of nineteen-year-old German soldiers can be called 'producing results' and the death of civilians by starvation and pestilence following an economic boycott is called 'collateral effects' at precisely the same time that one turns on a radio and hears the report of an arsenal of tanks that received a 'massive injury' or opens a book and reads about the government's hope 'to kill a hidden base'" (67).

20 C-130, named "Hercules," a transport plane capable of landing in rugged conditions and on short runways.

21 According to Miller's interpretation of the death drive logic, "Once death emerges, it cannot truly be canceled without destroying the entire world. The aim of the death drive—if it has one—is not merely to bring life to an end, but, more radically, to bring the entire world to an end" (15). Miller is mostly concerned with the disappearance of the archive, statues, museums, and intergenerational or intersubjective memory that sustain life. However, the idea he advances that the death drive means a cancellation of life's conditions of beginning invites an analysis of gender as well, an analysis that Miller does not engage.

22 Another perspective that informs opposition to women in combat is to say that men have always and everywhere been the fighters because of bodily differences. "[G]ender

58 Women in the War Story

roles in war are very consistent across all known human societies" (3), claims, for example, Joshua S. Goldstein. "In war," he goes on, "the fighters are usually all male" (10), and though women are sometimes participants, usually they participate only temporarily. (The next sentence begins with "exceptions to this rule" (10), and there are more exceptions than rules.) Genetics, testosterone levels, hormones, physical size and strength, as well as innate aggression are what feed this consistency, even though, Goldstein admits, there are caveats and divergences in the scientific evidence: "much of the human research on testosterone has studied criminals" (150), he asserts, for instance, or "the idea of aggression as a male quality" (135) is only prevalent for a particular type of aggression. Still, even the appearances of aggression are variable, and the category itself holds a diverse range of behaviors, aggression is produced in the stimulation of very specific areas of the brain, says Goldstein. The evidence Goldstein gives that combat instincts reside in males is that they also are manifest in "wrasse fish" (130). The dominance of war instincts in the body (even if the body is a fish), then, leads to the conclusion that war is primary and instinctual—it has always existed and still exists before injustices and inequalities because biology requires it. The male body underlies conceptions of war as inevitable, limitless, and without history.

23 On the flip side, the home front is the space of continuance, of the care of the spirit. Rebecca West's World War I novel, *The Return of the Soldier*, about a man on home leave with shell shock, for example, recounts an old romance that continues to rise up into the soldier's traumatized consciousness as hallucination: "This wonderful kind woman held his body as safely as she held his soul" (111).

24 This would-be warrior is in the process of discovering that his arms and legs have been amputated; his hearing, nose, and vision lost; and all that remains is his pared-down, working body-core-remainder.

25 "Suddenly everything went black, and a high-pitched noise from the netherworld enveloped Bergan. She lay in the dirt like a rag doll atop a blanket of blood, her arms extended and her legs forming the number four . . . Bergan's right thigh was a gaping hole, the leg attached by a piece of flesh the size of two thumbs to the rest of her leg . . . Her femur was broken and sticking out of the wound. Blood was already pooling in and around the wound, clotting in the sand like a ruby necklace. Bergan continued to scream" (244–246).

26 She complains that she could not have a career in the Air Force because women could not be trained to fly Apache helicopters and jets which, more resistant to attack, were usually used in combat missions.

27 Michael Hardt and Antonio Negri understand the computerization of work as the "homogenization of laboring processes" (292) marking the transition between Fordism and "Toyotism," making laboring bodies interchangeable. "From Marx's perspective in the nineteenth century, the concrete practices of various laboring activities were radically heterogeneous: tailoring and weaving involved incommensurable concrete actions. . . . With the computerization of production today, however, the heterogeneity of concrete labor has tended to be reduced. . . . The labor of computerized tailoring and the labor of computerized weaving may involve exactly the same concrete practices—that is, manipulation of symbols and information" (292).

28 "How many people had been shot by those weapons since she had written down their serial numbers? Twenty thousand assault rifles, multiplied by four years of warfare, plus however many times they had been fired" (348).

29 "It was a feeling of profound alienation, but it manifested itself as an almost physical sensation, as though there were literally a transparent barrier cutting her off from the rest of the world" (353).

30 "When the slayer is a woman, and especially a mother, whom we would expect to be a caregiver, the scene becomes more intense, drawing nearer to the essential nucleus of horror" (101).

Women in the War Story   **59**

31 Rachel Holmes has chronicled the discourse surrounding Winnie Mandela's role in the 1976 Soweto uprisings as engaged in such a narrative: "It is thus crucial to give proper scope to the political bond between the 'mother of the nation' and activist youth that had developed in the context of the 1970s . . . [T]he 'mother of the nation' had been regarded as an ally and protector of the interests of South African youth" (171). Holmes is concerned with the way this narrative ends up vilifying Winnie Mandela by making her seem unnatural or queer when she was alleged to have committed crimes against youth activists. She continues: "The overdetermining concepts of the heterosexual family and female sexuality are at the heart of the ways in which the practices and discourses of nationhood are forged, producing a double indemnity for women who are publicly associated with political power" (175). According to this analysis, women's combat promotes heterosexual norms *and,* simultaneously, disrupts them from the inside.

32 Goodell concludes her book with a "postscript" in which her creative writing professor interviews her. In it, she admits, surprisingly, that she does not recommend women's participation in the Marines. She attributes women's debilitating wartime trauma to "being female in an environment that was systematically hostile to females" (190) rather than to experiencing, witnessing, or engaging in violence and atrocity against an enemy.

2

FROM DECOLONIZATION TO BODY BOMBS

Tragedy, Feminist Political Theory, and the Female Militant

This chapter reconsiders the female terrorist of the current wars in relation to an older set of ideas surrounding female combatants in the mid- to late-twentieth century wars of decolonization, civil wars (like the ones in Central America), and anti-imperialist struggles. We have often heard that "one man's terrorist is another man's freedom fighter," condensing the issue to a matter of perspective. I argue here, rather, that the female combatant has gone through an historical transformation from "freedom fighter" to "terrorist" by committing acts of violence represented as in line with neoliberal ideology. In particular, I contend that the appearance of the female suicide bomber on the historical stage expresses an ideology of dispossession that feeds neoliberal forms of aggressive possessiveness. That is, neoliberalism envisions a liberal social contract dispossessing citizenship of rights and association much in the same way that a colonial state dispossessed the colonized of their culture in the political and symbolic exchange it imposed on those under its governance. Though both colonialism and neoliberalism meet with, on the surface, similar violent oppositional reactions, they each induce rather different political framing. I am not advocating or defending suicide bombing nor expressing any kind of agreement with it; rather, I oppose suicide bombing partly because I see it as the last desperate recourse for the extreme forms of political alienation that neoliberalism invests in its subjects.

Attributing the motivations of such so-called "self-sacrificial acts" to women depicted as submissive and desperate, this neoliberal re-alignment seeks to remake the politics of action and opposition into an agentless non-politics: an out-of-control spectacle of commitment, resentment, obedience, and blind emotion devoid of social project or connection. As Talal Asad suggests, "The stress should be not on violence as such but on spontaneous action when . . . political means are blocked" (47). Unbounded by social ideologies like national belonging or

From Decolonization to Body Bombs **61**

emancipation, the detonating body seems to answer to an internal command only, mechanically, like a weapon. As in Zoë Wicomb's post-Apartheid novel *David's Story,* the female combatant as an agent of decolonization disappears under an unresolved narrative, without burial, "dispelled by the comic behavior of the baboons" (181), leaving the movement bereft of political cohesion and social intention. As the power of the nation-state recedes before the intensification of a transnationalizing capitalism, violence does not translate into a struggle for or against a nationalizing vision with its political landscape or a connection to a community broader than immediate family. Rather, such militant violence by women equates with a violence that has been dehumanized, denationalized, and decommunalized. As such, it resists the narrative form of the nation; that is, it does not become part of a story or a project that progresses through change and time, expanding and maturing. Instead, the violent woman of the present is composed of an explosive life story, an atomized and emotional case history, where in a simplistic reading, her psychology is stamped exclusively by the stereotypes surrounding her cultural background, and her interior grief—without further inputs or reasoning—rules her actions.

The contemporary framing of the female militant replaces politics with sensation. Such stories of pure personal feeling reveal, displace, and misrepresent the tableaux of social alienation at the heart of everyday life under neoliberalism. As Bonnie Honig notes, speaking of the contemporary feminist interest in Antigone as a figure of personal pain and singular resistance, "it is difficult indeed right now to carve out room in late-modern Western democracies for protest or politics that do not slide into lamentation of singular loss or sovereign excess" (2013: 30). The sense of social isolation and pathos that is embedded inside of the lamentable life histories of individual female suicide bombers is likewise an expression of a deep-seated effect of neoliberal depoliticization, cultural and economic disenfranchisement for everybody. Explaining the causes of women's suicide bombings, Mia Bloom, for example, notices that the "lack of government programs for widows and orphans [in Iraq] leaves women with severe psychological issues" (218), including "mental illness" (219).[1] We are left senseless as the pain and anguish of our neoliberal detachments are absorbed onto the excruciating violence of the female terrorist body. The female militant is the explosive effect of neoliberal suffering that is seemingly marginalized as excessive or extreme by the same ideological system that produces it ubiquitously.

In keeping with Honig's critique of a feminist politics of lamentation, one might adventurously claim that Antigone is an early prototype of a female suicide bomber, as she chooses to die in blind submission to her gods, in defense of her family and its traditions, bringing others along with her. The feminist response to which Honig answers positions militant Antigone and her literary followers on the cusp of questions about the constitution of politics, human nature, and sovereignty in a postnational age. The reinterpretations of the Antigone figure from the mid-twentieth century on have been quite wide-ranging: on the one

62 From Decolonization to Body Bombs

hand, she orchestrates, says George Steiner, a symbolic resolution of the state seeking to "absorb this familial sphere into its own governance and order of values" (26), granting ethical substance to private domestic and local religious practices in which burial is central. On the other hand, as Freddie Rokem has noted of Bertolt Brecht's 1948 adaptation (just prior to the 1949 Berlin premiere of *Mother Courage*), she also reveals man's recognition of himself "becoming his own enemy and destroyer." Appearing at moments of historical need and resistance after Jean Anouilh resurrected her for the French resistance under Nazi occupation, Antigone's tragedy offers a way of thinking a relation to the political that questions the compromise with sovereignty that underlies the liberal contract. Antigone, in fact, as Honig and others have pointed out, continues to circulate as a literary figure that expresses changes in political relations produced inside an enduring literary record. That literary record is shifting: whereas this modern Antigone resists the sovereign state from within a shared symbol, from which she can demand recognition and be recognized, the neoliberal Antigone—like the female suicide bomber—cannot find common ground with the state's politics at all, not even in language; she thus seems to be without politics, unassimilable to the state. In sum, as I argue here, the *Antigone* is a play about political and therefore economic dispossession. What changes is whether Antigone's dispossession can be seen, on the one hand, as a moment of resistance which reflects sovereign power in it historical drive to represent an ever greater domain, or, on the other, as a sacrifice of the sovereign's bond.

In the liberal appropriation of Hegel's *Antigone*, Antigone's sacrifice is seen to be an exchange of her autonomy—and thus, also, the private autonomy of her familial and cultural devotions—for a broader belonging: her sense of personal love and duty does not remain outside of the interests of a public sphere defined by adherence to public laws, but rather is absorbed by the state, allowing the state to recognize itself in the hearts of its citizens. The Algerian feminist writer Assia Djébar, for example, situates her "new Antigone" (122) as mediating between power and the body: as the woman warrior clamors to bury her independence-fighter brother in a lament of mourning and loss, the Arabic voice of nationalized memory and storytelling is joined by a paternal voice, a French literary voice of romance, desire, and sexuality "armed to face the words of others" (127), and she becomes, through this hybridity, an artist, a lover, and a citizen. Yet, Djébar's Antigone obscures the ways that linguistic alienation operates within a broader social field.

By calling political relations into being as a "contract," liberal contract theory blurs the political with the ideologies of classical economic theory that assumes a consensual agreement where prices stabilize and reach equilibrium in their natural course. Citizen actions, though often selfish and seemingly independent, end up, in this theory, inadvertently and unintentionally promoting the prosperity of the sovereign system. As with the sacrifice of autonomy the individual makes in exchange for belonging to the sovereign and its protections, the economy—without necessarily deciding to care—is supposed to caringly resolve contradictions in line

From Decolonization to Body Bombs **63**

with the system, to mutual benefit. Just as liberal social contract theory invites the question of what is excluded from sovereign recognition, so the economic analogy invites speculation on how much abstracted reciprocal negotiations between presumptively "equal" economic actors require that the actors have already been dispossessed of their independent identities and expressions of value. The actors are, then, forced into accepting the terms of the contract. Antigone's story of reconciliation would be a projected back-story, from the position of the sovereign, that legitimates the representational power of the sovereign.

In such readings, Antigone's gender serves as the symbolic form of separation from the state that comes back into the state or as an antagonism that reflects the state to itself in its reconciled self-understanding. Antigone, R. Clifton Spargo remarks, carries the "radical signification implicit in the unrealized personhood of woman within the State . . . [O]nly a woman, by exploiting her relative autonomy from the public sphere, in which subjectivity is normatively dependent on a strict subjection to the State, proves capable of genuine individuation from sociopolitically bounded existence" (250).[2] Gender, that is, consistently inserts a break, the insinuation of a non-conformity or disagreement, reflecting the state back to itself. Though Antigone's interests and actions are, as Spargo continues, "out of sync with the *polis*'s restrictive construct of rights in the public realm" (251), her protest is still reciprocal: spoken *to* the state, in the language the state uses in its desire for recognition. "She stands," Spargo foregrounds, "in the political arena as though necessarily excluded from it, and in a voice charged by apoliticism denounces the injustices of the political realm" (258). Yet, Creon's power over Antigone is such that he need not hear her appeal (or even speak her language).

Whereas, on the one hand, the doubts about state sovereignty and justice that Antigone's situation raises might have provided a critical rejoinder to the modern state's excesses, its monopoly on legitimate violence, its inequalities, and its exclusions, the neoliberal moment, on the other hand, has changed the implications of Antigone's crisis: it has increased the vulnerability of the apolitical subject.[3] The neoliberal moment has made reappear, as Tina Chanter remarks, the theme of slavery that undergirds the play, where a woman residing within the territory of the state's rule has no recourse to the protection of or negotiation with its laws.[4] Antigone, says Chanter, cannot be integrated "into the story that Hegel tells about the necessary raising up of differences into a logic of contradiction that can be cashed out in terms of determinate negation" (30–31);[5] like a suicide bomber, she is thus—Chanter borrows from Lacan here—made into a "terrifying but profound monstrosity of formlessness" (30).[6]

Antigone's femaleness is thus employed in her various historical instances as a way of presenting degrees of dispossession of citizen care from the democratic sovereign relation, even to the point of introducing skepticism over the possibility of translating citizen wills into sovereign form at all, that is, of speaking the same language. Following on the trail of Antigone, recent literary instances of female insurgents use gender to reveal, as well, that such indelible imbalances in power,

64 From Decolonization to Body Bombs

also inherent in colonialism, are integral components of the liberal relation.[7] As Astrid Van Weyenberg proposes, the various revisions of the *Antigone* outside of Western contexts show the non-viability of debates like Creon and Antigone's in cultural and political settings where "no ethical equilibrium [can exist] between two equally justified claims" (265) because one side holds all the cards, and the other's vulnerability is pressing.

In particular, I compare here Indian-born novelist Joydeep Roy-Bhattacharya's rendering of an Afghani Antigone facing off against a U.S. Forward Operating Base [FOB] in *The Watch* against the traces of women independence fighters in Hélène Cixous' "Letter to Zohra Drif" and other Algerian texts. Like much of Cixous' quasi-narrative/quasi-poetic/quasi-philosophical autobiographical writing about Algeria, "Letter to Zohra Drif" is a reflection on Cixous' Algerian childhood from the perspective of Cixous' adulthood away from Algeria.[8] It—similarly to longer works such as "My Algeriance," "The Names of Oran," *Reverie of the Wild Woman, The Day I Wasn't There,* and *So Close*—follows a desire for memory that is erased by decolonization. The desire for memory weaves into a desire for Zohra Drif—the woman who blows up the milk bar in the Algerian war of decolonization as shown in Gilles Pontecorvo's classic film *The Battle of Algiers* and then becomes a senator post-independence. A ghostly character, shifting between presence and absence like *The Watch*'s Antigone, Drif appears sporadically in Cixous' Algerian autobiographical fragments as the object of desire (memory and identity) displaced onto a chain of substitutions by the imminent war. Whereas Cixous' narratives understand the invisible traces of women combatants as pointing to an unformed potential of future sociality based in metonymic connections and mutual recognition (a politics not necessarily tracing its lineage through states), *The Watch* foregrounds the threat of the woman's separation from state sovereignty as making her apolitical, an extension of neoliberal anti-statist resilience narratives.

An implication in the comparison between Cixous' Algerian works and *The Watch* is that the historical momentum of the female combatant takes shape in relation to her literary presence and, in addition, that literary form operates within the contemporary war scene.[9] Cixous, for example, calls the bombings performed by women as "this tragic play" ("Letter to Zohra Drif": 113) in order to show, as does Roy-Bhattacharya, that tragedy underlies the political relationships between invading states and dominated peoples in colonial wars. As Sean Kirkland demonstrates, tragedy plays out as a conflict between free will and determinism,[10] so the application of a tragic reading to contemporary geopolitics divulges that neoliberalism and its wars are stoking feelings of lost control and agency that find a literary equivalent in antiquity's spectacles of fate and divine and kingly power.

The two writers also offer readings of tragedy that contest Hegelian versions, where power is negotiated between the equal ethical positions of the prototypical state and the individuals it absorbs as citizens. While Cixous suggests that Antigone's politicization empties the state of politics, indicating that politics happens elsewhere, *The Watch* shows Antigone without politics: *The Watch* re-envisions that

From Decolonization to Body Bombs **65**

sovereign relationship as between the power of the state and the individuals it *conquers and cannot absorb* as citizens, individuals who are essentially without connection to that state and so without social connection at all. Where Creon's position in *The Watch* is therefore emphatically militaristic rather than representational as per the liberal social contract or the Hegelian dialectic, Antigone exists as outside of political relation, a pure violence incompatible with institutional forms, either sovereign or symbolic, of synthesis, compromise, articulation, or mediation that translate into the liberal promise. Even as it can attribute the failures of the social contract to the imperialist conflict, the imperial relation comes to be seen, through its *Antigone* analogy, as residing inside the liberal political project at its core, as its norm: seen through the lens of imperialist wars, the liberal social contract is shown to unbind the political body from the individuals it is supposed to govern. Liberalism's representational failures exile such individuals to the outside of politics—to the colony—where their only recourse is violence.

From National Struggle to Terror

In France as well as in Syria, Chechnya, Kurdistan, Iraq, Nigeria, and Palestine, the spectacular appearance of women as mass shooters, trained operatives, and suicide bombers has become a focus of media attention and global shock, as though the world has never before witnessed such women-perpetrated violence. In the so-called "War on Terror," women fighters have increasingly been recruited for terrorist acts. "[T]he number of female terrorists and suicide bombers has increased several hundredfold in the past few years" (ix), begins Mia Bloom in 2011. "It is now clear that women are the future of even the most conservative terrorist organizations" (xi).

Yet, the mass involvement of women in insurgencies and wars of liberation in the 1960s through the 1980s met with similar surprise and speculation. Demobilization in El Salvador, for example, revealed that oppositional forces in its civil war were composed of 30 percent women, with 15 percent (and less reliable data) in the much longer Guatemalan conflict (Luciak, 1–31). "By the end of the revolution," report Barbara Seitz, Linda Lobao, and Ellen Treadway, referring to Nicaragua, "about 30 percent of Sandinistas were women. They were visible at all leadership levels and came from all socioeconomic classes" (172). The mass mobilization in Nicaragua, the authors conclude, is attributable to the rise of feminism in the seventies in Latin America as well as to the Sandinistas' establishment of a women's branch as part of their mobilization (*Asociación de Mujeres Nicaragüenes Luisa Amanda Espinoza,* or AMNLAE—Luisa Amanda Espinoza Association of Nicaraguan Women); after victory, women "made up 50 percent of the popular militia units" (175). In a report on Peru's Maoist *Sendero Luminoso,* or Shining Path, Carol Andreas found that "Sendero Luminoso, since its inception, attracted women in much larger numbers than men" (20). In Columbia, "female composition expanded from approximately 20 percent of FARC [Fuerzas Armadas

66 From Decolonization to Body Bombs

Revolucionarias de Colombia—Ejército del Pueblo] ranks in the 1970s and 1980s, to 40–50 percent in the 2000s" (Mazurana, 155). In pro-Peronist and left-wing opposition groups in 1970s Argentina, "Female participation was large," reports Marta Diana, "and, in general, the numbers of women and men were pretty much equalized. There were whole zones that were exclusively female fronts" (my translation; 117). "[I]n Sierra Leone," Chris Coulter teaches us, "The number of women fighting in the various armed forces has been estimated at up to 30 percent" (12). Coulter goes on: "Women make up around one fifth of the armed forces in Eritrea, and almost one-third of the fighters of the Tamil Tigers in Sri Lanka are women" (15). Cynthia Enloe, too, points out that "by 1979 in Robert Mugabe's section of the Patriot Front, the Zimbabwe National Liberation Army . . . 300 or more of the 11,000 person fighting force were women" (1980: 48). Women composed 38.3 percent of the Bolshevik forces in 1917, she maintains, were "explicitly integrated" (49) in the Chinese Communist Party's Long March, and were enlisted in urban armed units during the Lebanese civil war.

The embrace of women fighters in struggles for independence and sovereignty in the mid- to late-twentieth century was generally seen as strategic for political aims. Tried and convicted as a combatant, even if her role in combat was never proven in evidence, U.S. citizen Lori Berenson professed that her involvement with Peru's *Movimiento Revolucionario Túpac Amaru* (MRTA) in the early eighties was "my way of saying, you know, I don't believe in this type of system . . . — this was when the U.S. was supporting death squads and supporting—you know, sending millions of dollars in military aid to bomb the civilian population of in El Salvador" (Amy Goodman). Generally, gender identities could be mobilized for organization and action.[11] "The process of 'recuperating' women," admits one of Marta Diana's informants, "was oriented around the exaltation of our feminine sentiments" (my translation; 151). Even negative news coverage asserted that the struggle was over control of the state as the central organizational form of political power, and women's involvement was needed for establishing sovereign power, in particular because of their role in the family as well as in political education: "Juana, since becoming involved in the organization, had advanced a lot," writes Carlos Penuin in an Argentine newspaper, *Somos*. "She worked as a teacher of ideology and as a combatant, indoctrinating university students and heading groups that threatened and extorted from professors so that they would include Marxist texts in the curriculum" (my translation; 14). The militants viewed their gendered bodies, according to Penuin, as a strategic tool for political ends, as they got pregnant as often as possible in order to elicit sympathy from the authorities, or seduced the police for the purpose of creating distractions.[12] Expressing ideological intentions through violence, women's participation in armed struggle meant that those ideological intentions were saturating the social landscape, the everyday, and the body.[13]

In most cases, at the end of the conflict, gender relations returned to much the same as they were before.[14] Yet, women's bodies in combat could be seen

From Decolonization to Body Bombs **67**

as offering a political opening, that is, a way of turning the violence of isolated engagements into an organized, social front. "Armed organizations publicize the role of women in their ranks," concludes Jocelyn Viterna about the outcome in 1980s El Salvador, "to portray their cause as so just that *even women* are willing to risk their lives, and the lives of their children, to support it" (original emphasis; 208). Frantz Fanon claims that the presence of the Algerian woman in the fight engenders the objective conditions under which human subjectivity takes a total new form. "[R]evolutionary war," he tells us, "is not a war of men ... The Algerian woman is at the heart of the combat ... [T]he effervescence and the revolutionary spirit," Fanon continues "have been kept alive by the woman in the home" (66).[15] For Fanon, the family is a pivot towards political involvement, but the new politics is born in the family's wreckage. Women's presence in the home makes them into the preservers and transmitters of consciousness and social relations that are set apart—and so, different—from the colonizing culture. When such women take up arms outside the home, they introduce a whole new temporal phase of social being, a difference that tears apart colonization and history alike by posing society anew. Women combatants promise, for Fanon, the bursting forth of a total new society on the historical stage.[16]

In contrast, explanations usually given for women's decisions to become suicide bombers include traits like subordination, family connectedness, mourning, romantic alliance, personal strife, religious dedication, and feelings of inferiority— traits related neither to political consciousness, to social belonging, nor to vision but rather to psychological trauma, dysfunction, and submission to control.[17] "[S]he came from a broken home," Mia Bloom describes Dzhennet Abdurakhmanova, a Chechen "Black Widow" who detonated a body bomb on the Moscow subway in 2010 in an act of retaliation, "and sensed that others in the traditional Kumyk society regarded her as inferior" (4). "Praise be to Allah," *The Guardian* quotes Hayat Boumeddiene saying in an interview in the Islamic newspaper *Dar al-Islam*. Wife of Amédy Coulibaly who killed a policewoman and four Jewish men in a kosher supermarket in the wake of the attack on the satirist magazine *Charlie Hebdo*'s offices in Paris in 2015, Boumeddiene encouraged other Muslim women to join her in the "land of the Califat" in support of their "husbands, brothers, fathers and sons" (Willsher). Boumeddiene did not commit suicide but disappeared, through Turkey, into Syria shortly after the *Charlie Hebdo* attacks, though international authorities searched widely to apprehend her.

The coverage insists that such female militants are acting in response to powers not in their charge, whether those powers be natural motions of the body or external institutions exerting pressures and threats. In fact, female militants merge institutions or belief systems into bodies, as their bodies operate mechanically almost as a pure expression of institutional will. Immediately in the wake of the shooting attack in San Bernardino, California on 2 December 2015, for example, investigators sought to affirm Tashfeen Malik's residency in Saudi Arabia, her enrollment in a Koranic classes at the Al Huda center of the University of

68 From Decolonization to Body Bombs

Multan—a religious university in Pakistan (with no apparent history of promoting radicalization)—, and her alliance with the Islamic State (ISIS, or ISIL) in order to read through these biographical markers the pathway for her radicalization. "She was a very hard-working and submissive student," reports one of Liam Stackdec's informants in *The New York Times*. "She never created any problems in the class. She was an obedient girl." Even those who were skeptical—without evidence provided, that Tashfeen Malik's one Facebook entry under a false name assured that she was under ISIL's control—still describe her as a woman without political motivations, whose actions are determined by external forces or commands. Rafia Zakaria in *Aljazeera America,* for example, reasons that her Internet marriage was most likely arranged by her parents, and she was probably confined to the home, under the strictures of her possibly abusive husband, Saudi-inspired religious conservatism, and U.S. immigration policy, which made her residency contingent on her husband's beneficence.[18] Neither Tashfeen Malik nor her husband and fellow shooter, Syed Rizwan Farook, are attributed political motivations; instead, their acts follow from their affiliation with non-nationalized militant groups governed not necessarily by religious beliefs, political theories, or aspirations to construct a different type of state and society but rather by force, command, and authority or by an undeterrable physical need for violence. According to Azadeh Moaveninov, also in *The New York Times,* non-religious Syrian women join the Islamic State as enforcers of Sharia law not because they necessarily agree with the premises of what they call The Organization, but rather because their families are at risk. They are provoked by "no normalcy or choice" even in decisions over their bodies, pregnancies,[19] work, associations, or freedom of movement. Unlike in the earlier descriptions of women combatants in national struggle or decolonization, gender here does not serve as an expansive quality that deepens sociologically a new political vision and connection but rather as a tool of manipulation and bribery, a way for The Organization to express its controls inside the very sensibilities of bodies.

Western interpreters of suicide bombing generally, as Talal Asad has remarked, search for personal—most often religious or pathological—rather than political motives that would explain the phenomenon of "horror" that suicide bombing, in the West, conjures: "Thus although it is the unlicensed act of killing civilians that defines the crime," Asad comments, "for journalists and security experts it is his [*sic.*] motive for doing this terrible thing that is of primary interest" (45). In keeping, "Is it possible that Wafa Idris, a paramedic in the Red Crescent, committed suicide this week on Jaffa Street mostly because her life was so miserable?" questions the Israeli newspaper *Kol Hazman* in 2002 (as cited in Issacharoff, 44). Issacharoff goes on: "The question always arises [in the media, about a female suicide terrorist] whether she had a romantic affair, divorce, personal distress stemming from rape, for example, or, needless to say, problems in having children" (43–44). According to a U.S. Army Intelligence report from 2011, women who conduct suicide attacks are likely to share the following characteristics: "dishonored through sexual indiscretion"; grieving and seeking revenge; "desire to belong"; infertility; suggestibility; and low self-esteem (6). The presence of women in the fighting forces of decolonization meant that the oppositional forces were spreading their political organization and symbolic challenge deeper into the social context—in a way of speaking, socializing their belief systems, their power networks, their actions, and their view of how the world could be shared with others, and so forming the possible ideological and material groundwork for state construction, or politics. The female terrorist, on the other hand, marks a political limit. She is egoistical, overtaken by her body's needs, self-obsessed, blinded by emotion and sentiment, obedient to God, family, and The Organization.[20]

My intention here is not to expose a religious difference or to insinuate a cultural, racial, or geographical essentialism. Nor do I want to vilify or blame religious motives that are determined to cause various forms of contemporary violence, where the frame of religion dictates the substance of judgments, ethics, or character. I find useful Talal Asad's line of questioning of the relation between violence and religion when he asks, "Is there, I asked myself, a religiously motivated terrorism? If so, how does it differ from other cruelties? What makes its motivation—as opposed to the simple intent to kill—religious? Where does it stand in relation to other forms of collective violence?" (1). Taking into account the way history and politics embed themselves into the way we see violence, I note, with Saba Mahmood, that such

> supposed descriptions of "religious extremism" enfold a set of judgments and evaluations such that to abide by a certain description is also to uphold these judgments. Descriptions of events deemed extremist or politically dangerous are often not only reductive of the events they purport to describe but, more importantly, also premised on normative conceptions of the subject, religion, language, and law that are . . . fraught. . . .
>
> *(66)*

Conjointly, I show that the concept of non-state or anti-state violence performed by women has changed as a result of neoliberalism's attack on states as the institutional ground of the social contract and political engagement. In other words, the anti-statism and apoliticality in neoliberal ideology inhabit how we frame women's violence today.

Antigone, on the Line

Traditional interpretations of the *Antigone* read the play as participating in an inaugural thinking about the compromise between the private individual and the sovereign state in social contract theory and democracy, with Creon representing the incipient democratic state and its laws and Antigone giving voice to the laws of kinship, native religion, and blood loyalty. In a liberal reading of Sophocles,

70 From Decolonization to Body Bombs

the exchange between Creon and Antigone culminates in Antigone's sacrifice along with the sacrifice of generations to come, contributing to the evolution of democracy in the state. After Antigone's death, Creon comes to sympathize with Antigone's perspective at least partially, so that the state can be seen as, in a Hegelian sense, effected by a general reconciliation with and absorption of its particular citizens as a part of itself.[21] Though George Steiner ascribes Antigone's popularity to humanistic concerns coming out of the French Revolution—such as exile, sexual estrangement, intimacy, and the public/private divide—, the surge of more recent Antigones in literature may be attributable to a recognition of a loss of control linked to a decline in sovereign responsibility. The *Antigone* understands sovereignty's failings as connected to the appearance of resistance and sacrificial violence in women in ways that contemporary literary authors are taking up as revelatory for present history. In recent interpretations, the relationship between the sovereign and the citizen collapses. The *Antigone* asks us to confront the question of whether this collapse is a political opening—i.e., the possibility of political action not consumed in the state's appropriations and juridical organization of power—or a political abandonment.

Of late, the *Antigone* has been read not only as interrogating Antigone's claims to recognition and inclusion by the sovereign state but also as posing the possibility of a viable non-sovereign politics, an ethics of social belonging outside of relations with the state, autonomous. Part of this move occurs by defining Creon's sovereign place as entwined in the symbolic as well as in the state, so that Antigone's claims appear as a problem of translation, that is, as an inability to translate Antigone's particular needs into terms that Creon can understand. The question of translation itself—whether any particular utterance can find recognizable equivalents in an alternate symbolic system—raises skepticism about any tie between the word and the world: that is, does an object appear in the world the same in one language as in another? Can the object be known in the same way if it is extracted from its linguistic surroundings and given others? Such poststructuralist interpretations of the *Antigone* configure citizenship through loss and dispossession because it is embedded in language. This turn is significant: it allows for a broadening of the way the political practice can be thought but leads to confusion in two ways: 1) confusion over how to evaluate differentials between levels, intensities, and types of dispossession; and 2) confusion over where the responsibility lies—or whether anyone at all is responsible—for the crises of nonbelonging—or dispossession—in contemporary forms of political bereavement.

Whereas, following Hegel, philosophical readings have used the *Antigone* to expose the limits of the modern sovereign project, in the twentieth century the *Antigone* has also provided a site for exploring subjectivities not bound by traditional sovereignty, or not unproblematically. Luce Irigaray, for example, has addressed how Antigone must be sacrificed in order to institute a symbolic gender complementarity necessary for the construction of the Western sovereign subject—a complementarity that exiles women from representation—,[22] while

From Decolonization to Body Bombs **71**

Kierkegaard sees in Antigone the birth of the modern subject who punishes herself rather than acting: alienated, self-absorbed, emotional, and isolated in the now-internalized pain and guilt inherited from her father.[23] Taking the issue farther, Judith Butler asks if Antigone can pose a politics completely free of state sovereignty: "whether there can be kinship—and by kinship I do not mean the 'family' in any specific form—without the support and mediation of the state . . .?" (2000: 5). Kinship, for Butler here, represents a challenge to state sovereign and symbolic power: a social figure that is not determined by an exterior imposition but is not totally autonomous. Kinship for Butler is an ethical relationship based in care, where the subject comes into being and acting at the same time as it is touched by the social: "*the sphere that conditions the possibility of politics without ever entering into it*" (Butler's emphasis; 2000: 2). That is, the social conditioning allows for the subject to be born as autonomous at the same time as it is socially conditioned through care; it is dispossessed of subjectness through a social connectedness that makes its subjectness.

Since the exchange with the sovereign happens through language, which can never totally capture what it means (and so is always, in some sense, dispossessed), Butler denies that Antigone comes to any resolution with Creon: "The symbolic is secured precisely through an evacuation or negation of the living person; thus a symbolic person is never commensurate with any individual who happens to occupy it" (2000: 14). For Butler, one of the predominant ways that Antigone challenges sovereignty is by using a language of reference for her kinship relations—like "brother," which could, in this case, mean her father—that does not operate as determinant: rather, the person answering to the referencing term has to change its frame in order to answer. What counts as grouped inside the kinship term—different than what the call intends yet responsive to the call—comes to be a social determination only through the call's indeterminate erring.

Though Butler's reading has the advantage of offering an understanding of identity based in symbolic forms and norming practices that do not need sanction from the state, it also dovetails with tendencies in public neoliberal rhetoric that marginalize politics by marginalizing the state. Butler envisions the subject as conditioned and formed by the social and its symbolic, and so always open to its impingements, outside of sovereign authority. This openness occasions the subject as responsible for others, but also as constituted by its relations to others and so unbounded and at a loss in its sense of self, its self-belonging:

> I am undone as a bounded being. I come apart, I find that I am my relation to the "you" whose life I seek to preserve, and without that relation, this "I" makes no sense and has lost its mooring in this ethics that is always prior . . . the "I" becomes undone in its ethical relation to the "you," which means that there is a very specific mode of being dispossessed that makes ethical relationality possible.
>
> *(* Towards a Performative Theory, *2015: 110)*

72 From Decolonization to Body Bombs

Can this emptying out of the "I" also be understood as a sort of abandonment, disenfranchisement, neglect, or obliteration?

Butler clearly does not intend this meaning. She continues, "To be outside established legitimate political structures is still to be saturated in power relations" (2015: 80). That is, contra Georgio Agamben and his theory of "bare life," exclusions still are social relations, sustained by "that dimension of politics that addresses the organization and protection of bodies" (2015: 119). Yet, can the social declare itself non-regulating and not responsible to the subject that it occasions? Bonnie Honig, for example, interprets Butler's opposition to sovereignty as potentially reducing the political to a pure solipsistic expression of inner tragic grief, alienation, and helplessness á la Kierkegaard: Antigone's "suffering cries," notes Honig, "mark an extra-linguistic, universal experience of human grief or the isolated solitude of deep human pain" (2013: 19). She goes on: "Lament . . . is not a basis for politics but is a sign of the partiality of our codes of grief and of the limited ability of our codes of grief to control or redeem our losses by embedding them in economies of meaning that are supposedly themselves impervious to rupture and interruption" (2013: 120). In Honig's view, with Antigone's pain and abandonment leaving no expressive capacity recognizable by sovereignty, "politics disappears" (2013: 20).

Butler says that even the subject's extreme isolation or alienation is produced by a social bonding. She bases this assertion in her stated conviction that politics needs bodies, and bodies are sustained through infrastructures and contacts that are socially mediated. Yet, unlike in Butler's depictions of power, in colonial situations, power's sustaining interests are divided from the interests of the bodies needing sustenance. In other words, Butler's vision cannot encompass situations where power's conditions are separate from the space of its applications. Though this type of division may usually define a colonialist relation, such disaffection may also always exist within liberalism's distributions of care and protection. Such estrangement is particularly evident when public representational power is usurped by private interests with no obligations to the public. In a dialogue with Greek anthropologist Athena Athanasiou entitled *Dispossession,* Butler is asked to address the ambiguities of her non-sovereign ethical and normative spheres in the face of, for example, refugee crises, growing statelessness, corporate deregulation, weakening welfare, debt, and labor flexibilization. "Dispossession" in one sense "establishes the self as social" (2013: 4), while in another sense it "establishes our vulnerability to social forms of deprivation" (2013: 5), to precarity, or, as Athanasiou names it, to "violent appropriation" (2013: 11). In other words, the body's connection to the social is what also makes it vulnerable and even unsustainable. Athanasiou offers this challenge: "Although the two senses of dispossession are bound to each other, there is no ontological, causal, or chronological link between 'being dispossessed' (as a primordial disposition to relationality . . .) and 'becoming dispossessed' (as an ensuing, derivative condition of enforced deprivation of land, rights, livelihood, desire, or modes of belonging). We should be wary of conflating

From Decolonization to Body Bombs **73**

or ontologically demarcating these nuances of dispossession" (2013: 5). Butler agrees with this assertion and links the confusion to the influence of colonialism on moral philosophy (8).

In what remains of this chapter, I compare two contemporary revisions of the *Antigone*. In both cases, Antigone the bomber resists imperial sovereignty. In the first case, Cixous' Algerian memoirs, the female combatant poses an alternative non-sovereign body in opposition to the imperial state by mobilizing translations: social symbolic systems and metonymic associations not restricted to state-bounded, possessive identities or origins. In the case of *The Watch,* on the other hand, Antigone is untranslatable: she counters the imperial state only through an absolute and explosive negation, an inability to form any political or symbolic relation in the face of the imperial state's power. The comparison shows that Antigone's opposition to sovereignty is invested with ethical grief and isolation that, without a political relation, erupts as pure violence.

Écriture **Algériance**

For the most part, U.S. scholars and students who know of Hélène Cixous think of her in relation to another figure of Greek antiquity, Medusa. In "The Laugh of the Medusa" and *The Newly Born Woman* (including "Sorties"), Cixous put *écriture féminine* on the critical theory map. I show here how the idea of *écriture féminine* develops out of a re-living of Antigone's tragedy in Cixous' Algerian experience before and leading up to decolonization.

Cixous writes herself into Antigone's character by referring to herself as "illegitimate," but where Antigone's illegitimacy is the effect of her father's transgressions and exile, Cixous' is the effect of her loss of French citizenship, her dispossession from sovereign belonging. Where Antigone, in Hegelian readings, has some kind of political relationship with Creon, who represents what will become the state (for Hegel), Cixous understands her Antigone as unbounded by the state. This "non-recognition" of Cixous—her statelessness—allows her to recognize herself in the faces of Algerian combatant women, similarly unbounded by the state, rather than in recognition by the state. The connection to the combatant women, through Antigone, politicizes Cixous, substituting for state recognition, in much the same way that *écriture* becomes a replacement as well as a supplement to an original, proscribed bond. Cixous' recognition of herself in the faces of the Algerian women fighters introduces the possibility of a political community outside of state identification, its laws, controls, and prohibitions.[24] The combatant woman cannot here be posed as an anti-politics; Cixous does not vilify all politics when she stands aside state politics. Even as we might want Cixous to have a greater analysis of inequality as part of her language project or to seed the imagination for alternative institutions, her emphasis on tracing social relations through the lens of language, like Butler's, allows us to imagine symbolic and political relations—perhaps incipient institutions—other than those normalized

74 From Decolonization to Body Bombs

by the modern imperialist state with its policies of exclusion and its monopoly on the means to violence.

"The Laugh of the Medusa" is a feminist text calling women to write their selves. In it, Cixous says that women are barred from their bodies, "a world all her own which has been secretly haunting since early childhood. A world of searching, the elaboration of knowledge, on the basis of a systematic experimentation with the bodily functions" (334). Writing, or *écriture,* answers to this secret-ing of bodies with waves of substitutions that never lead back to the missing body but produce constantly mobilizing, emancipating, and re-mashing textual motifs, metaphors, metonyms, sounds, and language forms in its place. Because the origin of meaning has been barred off, meanings tend to proliferate within words, allowing combinations and recombinations in both syntactic and symbolic dimensions. An example is with her use of the French word *voler:* "Flying is women's gesture," she writes, "flying in language and making it fly" (343). Woman can be known through bodily gesture or movement but not as body itself. So, *voler* indicates the aerial mobility and shiftiness of women's language but also and at the same time—"we've lived in flight, stealing away" (343)—*voler* is to steal: taking something that seems to belong elsewhere, giving it a new provenance, a new lineage, repossessing it. Neither meaning overcomes the other but rather mixes with it. Perhaps a form of stealing or at least an antidote to property, the translation leaves the ground behind but not completely; it leaves a trace. Translation reduces the quantity of reference points a word may possess in its original language—the translator must choose whether the replacement will be "to fly" or "to steal"—but also opens the word up to a new set of reference points and associations in the new language territory; it offers combinations and linkages between geographical language worlds, where each meaning recreates and augments the others without collapsing into them.[25] Women's writing, then, is a language that works by amalgamation and reinvention of meaning, mixing points of reference so that they are no longer "proper," singular, or attributable.

The reception of Cixous' work follows the path of *écriture,* barring access to its origin as its interpretive contexts multiply. Cixous' translator Peggy Kamuf calls it an "irony" that the translated text of "The Laugh . . ." was the "uppity offspring" (128) through which Cixous became identified with "the American-born idea of 'French feminist theory'" (128), against Cixous' intentions. This is especially ironic, says Kamuf, because "Cixous writes, like her mentor James Joyce, untranslatable texts" (129), so that the original is always lost: the text's meanings escape from its parental snares and pluralize into unintentional varieties: "She writes in tongues, you could say, but above all it is her principal idiom of French that is detonated by all the little bombs of her sentences" (129).

In fact, the American reception of Cixous through "The Laugh of the Medusa" cements an interpretive line that excludes much of its intellectual progeny, especially, for my purposes here, a line of reflective reminiscences on her childhood

From Decolonization to Body Bombs **75**

in Algeria. "In the Casbah," she writes in "Letter to Zohra Drif," "the oldest of Algiers's cities, the most folded up, the convoluted one, the cascade of alleyways with the odours of urine and spices, the secret of Algiers, and, if I had been able to name it then by its hidden name, I would have call it the savage genitals, the antique femininity," she says, "vaginality" (107). Algeria shares the secrecy attributable to the unrepresentable woman's body.[26] Many of these works on her Algerian childhood invoke the memory of Algeria as set adrift (like women's bodies in *écriture*) and the violence of decolonization barring the possibility of a retrieval or return: "From Algeria my love my terror I am liberated by the Algerian that is being born . . . It is this combat . . . that liberates me at last: I can go my way without the dread, the shame" (106). Just as *écriture* moved beyond bodily shame, sometimes violently, here Algeria is lost to memory through violence, but, like translation, the violence in that repression also creates new possibilities for identification and association.[27]

Cixous does not name Antigone when she is tracing out her Algerian past just as she cannot retrieve Algeria itself in her memory. "[F]or these brutal mists, these vanishing museums and churches, these sudden doglegs in the avenues, perhaps they were my fault, my misdoing" (*So Close,* 15), she writes, attributing the fading vision of Algeria to her near-sightedness. Antigone's apparent absence, however, does not stop Antigone from having notable effects, particularly through her loss of parentage and origins of belonging that Cixous borrows into her own autobiography. In "Sorties," Cixous notices, for example, allusions to both Greek and Shakespearian tragedy inside the repression of women's speech (the Unconscious), a panoply of tragic heroines besides Medusa that do not include Antigone: Clytemnestra, Helen, Medea, Ariadne, Dido, Penthesilea the Amazon queen, and, most decidedly, Electra, the sister who is dedicated to her brother despite his murderous acts. Of Electra she writes in "Sorties," "woman who looks after the family and its traces in her bosom and in the earth is the one who guarantees the burial" (*Newly Born,* 109). Cixous' descriptions of her political and national status in Algeria—as a Jew and a woman, in exile—are continually paralleling Antigone's plight. "I left my father there to mix his dust with that dust" (154), she says in her essay "My Algeriance," just as Antigone followed her father into exile and saw him die there. In death, her father sometimes returns, as does Antigone's, in the form of conscience, inhabiting her brother's often war-like reaction. In her Algerian memoir *The Day I Wasn't There,* after her "tragedy" (53)—when her infant child dies during her absence—, Cixous mourns the death of the brother she knew as he turns into another, angrier brother who wages war both on her and on the other brother he once was: "At war I hear the screech of missiles" (53). While the burial scene of the son merges into the memory of the father whom "none of us buried" (83), the brother is simultaneously brother, son, and angry father, upsetting categories of Cixous' self knowledge, a situation—like Antigone's—that she refers to variously as "banishment" or "exile." In the section called "The Burial," she calls this new, angrier brother—"the most warrior of the family" (82)—"a traitor" (82).

76 From Decolonization to Body Bombs

Cixous and Antigone, I would argue, have considerable conceptual and thematic overlap.

Yet, not the loss of the father, but the loss of the father's nation prompts Cixous to refer to herself, like Antigone, as "*The illegitimate*" (original emphasis; "My Algeriance," 162). Though a Napoleonic decree—the 1870 Crémieux decree—gave all Jews citizenship in the French North African colonies (the sweeping policy of naturalization already began to erode as early as 1871), the Vichy regime abrogated the decree in 1940, causing Cixous' father—a soldier for France serving as a doctor—along with his family, to lose French citizenship and yet not be granted citizenship elsewhere. For Cixous, this confusion of her relation to the state—this exile, or statelessness—compels her to refer to herself as, like Antigone, of questionable parentage: "a certain Jonas Cixous native of Gibraltar and interpreter for the French army was made and unmade 'French'. . . we the Jews, the forever-illegitimate, we were legitimate? Unstably but all the same legitimate" ("My Algeriance," 163). Cixous' reference to her French ancestry and Jewish illegitimacy through the personage of an interpreter is not a negligible detail. Cixous understands her father's death as multiplying her language access: "When I was ten," she reflects in "The Names of Oran," "my father gave me the last gift: he gave me two teachers, one of Arabic, the other of Hebrew, and then he died" (191). This multiplication of language forms affects kinship terms as well. Just as Antigone is daughter to her brother and sister to her father, Cixous belongs to what she does not belong by the nature of her father's name. "I alone in the Clos-Salembier [the place they lived in Algiers, outside of the French quarter]," confesses Cixous in *Reveries,* "was on both sides, as brother on my brother's side and as girl without my brother who in this case should never have been my sister" (24). Without French citizenship, Cixous experiences a loss of identity and a confusion of kinship, a "paradox of this passport" that she calls "passporosity" ("My Algeriance," 155) because she is welcomed into the state that at the same time dispossesses her. The refusal of the French state to grant legal recognition turns Cixous into the daughter of Oedipus, an Antigone without identity and without name.[28]

Cixous refocuses the politics of the *Antigone*, using gender, memory, and language, instead of states, as politicized social relatedness. Unlike for Antigone, gender for Cixous is not stamped into place by state codifications: rather, identity bars off the state as it passes through metonymic chains, mix-ups, journeys, flights, and crossings. Antigone's disconnection from her name and her nation does not mean that this Antigone is cursed with a tragic, sacrificial destiny. Instead, this expulsion from citizenship allows her identifications to switch from the state to the state's dispossessed others, most immediately the Arabs, banished Antigones as well of confused parentage.[29] The same 1870 law that expelled the Jews from French citizenship also expelled the Arabs: "Who has right?" she protests. "Rights, laws, vacillate, pivot. What is the law? How is it, I asked myself, that the 'Arabs,' the earliest 'arrivals' in this land, are precisely those who were excluded from citizenship? *The illegitimate*" ("My Algeriance," 162). Both Jews and Arabs were banned from

From Decolonization to Body Bombs **77**

attending French schools by the 1940 Vichy decree, relegating the proportion of Jews matriculating even after the Allied victory,[30] while Arab children also were few ("Inside there was only Algeria without Algerians" (109), Cixous writes of her school in "Letter to Zohra Drif").[31] When three young Muslim girls arrived at Cixous' lycée, "We were laughing. I was with them. I was attached to their presences" (*Reveries,* 85), she recounts. She sees them as future combatants, and the violence they unleash will unleash in her a violent and detached language, dispossessed of assigned meaning and taken up by movement and redefinitions, other linkages. Though, as Gayatri Spivak remarks, "one does not hear [Cixous'] name in activist circles in Algeria" (1993: 159) and "her take on the complexity and hybridity of so-called postcolonial nations is shaky" (1993: 159), Cixous' relation to Algeria, for Spivak, is as an exile for whom the "enabling violation of imperialism laid the line for a woman's alliance" (1993: 161) or a pluralization of struggle.

In Althusser's account of hailing citizen-subjects, the state calls citizens to turn their face towards it; in Cixous, the excluded subject extends the call for identification: "I looked all my Algerias in the face" (*Reveries,* 85), Cixous continues. "I needed them, from behind the bars, I called out to them silently and hopelessly" (*Reveries,* 85). One of them was Zohra Drif and another, Samia Lakhdari, was also a combatant in the 1957 Battle of Algiers. Cixous recognized in the faces of those denied by the state the projection of what was to come, the imagined future that would reorder the present of dispossession: "I had a feeling of community. With them," she remarks. ". . . It would have been in anticipation, a declaration of love for the future still well hidden behind the foliation . . . my hands held out toward my kind, on the other side . . . There was no *us*" ("Letter to Zohra Drif," 110–111). The break in the first sentence—separating the subject who declares herself part of a community from the community that she declared herself a part of—insinuates a break in time between the split subject in the present and some unalienated reconciliation that is deferred: there was no "us" yet. Yet this break in the sentence is not an exclusion; this future also inhabits the present as a displacement. The future Algeria that she sees in the girls' faces multiplies her own names and identities, the writing of her self: "I was born Hélène," she writes in "Letter to Zohra Drif," "but a bit of Zohra in me had never stopped chafing at the bit" (108). Their violence is in her language. While Antigone, in Hegel's version, politicizes the state by seeking a singular recognition for her identity within it, Cixous politicizes those to whom the state denies recognition, recognizing them in herself and herself in their violence.

Cixous' Algerian writings are steeped in cravings for a return that can never be: a return to childhood, a return to her father, a return to Zohra Drif, a return to Algeria. Where this sense of loss takes the form of a lost letter in *Reveries*—a letter written in the middle of the night, that continues missing, so that in the morning "I [Cixous, its 'author'] could find only half a sheet" (4)—, *So Close* is framed through Cixous' pressing intention to write a letter to Zohra Drif, a letter that never happens because it cannot: Cixous does not have her address; a letter

78 From Decolonization to Body Bombs

cannot arrive without "proper" administrative reference and destination. As with *écriture féminine*, Cixous flies away on a journey to Algeria and finds substitutions, many other objects of desire that do not satisfy the original demand and so moves on. Cixous' journey is a translation, a constant but violent wrenching away from an original territory driven by a call from future resemblances: "What do I have in common with Zohra," Cixous asks herself while planning her letter that never gets written, "except the silent weight of fits of anger in the classroom, I will open the door, we can blow up the door, everything impossible will be easy, I will write: I am amazed I see the just person, which I will never be, I see her resemblance with you, I am not against blows from a golden lance and the exultation of bombs" (*So Close*, 13). The disappearance of the first letter leads Cixous to forge multiple letters with multiple destinations: "[T]hrough an abundant flow of dreams and the chaos of civilizations Algeria had sent me a sea of traces, visions, relaying packages across thousands of obstacles" (*Reveries*, 4). Algeria is a site of linguistic abundance: "All the beach-words, the theater-words, the street-words were both strange and strangers, and . . . they fluttered in the form of magic, incantatory verbal spirits . . . the words, being musical houses where sorceries kept watch" ("The Names of Oran," 184–185). Letters that do not arrive, Cixous says she learned from Derrida, are "are veritable bombs" (*So Close*, 15).

Zohra's violence as *écriture* subverts the state, repressing the state as an origin of political relations by inhabiting a political relation beside it. Politics becomes more embracing when it loses its singular parentage, its heritage and proper reference: "So apparently," Cixous specifies,

> there was France and the other, another than France? In Algeria, and more specifically at the Lycée Fromentin where I thought I was in a piece of France that was more representative of the France-Thing, more adherent to the spirit of France, than an embassy, *each utterance* having born anymore than anyone else in my families, and yet where flowed the language that I desired to adopt the most in the world, which I adored for its paradoxical riches, its deep sources of amphibology, its winks, its duplicities.
>
> (*So Close, original emphasis; 18*)

The violence of decolonization is linked to *écriture* in that it allows Cixous to imagine political connections more like a language (here, Arabic), not recognized in the name of state bureaucracy, ownership, and citizen control like the name of the feminine body could not be recognized in its parentage, definition, essence, or symbolic placement. This violence demands a politics not of exclusion but of adding-on.

I am not suggesting that *écriture* offers some kind of vision for an alternative to the modern state where the combinations of people could mix freely like language, devoid of barriers or institutions of power, in a multicultural euphoria. Nor am I suggesting that the violent exclusions through which the modern state

From Decolonization to Body Bombs **79**

operates can be dismantled through metonymy or resolved like a translation. The many criticisms of deconstruction for its political evasiveness are not so easily rejected.[32] Rather, instead of a liberal contract—where you surrender rights and freedoms in exchange for care and security—, Cixous' *écriture* wants to rewrite a political relation beyond a symbolic of sacrifice, one of abundance. Here, care as combination replaces sacrifice and exclusion as the underlying conceptual organization of the political.

So Close—describing Cixous' journey towards the memory of Algeria—just about ends on Cixous' father's grave in Algeria, but it does not end there. Having remembered Zohra on the grave of her father, Cixous travels on to visit the Clinic d'Isly, where her mother served as a midwife, even after independence, until the more radical factions within the FLN (*Front de Libération Nationale*) shut it down in 1971. At work, her mother oversaw not exclusion, forgetting, and sacrifice but rather a continual extension of a long list of bodies with names: "[t]he Clinic had two doors that were always open . . . she excels at delivering, but it isn't only the births that count, in addition there are all the stories" (*Reveries*, 62). The clinic is an opening towards sharing the world with others. The separation from the father/state—decolonization—allows political mobility, the sense that identities are not secured in the divisions that the state enacts through bureaucratic and territorial placements and controls, but rather in the constantly changing politicization of unrecognized similarities and common belonging.[33] In her resemblance with Antigone, the woman combatant, then, mobilizes not a critique of politics *per se* in the guise of the state as the total representative of the political and of the community—as neoliberalism would have it—, but rather a protest against *this* state, the one that blindly denies, through imperialist practices, the political connection of care between its citizens in identifying the stories that they tell about their selves.

The Watch

In Cixous, colonial alienation creates the conditions for translation as politics. In other words, the lost object of identity—the untranslatability of original experience—makes possible resemblances and associations that are other to primary identification and mobile. A new neoliberal context, however, treats the isolation of the untranslatable subject as a loss of the political altogether. For neoliberalism, untranslatability means that the subject is beyond the mechanisms through which the subject expresses needs and the sovereign responds to this call by administering care in kind; with such a breakdown in symbolic exchange, the subject can only confront the sovereign in a relation of unsignifiable violence. Neoliberalism's crisis of care is founded in the state's capitulation to capital, where the state's administrations of care are increasingly limited. Without any meaningful recognition by the state, the neoliberal individual is emptied out, annihilated, depoliticized. This conclusion makes visible a devastating consequence of liberalism's self-understanding: liberalism excludes objects of care that fall outside of

80 From Decolonization to Body Bombs

the sovereign's definitions, even designating certain bodies as unintelligible and so not-to-be-cared-for, or disposable. Its production of disposable bodies makes it possible to understand neoliberalism as the heritage of a colonial historical context.

In *The Watch,* an Afghan woman, Nizam (but also called Antigone), approaches an isolated U.S. Forward Operating Base [FOB] and demands to bury her brother, Yusuf, a warrior who led armed militants in an attack on the site during a brutal sandstorm. In the firefight, the U.S. force killed seven Afghani tribesmen they believe are Taliban (the lieutenant refers to this event as the *Seven Against Thebes*). It turned out, however, that they were not Taliban but kin in a wedding party that had been obliterated in a drone strike months before when the local governor had, in likelihood deceitfully, claimed that all the participants were insurgents so that he could call in an American strike on his enemies. Among the attackers was Antigone's only surviving brother. Though losing her legs in the drone attack, she crosses the mountains along a twenty-three kilometer ancient path in a cart that she guides by pulling on the ground with her hands, intending to demand the return of her brother's corpse for burial. The U.S. command, however, as proxy for the Afghani authorities, refuses to return the body, planning to display it on television in order to project strength.

Already, then, the question of sovereign authority is under scrutiny. The imperial relation imperils reaching agreement on a course of action. The Afghani government does not hold the country, and the American forces begrudge the preposterous plan even while obligated to defend it. Afghani sovereignty seems to depend on an inflated media image, and at one point the first sergeant even suggests that the corpse itself is unnecessary when photographs of the body alone would suffice (200). Sovereignty is shown not as establishing relationships with those calling for recognition from the outside but rather as coming to balance uneasily its own internal conflicts as much as possible given the shakiness and arbitrariness of its hold on the occupation of hostile territory. At one point, the second lieutenant says to the captain, "With all due respect, Sir, the boundaries of our actions are leading to our losing good men to save the asses of a bunch of mofos in Kabul who're making out like they're on Wall Street" (271). This Wall Street analogy projects colonialist conquest as corrupt and destabilizing financial speculation rather than as a system of command and control.

The novel applies four principle formalistic devices to convey the sovereign crisis brought to bear in the colonial encounter: 1) unlike for Cixous, the colonized is in a situation of dependence; the imperial state has something that Antigone needs and must demand from it, and this antagonistic bond cannot be broken because the imperial state has exclusive control over the fate of the needed object; yet, the state cannot capitulate to satisfy the demand and still maintain its precarious hold on power; 2) the Creon function—or the incipient state body—is internally split by a hierarchical division of labor that likens it to a vast corporate machine; 3) this sense of internal rupturing and indecision not only

From Decolonization to Body Bombs **81**

forwards the plot but also shapes the formal patterns of speech, where punctuation shifts make characters' utterances seem not to belong to those characters properly or exclusively; this device also projects a feeling that the characters are not bounded individuals acting through individuated consciousnesses but rather blended together in an overall symbolic structure that moves them all; and 4) a translator stands at the center of the communications between the outpost and the territory it is supposed to bring under control, and, unlike the artillery and firearms, the translation often misfires; the command therefore operates on false information, mistaken judgment, and unsure or aberrant decision-making. Unlike for Cixous, where translation adds on the meaning-systems of the new language, hiding a view of the original, the translation leaves Antigone outside the symbolic relation. "I am a woman in their man's world," announces Antigone, "and they do not know how to proceed" (8). As none of the soldiers on the base are women, and women—often from broken relationships—only enter the narrative as distant memories fading in and out of consciousness, Antigone's gender allows her only an unrealized relation to the symbolic as to the state, a dispossession from the political as from representation.

The allusions to Sophocles' tragic play are not subtle: the medic goes to movie night for the screening of the 1961 *Antigone* starring Irene Pappas, when he falls asleep and the movie plot continues on as his dream, his wife in his dream touching him on the shoulder as Antigone touches Polyneices (68). Further on, the Vassar-educated first lieutenant, Nick Frobenius, has a copy of Sophocles' *Antigone* that he lends to the captain just before he (the lieutenant) dies in the crash of an emergency helicopter lift, inspiring the captain's retaliation after the lieutenant's death. As well, the chapter names and character types self-consciously repeat the figures of the classical drama as shaping confrontations in the current war.

The differences from Sophocles are also substantial: for one, the role of Creon is played as an institution organized by a chain of command instead of as an individual psychology or even the representation of an idea (as Hegel interprets it). As the captain remembers what the first lieutenant told him about the play:

> It's the age of Creon. 'Cept that he's here, and there, and everywhere. He's the government and the corporations and everything else that matters, and he's totally faceless. He's a machine, a system, he has his own logic, and once you're part of that, it really doesn't matter if you're a grunt or a general: you're trapped in a conveyor belt of death and destruction. And that's the saddest thing. The saddest thing is that we're part of Creon. We're all compromised and there's nothing we can do about it.
>
> *(258)*

Creon has turned into a self-propelled administrative apparatus. There is no process whereby an oppositional Antigone resists and then is understood as the state is brought into line with its new stage of history, as in Sophocles' or Hegel's

82 From Decolonization to Body Bombs

Antigone. Creon's outer appearance that Antigone confronts emanates resolution and singular decision—the walls of a fort, guarded by snipers—, whereas decisions inside the fort are anything but singular and resolute, passing through social conflict within and between nations, classes, geographical origins, interests, ranks, points of view, narrative divergences, memory backflashes, emotional outbursts, dialects and jargons, character backgrounds, and character development. Whereas Antigone in her opening chapter relates the whole story from beginning to end, with gaps of incomprehension to allow, from inside the fort, twists and turns in the plot that she does not see and cannot fathom, the side of the U.S. military is recounted in a series of point-of-view chapters, each temporally-bound in a particular character's voice-perspective repeating a missing piece of the tale. Time is broken up, moving forward in pieces and then going back to try to fill in the fissures in other perspectives by inserting still other perspectives. The novel offers no point where the entire objective scene can be rationalized, imagined, reconstructed, and represented.

While sovereign power divides along administrative lines (as in Ariel Dorfman's novel *Widows*), the lines themselves are divided according to tasks: a medic, for example, administers care, with the support of the enlisted men who agitate to bring Antigone food and provide medical care, while the captain and his fellow officers build security through command. The debates inside the base review a range of military ethics from security to humanitarianism without ever unsettling the conviction of the right to rule. The conflict, then, focuses on whether Antigone should be an object of security or care. Yet, Antigone refuses their food, as their gift cannot translate into her body: "I leave the food untouched. Soon the ubiquitous crows congregate. I wheel my cart away and the bowl disappears in a blizzard of black wings" (23). Where the female position in the *Antigone* might have once been out of sync with the expression of sovereign force as Sophocles suggests, historically gendered positions of relational care, on the one hand, and, on the other, rule-following force turn here into differential military ranks, functionalities unified in a system even while expressing friction within that system. Care has been absorbed within the military state at the outset rather than through a dialogical process as Sophocles and then Hegel understand it. "It's good to belong to an organization that cares about the finer points" (273), finally admits the captain, aligning the values of care, kinship, and blood loyalty with the military's propensity to violence and leaving the Afghani Antigone of *The Watch* outside the sovereign symbolic system of her tragic origin.

Unlike in Sophocles' *Antigone* and differently than in Cixous' Algerian works, the problems, tensions, and divisions of sovereignty in *The Watch* are absorbed inside of the sovereign instead of externalized in a separate figure, a rational challenger. In keeping, the narrative form also pulls together all sides of a discussion into a single personality by omitting quotation marks. Though the plot advances through dialogues, the characters' speeches do not break off into isolated enunciations captured between quotation marks, each belonging to different

From Decolonization to Body Bombs **83**

characterizations or voices facing off one against another. Instead, they follow one from another as though objectified through an omniscient narrator, a sequencing line, or over-view, the first person joining other first persons in a stream of indirect discourse that break apart the articulation of "I." As other first persons interject, the proper particularity of the subjective enunciation is absorbed into the generalized voice. The foundation of sovereign authority is emptied out in a sequence of citations without limits. Similarly, the author himself is a singular creator of a text that precedes him, a modern Indian-American whose subjectivity continues the molding of a classical Greek play from fifth century B.C. Citation is belonging to the sovereign.

Antigone starts the book in her position alone on the edge of the text and outside the Base, looking in without understanding, just as the American command watches her under spotlights, from binoculars, or through their rifles' sight, their view blocked by her burqa, her cart, or the brightness of the sun. As her body is partially obstructed from view, Antigone's speech never reaches any sort of compatibility with sovereign command. Her language is non-transmittable: no one else on the base knows it. Antigone's sister in the chapter entitled "Ismene"—who, in Sophocles' play, refuses complicity in Antigone's defiance of Creon's decree—is played by the character of Masood, a translator in the employ of the U.S. military.[34] Whereas the standard reception of Ismene reads her as sympathetic but weak and, in the end, Antigone's betrayer,[35] Masood struggles unsuccessfully to ingratiate himself to Antigone—who is Pashtun where he is Tajik. He coaxes her to admit their similarities—his family also died but under Taliban fire—, but she rejects his offer of kinship and resemblance, insisting she is loyal only to her own origin: "My loyalty is to my brother and the memory of my family" (24). Ismene is not the one who refuses complicity with Antigone's defiant act, as in Sophocles, but rather the one, without a shared symbolic, for whom complicity is not even possible.

Knowing only parts of both Creon's language and Antigone's means that Ismene-Masood is denied access to symbolic meaning on both sides. Ismene falls outside the symbolic forms of identification through which the American troops interact because of his cultural references: when he says "Ozymandias," for example, the sniper Specialist Simonis hears "Ozzy Osborne" (112). Specific cultural references only serve to block understanding. Likewise, Ismene misunderstands sovereignty in its American terms: "You represent democracy, freedom, and the rule of law, your task is truly noble" (109), he eagerly declares to the men, only to meet with their resentment. "I don't do politics" (109), says one, in anger, or "I'm simply doing my job, like you're doing yours" (160), retaliates another. Whereas Ismene translates sovereignty as an ideal to follow, a total politics and a symbolic identification to embody, the American soldiers uphold it as mechanical, an administrative tool of empire as empty as an image of a corpse on television, or an objectified routine. Like Antigone, whom the officers cannot determine as a woman or a man because she is covered by a burqa, Ismene's continual communicational misdirections—his inadequate grasp of their symbolic system—make

84 From Decolonization to Body Bombs

his kinship obtuse to the American troops as they negotiate divorces or think about naked pin-ups and sensual memories: "Fruit's as gay as Father Christmas," says one of the enlisted. "Fuckin' loud and queer" (117). His cultural isolation, like Antigone's, moves him out of line with the symbolic of kinship that mirrors the sovereign relation in Hegel.

Likewise for Antigone: the total annihilation of her kin puts her in an unrecoverable position in terms of the symbolic. As a covering, the burqa operates similarly to translation. Like translation, the burqa hides the meaning of Antigone's story by making uninterpretable the wounds on her body: missing legs, bloody hands, and gender. "What d'you think, First Sarn't?" asks the Captain, "Man or woman beneath the burqa?" (126). Unlike for Cixous, where the inaccessibility of the original meaning allows a proliferation of meanings in alternative connections and contexts, Antigone's untranslatability isolates her totally, empties her out. The secret-ing of her body under the burqa does lead to a series of guesses as to where she came from and why, but none of them resemble Antigone's story. Her history, like her gender, is hidden under the sovereign's errors in interpreting her cultural references.

Antigone is, in fact, in extreme physical and emotional pain: the text intimates that her corporeal suffering explains her behavior fully. Likewise, the reasons for the persistence of her demands are erased from the sovereign's narrative. The background of why she may have dragged herself over the mountains—of what her life was like before she came under the crosshairs of a U.S. drone, of how she was dispossessed—disappears as the burqa becomes the only available evidentiary sign. This disconnection of Antigone's story from her social and political circumstances—the non-translatability of her account—disorients the U.S. directives as the officers misconstrue her political motives and interpret her presence as due to someone else's decision. Unable to trace her intentions, the captain, for example, considers her as a decoy or diversionary tactic put in place by an invisible foe in order to distract the U.S. surveillance from detecting other imminent threats.

The paranoid question of what lies beneath the burqa circulates among the troops and calls for a response but also makes a response impossible. The platoon does a complete body search, forcing Antigone to remove her burqa, to stand naked on her leg stumps before a group of men, to turn around, and to lie down and spread her legs (16), but they find nothing. Nothing appears to have preceded the covering. Like the burqa, the paranoid U.S. speculative story replaces the hidden object—Antigone's body. "So their kinetic ops agent is a girl in a makeshift go-kart?" (134) asks the second lieutenant, referring to the Taliban who, he wrongly thinks, must have sent her.

For Cixous, a barrier against translation and prescribed identification opens a multiplicity of alternative political connections. The burqa here, however, proves the truth of U.S. expectations. She carries a weapon; she is a suicide bomber. The examination misses the point: she is, indeed, hiding a weapon beneath her covering, a knife, but they never discover it. While, in line with her own cultural

From Decolonization to Body Bombs **85**

practices, she uses the knife to sacrifice a lamb in order to give it as a gift to the command post in gratitude for the offers of care extended by the enlisted personnel, the captain sees its flash as aggressive and quickly convinces himself that he was right to have distrusted her all along, that she like her brother threatened the survival of the post. He abandons his intentions to give her medical assistance. A simultaneous movement spotted on the surrounding hills signals danger. The captain concludes that her kin or fellow tribespeople are finally preparing an attack, and that she, too, will detonate. The sniper, under orders, shoots to kill. "We hear the bullet whistle past," notes the captain, "and then the girl's falling backward with a bright red explosion where her heart used to be" (279). As the movement on the hills turns out to be a dog running wild, Antigone's whole story becomes one of isolation, personal pain, misunderstanding, and abandonment.[36] There are no cells in the hills, no nationalists, no Taliban, no family. As with her brother, Antigone is rendered a body of pure spectacle with no social attachments, like a television image dispossessed from a cultural content, identity, or belonging that is out of sync, untranslatable. The sovereign's misunderstanding has the final say. Antigone explodes; in the process, her body reveals, underneath the burqa, only the effects of sovereign violence at its core.

Conclusion

All this is not intended to provide a moral excuse for suicide bombing or to make a claim that suicide bombers are simply misunderstood, but rather to suggest that the female suicide bomber cannot be as surprising as some media pundits proclaim: she is already embedded in the Western imaginary as the possibility of failure in the symbolic exchange the social contract orchestrates. In addition, the suicide bomber is positioned within representations of the current war as the social contract's last grasp at viability under neoliberalism: isolated in her emotive expansiveness, without agency, totally obedient and yet just as totally responsible for her acts and decisions, injured to the point of near immobility and yet responsible for her own pain, guilty without cause and yet responsible for her total criminality.

The Watch replicates the liberal social contract by dramatizing an encounter on the frontier of the so-called "War on Terror." The U.S. invasion of Afghanistan proves an apt site for the Antigone to take place in light of the play's Hegelian interpretation as a founding moment for modern sovereign power: the novel brackets the birth of Athenian democracy against the founding of a failing Afghani state. The colonialist setting makes visible not only the social contract's presumption of inequality, not only the sovereign's need of violence, not only the instability inside sovereign power, but also, even more emphatically, the dispossession or sacrifice of the individual at the center of the political relation with the sovereign in liberalism.

Such political dispossession of the individual can translate into symbolic failure. Describing the impasse of contemporary politics, Zygmunt Bauman notes:

86 From Decolonization to Body Bombs

"There is no need for dialogue, since there is nothing to talk about: the subjects have nothing to say which could possibly be of value to the business of power, and the powers-that-be have no further need to convince, convert or indoctrinate their subjects" (88). This comment aligns with Antigone's relation to the U.S. military in *The Watch*. While the *Antigone* may once have presented an allegory of the state where the state absorbs its opposite, the increasing dispossession of some individuals tends now towards greater tragedy. Language is lost to representation. The neoliberal sovereign cannot translate Antigone's demands or her pain. This kind of tragedy emphasizes total isolation and a loss of political agency, reviving the classical tragic themes of fatalism within the contemporary political relation and reducing politics to lamentation.

Poststructuralist thought allows us to understand dispossession as not just a loss of a sovereign relation based on a sacrifice for the sake of security but also as a loss of symbolic belonging and social connectedness, a loss that augments insecurity. Yet, poststructuralist revisions of the liberal political relation run the risk of having no normative ethical standpoint from which to judge the effects of dispossession as a loss of sovereignty or the repercussions of an apoliticism lived as personal lamentation. In its focus on thinking of the emergence of the subject through language, poststructuralism has sometimes marginalized sovereign power beyond the terms of its own critique. Athena Athanasiou, in her conversation with Butler, raises this question of how to judge and even resist neoliberal regimes' allocations of precarity and disposability to certain bodies that do not fit its recognizable symbolic forms of personhood increasingly defined through property regulations that are more polarizing than ever. Athanasiou uses as examples events happening on a global scale: agricultural appropriation, colonial occupation, capital crisis management, environmental destruction, security regimes, policing of migration, and "economies of abandonment" (31) like the War on Terror. In response, Butler reflects again on the possibility that such dispossession is itself a form of resistance:

> It seems to me that there is a presence implied by the idea of bodily exposure, which can become the occasion of subjugation or acknowledgement. The coercive exposure of bodies at checkpoints or other sites of intensified surveillance can be one instance of the former. The body must arrive, present itself for inspection, and move only according to the motion and speed required by the soldier or machine . . . But similarly, when acts of resistance happen at the checkpoint, when bodies show up or move through in ways that are not allowed, or when communities form on either side to limit and counter military practices, a kind of presence occurs.
>
> *(*Dispossession*, 13–14)*

Butler acquiesces to Athanasiou's line of questioning but without acknowledging that she is setting up normative terms. Privileging an Antigone whose words

From Decolonization to Body Bombs   **87**

and body motion can be interpreted in sovereign terms, she does not detect the suicide bomber without a passport who haunts this meeting at the checkpoint. As Butler sets up this scene of confrontation, there is no place for imagining bodies' symbolic exchange as proposed in *The Watch*. Where does a politics of self-destroying bodies fit in? Is suicide bombing a revelation that the liberal social contract is formulated inside the colonial encounter that exposes its failures and limits?[37] Is suicide bombing showing that the social relation of interdependency and symbolic exchange can, does, and must fail? Does suicide bombing intensify and polarize even more the already polarized liberal political relation between the unheeding sovereign and the self-sacrificing individual?

In other places, Butler provides a strong and much needed articulation of the ethical stakes in the social disinvestments of neoliberal forms of dispossession. "[E]veryone is dependent on social relations" (2015: 21), she begins her book on protest, and "none of us acts without the conditions to act" (2015: 17). Any intention to escape from current social conditions must, insists Butler, take into account that these conditions give us life; there is no stepping outside of these conditions. Yet, neoliberal rationality, she continues, by establishing the conditions for the subject's deepening sense of isolation, establishes "every member of the population as potentially or actually precarious" (2015: 15) and dispensable. "Under contemporary conditions of forced emigration and neoliberalism," she notes, "vast populations now live with no sense of a secure future, no sense of continuing political belonging, living a sense of damaged life as part of the daily experience of neoliberalism" (2015: 202). We are all Antigones, left with little political recourse outside of senseless violence, self-annihilation, dispossession, and lamentation.

The suicide bomber makes spectacularly visible an absence of care—the body, bereft of associational bonding, coming apart. Dispossessed individuals—individuals without any political recourse but violent self-destruction—are bodies saturated in neoliberal power, with social conditioning ideologically denied and material supports being withdrawn under the ideological proviso that such lack of support proves an individual's own failings. In the recent past, decolonizing nationalism—a relation to a not-yet-realized hegemonic formation breaking from the sovereign state (often expressed in kinship terms)—may have inspirited ways of associating not premised on sacrifice but on political resemblance, abundant care, and transformative belonging, one that did not remit us to what neoliberalism wants for us now: a total political deprivation, symbolic detachment, violent enforcement, and the evacuation of the living person. The next chapter explores further a needed acknowledgement of a relationship between bodies, care, and politics. In Hannah Arendt's terms (that Butler draws on), the body represents a person's relationship to the world she shares with others, a world that is politicized in response to that body. In this, the political understanding of the body, for Arendt, cannot be reduced to an expression of pure violence on one side and lamentable need on the other but must be centrally part of constructing the world we inhabit together, thinking of the future.

Notes

1 As well, in a report by the Institute for Strategic Dialogue about why Western women have joined the Islamic State [ISIS, or ISIL], "Till Martyrdom Do Us Part," Erin Marie Saltman and Melanie Smith explain that the most common motivational factors are "feeling isolated socially and/or culturally" (9) and "[f]eeling isolated within Western culture" (9) as a result of discrimination against ethnic differences and a lack of any national or international response to such discriminatory practices. According to this report, ISIS promises such women, instead, a sense of belonging and an active role to play in the caliphate by being a wife and a mother (14): "Women within our dataset consistently speak of the camaraderie and sisterhood they experience within ISIS-controlled territory. They discuss the feeling of belonging, of unity and community" (15). The report also remarks that women often feel disappointed. The report is based on an aggregation of profiling data accumulated from social media. The *New York Times* also reports on an American teenager recruited over social media, indicating that ISIS not only looks for lonely teenagers but also makes them feel lonelier as part of their recruiting process: "We look for people who are isolated," said one former recruiter. "And if they are not isolated already, then we isolated them" (Callimachi).

2 As Tina Chanter notes, as well, of literary interest in Antigone from the nineteenth century on, Hegel positioned Antigone as a threat to the state in its origin, not only because women were "representative of the private, domestic, and civic sphere, as opposed to the public, political, and civic sphere" (xi), but also because he saw their political demands as disruptive to "the narrative of civilized, masculinized, and progressive rationality" (xi), which formed the basis of the modern, sovereign state.

3 Neoliberalism is a system, says Aihwa Ong, "through which governing activities are recast as nonpolitical and nonideological problems that need technical solutions" (3).

4 "If the way in which the difference between women and men was conceived as intricately bound up with the differentiation between citizens and non-citizens, . . . so too the citizen-alien binary was very much informed by the free-slave binary" (xxvi).

5 Susan Buck-Morss convincingly and provocatively raises the spectre of colonialism and slavery in the Hegelian version of the liberal contract in contrast to a neoliberal reading. Hegel, she notes, gave up on Hobbes' tale of the state of nature as the natural freedom that the state must uphold. In its place, Hegel's dialectical account of freedom, Buck-Morss attests, is based in the social advance of freedom in the Haitian revolution, a freedom that the slave cannot surrender while remaining human: "Those who once acquiesced to slavery demonstrate their humanity when they are willing to risk death rather than remain subjugated" (2009: 55). Sovereignty would mean protecting that freedom. Buck-Morss laments that two centuries of Hegel scholars have neglected to account for this association with freedom "*in the world*" (2009: 61) that he learns by reading the news from Haiti.

6 Speaking of suicide bombers, Adriana Cavarero remarks, "What is unwatchable above all, for the being that knows itself irremediably singular, is the spectacle of disfigurement, which the singular body cannot bear. As its corporeal symptoms testify, the physics of horror has nothing to do with the instinctive reaction to the threat of death. It has rather to do with instinctive disgust for a violence that, not content merely to kill because killing would be too little, aims to destroy the uniqueness of the body, tearing at its constitutive vulnerability" (8).

7 *L'attentat* (*The Attack*), for example, by the Algerian police-novel writer Yasmina Khadra, tells of an educated, professional-class Arab-Israeli woman—living in "a splendid residence in one of the most exclusive neighborhoods in Tel Aviv" (22), winning recognition for service to the Israeli state—who blows herself up on a busy street, unable to reconcile her Israeli existence with the loss of nationhood for those she identifies as her people (For a more extensive discussion of Khadra's *L'attentat* in the

context of her other works, including an Algerian police series published under a different name and a different gender, see my "Military Literati: Yasmina Khadra and the Veil" in *Policing Narratives and the State of Terror*). Athol Fugard's play *The Island* stages anti-apartheid fighters performing the *Antigone* in drag while serving their terms as prisoners at Robben Island: "The law is no more or less than a shield in your faithful servant's hand to protect YOU!" (74), the actor playing Antigone improvises before her Creon. The Argentinean feminist playwright Griselda Gambaro has her Antigone in *Antígona Furiosa*, an abstraction of the Madres of the Plaza, perform from inside a cage, hanging from the gallows, as "[s]itting together at a round table, two men dressed in street clothes are having coffee"(137) outside the cage. Ariel Dorfman disguises his critique of the disappearances in Argentina and his native Chile by relocating the conflict to Antigone's native Greece during World War II, as widows and family members battle against the Fascist armed forces to bury the tortured bodies washing up on their shores.

8 Jennifer Yee attributes Cixous' outsidedness and exclusion in these Algerian narratives to her self-positioning as "a Third party, the outsider who is innocent and yet implicated in the colonial system" (189). This reading neglects to note that the critique (and deconstruction) Cixous is staging against the Enlightenment's version of objectivity, transcendence, and "disinterested" critique.

9 As George Steiner writes, "Even more pervasive, and altogether impossible to index, has been the role of the matter of Antigone in the actual lives of individuals and communities. It is a defining trait of western culture after Jerusalem and after Athens that in it men and women re-enact, more or less consciously, the major gestures, the exemplary symbolic motions, set before them by antique imaginings and formulations" (108).

10 "Some see tragic action as fundamentally unconstrained and, thus, punishable, by which they mean that the action arises from an internal space of free choice or decision. Others see tragic action as the work of the gods or an abstract divine power or fate, thus locating the source as external to the protagonist" (52). Kirkland's point is that within the Greek classical context, the opposition between these two positions was less, if at all, relevant than it became under modern political and philosophical thought. The blending of these two positions, however, seems dangerous in a neoliberal perspective where power boasts of total technological, ideological, and economic mastery (as in colonialism), making self-determination ever more necessary to defend.

11 For example, as Jocelyn Viterna convincingly demonstrates, women in El Salvador were recruited into the FMLN [Frente Farabundo Martí para la Liberación Nacional] when the guerrillas offered them protection from the sexual aggressions of the Salvadorian army. The guerrillas thereby espoused in their recruiting efforts conservative sexual values, placing a sacred premium on female purity where "joining the guerrillas therefore became an important way that women could defend their identities as good young women" (54–55). "[D]iscussing how the Armed Forces cut fetuses out of pregnant women's bellies," Viterna elaborates, "was one of the most effective ways for Salvadorans to demonstrate why the FMLN was 'good' and why the state military forces were so very, very evil" (76). She goes on, "they [the FMLN] increasingly relied on gender narratives instead of political narratives to guarantee recruitment success" (75).

12 As well, women combatants would consider the gendered body as part of a decision about the direction of their political involvement. "The possibility of having children," Diana's informant continues, "was complicated for us. We wanted them, and at the same time we knew it would be difficult. On the other hand, we knew that our struggle was also for them" (my translation; 137). Or, "My terror as much as the other militants' was what would happen to our children if we were caught," confesses another informant, "... but I also knew that I was giving them the living example in accordance with an idea" (my translation; 123).

13 Feminist anthropologist Begoña Aretxaga has made similar claims about the struggle for independence in Ireland. Exploring women's involvement in the resistance, she

90 From Decolonization to Body Bombs

notes: "The house was far from being a secluded female space . . . The logistic structure of political violence is articulated . . . through a web of intimate relations" (52–53). Nell McCafferty's novel *Peggy Deery: An Irish Family at War* also shows that postcolonial violence infiltrates daily family life in its minute detail: "The police moved into her bedroom, where one of them felt the sheets and said that both sides of the double bed were warm" (110), McCafferty describes the police search for Paddy Deery, who had been involved with the violent arm of the Irish Republican Army (IRA). Encountering police investigators in pursuit of her husband, Paddy's wife Colette "felt she had nothing to lose, since all was obviously lost anyway: Paddy had left his socks and shoes on the floor" (110). Sociologists working in Palestine have, like Fanon, observed that the marginalization of women's participation in violence has meant a depoliticization of civil society and a loss of momentum towards a reconstructed future, particularly in the postcolony. Penny Johnson and Eileen Kuttab have shown that whereas the violence in the first *intifada* occurred in the communities and neighborhoods and therefore included women as defenders of their homes, the second *intifada* took place as direct militancy mostly at border-checkpoints rather than in neighborhoods, minimizing the role of women. Women's invisibility in the second *intifada* is, they note, "exemplary of a larger absence of civil society" (24) and of a general "decline in political activity" (25). As Nadia Latif argues, the constructed separation between women and violence has meant a focus on violence as remarkable rather than routine, obscuring the ways that many experience violence throughout the social, including "malnutrition, lack of access to potable water, sanitation and adequate health care, low wages, hazardous living and work conditions . . . impoverishment and under-development" (25).

14 Mazurana claims, "[O]nce wars ended, women in armed forces and groups were expected to resume their traditional roles" (154). Of women combatants in Sierre Leone, Chris Coulter writes, "The violence they committed was not emancipatory and in most cases was not perceived as meaningful in any ideological sense, . . . nor were they motivated by any promises of improved status for women in postwar society" (139). "The national project," summarizes Begoña Aretxaga about Ireland, ". . . was predicated on a rejection of modernity, not on its national adaptation. . . . In doing so, Irish nationalism, perhaps more than others, remained trapped within the framework of colonialist false essentialisms. The consequences were enormous for women who were erased from the professional and intellectual life of the country" (150). Analyzing the Algerian Charter of Algiers, the National Charter, and the 1976 Constitution, Marnia Lazreg notes that "The lack of appreciation at the political theoretical level of the significance of the category 'women' on a par with the categories of 'peasants' or 'workers' meant the erasure of women from the government's political agenda. Women could only exist as wives, mothers or daughters of men" (149). "Although there were important changes in gender relations," Ilja A. Luciak observes about Central America, "on the whole, the subordination of women prevalent in prewar society continued" (10). Addressing the mobilization of gender categories in the Argentinian Madres de la Plaza protests, Diana Taylor concludes, "The Madres played into a national fantasy predicated on sexual difference that explains male potency and dominance and the female's lack thereof. Much as the military's performance was a display of virility, the Madres' spectacle was a public display of *lack*. They made it evident that they had no previous political identity or background, no expertise—they were just housewives; they had no power, no weapons, just absence, missing children. . . . The role did not allow for their politicization. Rather, the maternal role once again relegated the women to the subordinated position of mediators in an old drama. . . ." (original emphasis; 203–205). In the case of Pakistan, Veena Das has argued that the Partition restored the gender order by recovering women who had been abducted and held: "The state of war, akin to the Hobbesian state of nature, comes to be defined as one in

From Decolonization to Body Bombs **91**

which Hindus and Muslims are engaged in mutual warfare over the control of sexually and reproductively active women. The origin of the state is then located in the rightful reinstating of proper kinship by recovering women from the other side" (21).

15 Not everyone has agreed with Fanon that women's participation in struggles for decolonization has meant the politicization of women within civil society. As Marnia Lazreg has pointed out, the idea that "the burden of a revitalized native society was to be borne by women" (87) was central to decolonization throughout the history of the Algerian movement, even as cultural and religious tendencies still subordinated women, a situation that became clearer after independence. "It is clear that women's participation in the war was instrumental to its success. Yet, with a few exceptions, the nature of this participation fit in a 'traditional' pattern of gender roles, where men held positions of responsibility and command, and women executed orders" (124). According to Lazreg, the degree of women's subordination varied according to urban and rural differences, as well as differences in education and class origin.

16 Feminist critics have commended Fanon for his criticisms of nationalist politics, which place women outside of nationalist struggles for the purpose of maintaining a sense of pre-modern belonging and tradition. As Madhu Dubey, for example, has commented, "some nationalist ideologies . . . employ women to embody the corrupting threat of emancipatory possibilities of modernization" (3). For Dubey, Frantz Fanon challenges this tradition through his "vehement refusal to center national identity around a static cultural tradition located in the precolonial past" (9). Dubey is here criticizing, among others, some of the subaltern studies scholars—like Partha Chatterjee and Dipesh Chakrabarty—who have adopted a linear view of nationalist history that is distinctively gendered, with masculinity underlying the forward motion of history and progress, and femininity defending tradition. Anne McClintock, too, faults nationalism for its symbolic placement of women in the stagnant, prehistorical role of maintaining traditions: "[T]he temporal anomaly within nationalism—veering between nostalgia for the past and the impatient, progressive sloughing off of the past—is typically resolved by figuring the contradiction in the representation of *time* as a natural division of *gender*. Women are represented as the atavistic and authentic body of national tradition" (358–359). McClintock lauds Fanon for not relegating women to a time before the nation, an ideal that is past, and also for rejecting the narrative structure of the nation as family. The problem with Fanon, for McClintock, is that women are invited by men into the nationalist struggle that men already inhabit: "Theirs is a *designated agency*—an agency by invitation only" (366).

17 Like the female suicide bomber, Antigone's politics, says Honig, is lamentational, exemplified, for instance, when she compares herself to the mythological mother Niobe who loses her children in a dispute with the goddess Leta (as Antigone loses her potential children in a dispute with the sovereign Creon) and then is abandoned in the form of a stone that forever sheds her tears: "The rains never leave her, the snow never fails, as she wastes away. That is how men tell the story. From streaming eyes her tears wet the crags; most like to her the god brings me to rest" (lines 888–891). Antigone and the chorus reject this assertion that fate and divine intervention cause her grief. For Honig, feminist political theory's turn to questions of grief, instigated by Antigone, "captures and mirrors modern romantic and liberal imaginations" (2013: 55), a "certain left melancholy" or "self-indulgence" (2013: 55) that poses a "post-political ethical universalism" (2013: 59) against the state as the site for doing politics. Niobe is an important figure in the next chapter.

18 "As with many American men who search for wives abroad, it is likely that Farook was insistent on procuring an immigrant wife who, accustomed to the strictures of a conservative father, would acquiesce to his domination. . . . Male oppression is pushed out of this tale of mass carnage because it does not have the cachet of intrigue that gets journalists' blood pumping and the war drums beating. The details and dynamics of the

92 From Decolonization to Body Bombs

marriage and the powerlessness imposed by the immigration status of one spouse over the other do not generate much interest."

19 "The Organization also cast a long shadow over her marriage. Though Aws had always wanted a baby, Abu Muhammad [her husband] asked her to take birth control pills, still available at Raqqa's pharmacies. When she pressed him, he said his commanders had advised fighters to avoid getting their wives pregnant. New fathers would be less inclined to volunteer to carry out suicide missions."

20 Benedetta Faedi Duramy's book about women in armed conflict in Haiti contests that women only join armed groups when they themselves have been victimized: "female aggression is principally employed as a coping response to previous victimization and as an adaptive strategy to the daily hardships women and girls face in the context of armed violence" (119). According to Duramy, armed militias used rape as a political tool after the coup that ousted Jean-Bertrand Aristide in 2004. As a result, women could not return to their families, and the family fabric of Haitian society unraveled. These stigmatized women had no option but to take refuge with oppositional gangs, where they sometimes engaged in armed action but mostly against their will: "girls are often forced to join the gangs and become concubines of their members because they fear retaliation against themselves and their families. However, in many cases, lacking food, work, and money to pay their school fees or hospital bills, they choose to affiliate with the armed groups in the hope of better prospects" (76). Their motivations are interpreted as individualistic, therapeutic, and purely emotional: "three major factors that motivate women and girls to engage in criminal and community violence are their need to protect themselves and their families, their resentment towards state negligence and denial of their plight, and their dysfunctional desire to attain personal and social respect through retaliation" (15). Not only does it seem unlikely that a militia could sustain itself without some form of consent or buy-in from participants, but also the groups are constantly referred to as "gangs" or "criminals," groups concerned with committing acts of illegal violence, but not "movements," socially embedded groups with political intentions. Though the women Duramy studies do not wind up as suicide bombers, Duramy, whose stated project is to advise the United Nations and other international relief organizations in neoliberal reforms, assumes that their motives cannot be political and their choice of violence can result only from personal trauma. This is much the same pathway that generally pops up in descriptions of suicide bombers.

21 Referring to the Madres of the Plaza de Mayo movement in Argentina as an appropriation of the *Antigone,* Diana Taylor has argued, "[T]he *Antigone* plot specifically raises questions about political leadership and mis-rule, about the conflict between the so-called private and public spaces, about public fear and complicity" (209). Though praising the Madres for accomplishing a take-over of the rhetoric surrounding the dictatorship, Taylor still criticizes the movement for a conservatism around gender roles, fashioning themselves, in line with the *Antigone,* as lamenting mothers representing the sanctity of the domestic private sphere.

22 "Without friends, without husband, without tears, she is led along that *forgotten path* and there is *walled up* alive in a *hole* in the rock, shut off forever from the light of the sun. . . . Thus the sister will strangle herself in order to save at least the mother's son. She will cut off her breath—her voice, her air, blood, life—with the veil of her belt, returning into the shadow (of a) tomb, the night (of) death, so that her brother, *her mother's desire,* may have eternal life" (Irigaray's emphasis; 218–219).

23 "If the individual is isolated, then he is either absolutely the creator of his own destiny, in which case nothing tragic remains . . ., or the individuals are only modifications of the eternal substance of existence, and so again the tragic is lost" (158).

24 I am here referring to some of Rey Chow's insights into the relationship between women and political community in her analysis of Fanon. Chow understands Fanon's perspective on combatant women in "Algeria Unveiled" as reifying and essentializing.

From Decolonization to Body Bombs **93**

In that famous essay, Fanon sees the French and the Algerians as totally opposed and mutually exclusive in their Manichean corners, without any possibility of mixing into a broader political community. The woman combatant can only belong to the Algerian nation where she finds her place within the kinship structure, and, as such, she is desexualized. In contrast, Chow indicates, *Black Skin, White Masks* offers a view of women as traitorous because they are sexualized: "Women, because they have the capability of embodying physical contact—of giving material form to 'touching,' to the transgressions of bodily boundaries—in the form of reproduction, are always potentially dangerous" (39). Chow, therefore, sees Fanon's female combatants as lacking agency and his women civilians who seduce French soldiers as having an agency "that could break down all boundaries and thus disrupt social order" (39). Cixous restores the combatant woman's sexuality and sees that combination as integral to political community formation.

25 Cixous' ideas on translation dovetail with Derrida's. Glossing the story of Babel, its confusion of tongues, and its lack of completion, Derrida writes, "[T]he Semites want to bring the world to reason, and this reason can signify simultaneously a colonial violence (since they would thus universalize their idiom) and a peaceful transparency of the human community. Inversely, when God [the unrepresentable, the untranslatable] imposes and opposes his name, he ruptures the rational transparency but interrupts also the colonial violence or the linguistic imperialism. He destines them to translation. He destines them to translation, he subjects them to the law of translation both necessary and possible; in a stroke with his translatable-untranslatable name he delivers a universal reason (it will no longer be subject to the rule of a particular nation), but he simultaneously limits its very universality: forbidden transparency, impossible univocity. Translation becomes law, duty and debt" ("Des Tours de Babel": 174). As with Cixous' unrepresentable woman's body, Derrida's barring of access to God means that the word takes on multiple meanings at once, breaking from one meaning center while adding on another, without it ever bound to an origin.

26 Just as *écriture feminine,* in "The Laugh . . .": "we've lived in flight, stealing away, finding, when desired, narrow passageways, hidden crossovers" (343–344). The "militant" (340, 341) is already inside *écriture,* "an explosion . . . *in language*" (343), "herding contradictions into a single battlefield" (339).

27 Robert Young has remarked on the importance of Algeria to the deconstructive project: "Many of those who developed the theoretical positions subsequently characterized as poststructuralism came from Algeria or had been involved in the war of independence. Fanon, Memmi, Bourdieu, Althusser, Lyotard, Derrida, Cixous—they were all in or from Algeria" (413). For Young, this connection is significant because the split subject, or the decentered subject, that characterizes certain forms of poststructuralism can be historicized through decolonizing violence: "Violence makes the subject double, doubly subject, simultaneously subject and object, an outsider to his or her own being . . . [I]t is by becoming a subject of violence that the dehumanized colonized subject becomes a subject for the first time" (294–295).

28 Much scholarship on Cixous and her Algerian experience reduces exile to an aesthetic question. Cixous' loss of identity, such arguments may suggest, underlies the heterogeneity of linguistic usage or the hybridity of narrative form. Claire Boyle, for example, attributes Cixous' unconventional syntax to her challenge to the autobiography genre where there is a "lack of knowledge circulating about the autobiographical self" (72)—a self that others cannot know—which she terms "misrecognition." Likewise, Lynn Penrod sees the very idea of *écriture* an expression of exile: "For the place of exile is also the place and space of writing" (138) and "the feeling of banishment, of exclusion threads through her work" (144). In these readings, *écriture* relates to sovereign expression rather than state sovereignty.

29 Relatively few Algerian Muslims took advantage of the French offer of citizenship in 1870, partial though it was: "Because naturalization implied relinquishing their legal

94 From Decolonization to Body Bombs

status as Muslims [*status personnel*], the acquisition of French citizenship by Muslims was interpreted by their coreligionists as apostasy" (Weltman-Aron, 139).

30 Cixous says that 1 to 2% of Jews were included as "alibi or hostage Jews" ("Letter to Zohra Drif," (108)). Weltman-Aron: "The *numerous clausus* targeted professors and university students at first, but the measure was later applied to primary and secondary schoolchildren, despite the fact that such application was not required by any legislative text . . . the *numerous clausus* was not completely abolished until March 1943, while the whole anti-Jewish legislation was only dismantled in October 1943 . . . The measure of discrimination excluding some, but not all Jewish schoolchildren, made it particularly incomprehensible to them, while bringing few advantages to those who were kept as students, and whom Cixous names 'alibi and hostage Jews' . . . Cixous even claims that some schools, such as her *college,* the Lycée Fromentin in Algiers, seemed to perpetuate secretly a form of *numerous clausus* well after the war" (139–140).

31 Weltman-Aron, 141.

32 See, for example, Anne McClintock and Rob Nixon for a heated presentation of some of these arguments. Although their debate with Derrida might seem of a generation ago, these sentiments continued on. McClintock and Nixon denounce Derrida for declaring the word *Apartheid* as the "last word of racism" and describing it as excessive, without foundation, containing its own destructive opposition. McClintock and Nixon argue back that Derrida removes the historical sedimentation of the word, "a severance of the word from history" (341), as well as a disregard "to the protean forms of political persuasion" (352). The politics and powers of any particular situation will, of course, control and even block the way language develops uses. Derrida responds by saying that the difficulties the *Apartheid* regime had of convincing the world it was right meant that history was also splitting apart the regime's language: "Those in power in South Africa have not managed to convince the world, first of all because, still today, they have refused to change the real effective meaning of their watchword: *apartheid.* A watchword is not just a name. This too history teaches us" ("But Beyond . . .": 362).

33 Cixous does meet up with Zohra Drif during her stay in Algeria. At this point, Zohra Drif was already pursuing her political career, tracing her lineage as a combatant and a politician to women fighting against the initial, nineteenth century French invasion: "They [women] have always actively participated in the resistance against the occupation," Zohra Drif says in the documentary, *Remembering History,* included in the DVD boxset for *The Battle of Algiers.* "I was always deeply involved with my country and my people." Zohra Drif did not consult with Gilles Pontecorvo during the making of *The Battle of Algiers.*

34 Translators and interpreters have become significantly more central to plotting the contemporary war story than in prior wars. Translators occupy a liminal position in war texts, responsible for the cultural understandings and, more often, misunderstandings received by each group about the others and drawing attention to non-translatable aspects of the violence that influence the war's trajectory. Translations serve as communicational breakdowns. Works, besides *The Watch*, that develop and dramatize the translator role, giving it a personality, a background, motivations, and psychological depth include: Helen Benedict's *Sand Queen*, Gayle Tzemach Lemmon's *Ashley's War*, Michael Pitre's *Fives and Twenty-Fives*, Matthew Gallagher's *Kaboom: Embracing The Suck in a Savage Little War*, Helen Thorpe's *Soldier Girls*, Kayla Williams' *Love My Rifle*, and Phil Klay's "Psychological Operations" in *Redeployment*, among others.

35 Honig notes, "Perhaps no element of *Antigone's* reception history is more settled than the belief that Antigone's sister, Ismene, is an anti-political character who lacks the courage or imagination to act when called upon to do so" (2013: 151). Honig challenges this standard interpretation in line with her view that the apolitical needs to be politicized.

From Decolonization to Body Bombs **95**

36 The U.S. personnel, too, are isolated in an outpost, and their families, too, are fading in memories, only sustained in the ephemerality of a film strip caught up in a dream.

37 Part of the confusion here may be attributable to a lack of clarity over whether Butler is posing the relation between the subject and the social in descriptive or prescriptive terms. She insists that she is talking about the way norms work, not the ways she prefers them to work; yet, she also insists, with a nod to Arendt, that violence cannot be political because politics is always constructive. Nonviolent resistance, she says, "does not just say no to a violent world, but crafts the self and its relation to the world in a new way, seeking to embody, however provisionally, the alternative for which it struggles" (2015: 187). Nancy Fraser's criticisms of Foucault would apply here to Butler's more Foucauldian moments and her suspicion about norms: "On the one hand, he never directly pronounces in favor of rejectionism as an alternative to dialectical social criticism; but, on the other hand, his writings abound with rhetorical devices that convey rejectionist attitudes . . . it is not surprising that Foucault fails to distinguish among the various sorts of rejectionism . . . On the contrary, he tends to conflate conceptual, strategic, and normative arguments" (37). Also, she inherits from Arendt the problem of claiming that politics is non-violent even though, unlike Arendt, she includes a critique of sovereignty, maintaining that sovereign power is the power of violence, and that other forms of power may have other configurations. Arendt, on the other hand, wants to find a non-violent configuration of sovereign power, as I explore in the next chapter.

3

A CRITIQUE OF VIOLENCE

In the Age of Mechanical Drone Warfare

When, in 1968, Hannah Arendt posthumously published her friend Walter Benjamin's essays in *Illuminations,* she excluded his now-famous, enigmatic work, "A Critique of Violence." "A Critique of Violence" (1921) exhibits Benjamin's philosophical investigations into the role of violence in modern state sovereignty and inherent in its law, and the construction of an alternative understanding of violence—or revolutionary violence—outside of the framework of the modern state. Increasingly relevant today, when violence plays an increasingly central role in spreading markets and controlling populations and when state sovereignty is increasingly undermined by corporate and financial interests, the essay touched on many of the issues that Arendt herself addressed in her opposition to totalitarianism as well as in her theorizing on the politics of the revolutionary tradition and its outbreaks in her time. Arendt never gave any reason for the essay's omission in her collection but spent a considerable part of her career reflecting on the relation of violence to politics in ways that respond to Benjamin's critique, though without any references to it.[1]

Arendt and Benjamin were both interested in a critique of historical materialism, which would divorce thinking from being and open towards an unpredictable contingency not absorbable into a predetermining narrative of progress or causality that denies politics. As Seyla Benhabib puts it, like Benjamin, "Arendt is not concerned to establish some inevitable continuity between the past and present that would compel us to view what happened as what *had* to happen. She objects to this trap of historicist understanding and maintains that the future is radically undetermined" (original emphasis; 2012: 40). Arendt is not interested in inevitability or reconciliation. She thought, for instance, that saying that historical events preceding the Holocaust meant that the Holocaust had to have happened meant treating temporality as determined in retrospection, and she understood

A Critique of Violence **97**

this interpretation of historicity as a washing out of the human potential for freedom and action. As she notes in *A Life of the Mind*,

> A thing may have happened quite at random, but, once it has come into existence and assumed reality, it loses its aspect of contingency and presents itself to us in the guise of necessity. And even if the event is of our own making, or at least we are one of its contributing causes—as in contracting marriage or committing a crime—the simple existential fact that it now is as it has become (for whatever reasons) is likely to withstand all reflections on its original randomness.
>
> *(1971, "Willing":138)*

In some ways, Arendt's view that *nothing in history had to have happened* as it did is a statement of divine-like, democratic agency and optimism in the face of overwhelming odds, where history—as it is for Benjamin—is shaped by those who live it rather than to mechanical processes, historical inevitability, fate, or state-sanctioned legal enforcement. In this, both Arendt and Benjamin were engaging in a fundamental post-Hegelian unraveling of a tradition of causality—or instrumental-reasoning—which connected means to ends, onto which Arendt cast the term "violence," and both sought alternative possibilities for thinking about action, politics, and power that would not be governed by a pre-existing and determining concept. For Arendt, violence was instrumentalizing and therefore depoliticizing.

Within Arendt's version of some of Benjamin's methods and insights in "A Critique of Violence," she rules out a central character in Benjamin's vision: the legend of Niobe. In this chapter I argue that Arendt's avoidance of Niobe has philosophical importance for her work: for Arendt, gender cannot be trapped in the means-ends logic of war culture, historical necessity, market calculation, or sovereignty. Because bodies are political, that is, always coming into the world as no one has before, gender breaks out of historical time and interrupts the meanings imposed by historical necessity, advancing a logic of freedom. In other words, gender for Arendt cannot be thought outside her version of politics; in fact, in some readings it can be said to constitute her version of politics. I show how Arendt's analysis of gender frames her conceptions of life, thinking, and judgment (or spectatorship) whose outcome cannot be deduced by its form or its prior appearances: gender is a pure means without ends.

"A Critique of Violence" is a critique of the violence within the law as well as a messianic prophecy about the revolutionary violence that would destroy the law. Benjamin rejects the means-ends logic of both natural and positive law, as well as of law-making (foundational) and law preserving (police) violence. He sees these forms of violence combined in what he calls "mythic violence," a "manifestation of the gods" (248) or a "fate-imposed violence" (247) that sustains state sovereign power. As it liberates the means from the ends, "mythic violence" gives way to the

98 A Critique of Violence

messianic moment, the utopic, redemptive insertion of "divine violence" (Hebraic law over Greek law).[2]

Niobe's plight takes its place in Benjamin's story as a parable for "mythic violence." Mythologically, Niobe brags about having fourteen children, more children than Leto, who only gave birth to Apollo and Artemis, twins fathered by Zeus; in revenge, Artemis kills all Niobe's children and turns Niobe herself into living stone—to endlessly shed tears, speechless and childless—and, by this act, establishes the law. As Benjamin describes it,

> Violence therefore bursts upon Niobe from the uncertain ambiguous sphere of fate. It is not actually destructive. Although it brings a cruel death to Niobe's children, it stops short of claiming the life of their mother, whom it leaves behind, more guilty than before through the death of the children, both as an eternally mute bearer of guilt and as a boundary stone on the frontier between men and gods. If this immediate violence in mythic manifestations proves closely related, indeed identical, to lawmaking violence, it reflects a problematic light on lawmaking violence, insofar as the latter was characterized above, in the account of military violence, as merely a mediate violence.
>
> *(248)*

Maternal retribution—like mediate, military violence, instrumentalized by guilt— is as though fated, and the cycle of fated violence will, for Benjamin, only be broken by a redemptive non-sovereign violence, or divine violence.[3] Arendt will avoid the problem of conceiving of a non-sovereign politics, relinquishing any allusion to sacred power. For her, mythic violence is apolitics, instrumentality and fatedness, and politics, in opposition, is the release from the mythic.

The difference between the two approaches to the relation between politics and violence has to do with care. Whereas Benjamin equates care to material causality and violence, Arendt defines politics as care without violence, the care that it takes to share the world with others. Benjamin is using what he might call an *image*—the mother Niobe—to show that the law is bound up in an endless circularity whose outcomes are already embedded in its forms, repetition without escape. The punishment reflects the crime, absolutely; the law is a stone, or a weapon, held by fate; the past prescribes the future; the compulsion behind primal, maternal feeling assigns guilt just as the violence inside the law does; the eternal return of myth is replicated in the idea of historical progress towards modern state power. In the tale of Niobe, Benjamin is borrowing the attribution of freedom-crushing, putrefying guilt that one of his influences, Ernst Bloch, equates to worker subjectivity under the systemic rule of exchange, controlled by the levers of a laughing businessman, or the "purely technical system of administration" (239) found in modern bureaucracies: "The soul must assume guilt in order to destroy the existing evil, in order not to assume even more guilt" (242).

For Benjamin, fate and repetition determine Niobe's destiny, automatic, predictable, and unpreventable like a mechanical or causal process: "Niobe's arrogance," says Benjamin, "calls down fate upon her not because her arrogance offends against the law but because it challenges fate—to a fight in which fate must triumph" (248). Whereas Bloch explains that what breaks through the guilt that sanctions the law is Judgment Day, what Benjamin calls "divine violence"—a "bloodless" assault that interrupts Niobe's irresolvable grief—becomes manifest in an expiation that destroys simultaneously law altogether, a redemption through judgment.

Arendt sometimes seems to appropriate Benjamin's framings of violence and judgment in terms of her own politics of modernity and her philosophical readings of history. Following Bloch, Arendt reads judgment as a sovereign life in common, whereas Benjamin reads it as a divine flash that abolishes state sovereign power.[4] In Arendt's case, what Benjamin calls "divine power"—in her own words "the creation of new power" (*On Revolution,* 140)—occurs when each man's actions appear in a place where people come together to be judged and remembered in the presence of others.[5] In other words, Arendt takes maternal care out of its circularity and revises it into judgment, a love of the world.

By comparing Arendt's political modernity to Benjamin's critique of violence, this chapter deciphers Arendt's refusal to consider gender solely in a technological version of history as fate, a version of history that accepts the elision of violence to power. The chapter then goes on to discuss a contemporary Niobe story in Rick Rosenthal's 2013 film *Drones. Drones* stars Eloise Mumford as Sue Lawson, daughter of a four-star general and a recently commissioned U.S. Air Force lieutenant who, because of a physical handicap, gets assigned as a drone operator. Her main duty is to monitor inside the home of a family in Iraq as the members appear projected on a screen in a trailer at Creech Air Force Base in the Nevada desert. The patriarch of the Iraqi family, Mahmoud Kahlil, though not currently at home, is strongly suspected of being a major Al-Qaeda operative. Unexpectedly, the alleged terrorist returns to the site, and Sue, along with her enlisted teammate, Airman Jack Bowles, must contemplate the ethics of their possible actions in response to U.S. military command authority. The film re-engages some of Arendt's philosophical motifs—e.g., necessity, command (or compulsion), thinking, work, automation, causality, judgment, appearance, spectatorship, action—explicitly around gender and demonstrates how the technologized woman soldier displaces Arendt's freedom for a neoliberal age.

What is *essential* to retrieve from Arendt's reflections on politics and violence is the centrality of freedom. In a neoliberal context, the rhetoric of freedom has been seized by a right-wing corporatism and market fundamentalism that attribute freedom wholly to unfettered markets and individual consumerism, to uncaring and apolitics. Arendt, however, understands the philosophical tradition as revealing the opposite: that the logic of markets is constructed through a type of violence and means-ends logic that is incompatible with freedom and with

100 A Critique of Violence

politics. This means-ends logic is a type of apolitics that makes bodies into tools and determines a priori what kinds of bodies can inhabit the world with others. Arendt reminds us that freedom is too important to relinquish it to the masterminds of unfreedom. Unlike Benjamin, who wants, as Beatrice Hanssen has noted, "to show the mutual contamination and duplicity of two political traditions, those of power and of violence" (20), Arendt wants to find a way of thinking about power or politics as separate from violence, fate, determinism, causality, administrative logic, and force.

Mere Life

The status of women in Arendt's philosophical project is radically unstable, and feminist critics have noticed. The instability results from the way Arendt uses sites, symbols, and social narratives that traditionally relate to women's social positioning as pivots that allow her also to introduce her favored terminology in political discourse, words like freedom, world, public, human action, plurality, contemplation, and newness. In other words, Arendt refuses to submit gender to what Heidegger calls "the instrumental conception of technology" where "[e]verything depends on our manipulating technology in the proper manner as a means," a conception we cling to more fervently as technology (or gender) "threatens to slip from human control" (5). Gender is deeply politicized; its seeming instrumentalism is an effect of its politicization. For Arendt, the relegation of women's work to the private sphere during industrialization is an example of its politicization, its indeterminate outsidedness that counters mechanized culture.

Feminist scholarship has been particularly concerned with Arendt's disparaging of the private sphere and women's connection to biological life cycles as a threat to the politics of freedom. Hanna Pitkin, for example, laments, Arendt's version of necessity (or "economics") "is to be excluded [from the contents of public and political speech] because it serves the needs of the body, and the body is a threat to human greatness and freedom, an encumbrance that ties us to our animal nature, something shameful to be hidden in private darkness" (337). Though she tries to retrieve Arendt's thought for a postmodernist (or performative) feminist politics, Bonnie Honig agrees that "Arendt protects the *sui generis* character of her politics and the purity of her public realm by prohibiting the politicization of issues of social justice and gender" (1995: 135).[6] Such feminist critiques assume that women's differences—even if the differences are themselves archaic and oppressive—need to be recognized and affirmed, and that pejorative references to the private sphere are necessarily castigating to women. Rather than affirm this connection, a more vital version of feminism, it seems to me, one would want to disassociate women from being immersed in repetitive life cycles tied to bodies—as does, for example, Simone de Beauvoir—and, instead, to recreate gender politically—as does Arendt—, free from the causal repetitions determined by this version of social history.

Not all feminist critics have dismissed Arendt for noticing that women's immersion in biological life cycles and private life is not something to affirm but something that Arendt herself wants to replace with the possibility of politics. If Arendt interprets the body as outside politics because driven by compulsion, Judith Butler reads that such compulsion is an effect of politics: "What about the possibility," she writes, "that one might be hungry, angry, free, and reasoning, and that a political movement to overcome inequality in food distribution is a just and fair political movement? (2015: 47).[7] In effect, then, women's immersion in the biological life cycle and the private sphere is a congealing that hides the politics that creates the congealing. Butler goes on to "draw upon [Arendt's] resources" (2015: 75), holding onto Arendt's crucial insights about action and change through political gathering, understanding Arendt's conception of the gender and the body as in conformity with her own, as socially connective. Another feminist response has read Arendt as splitting the body into its politicized version and some more instrumentalized, violent version. There is a body, as Linda Zerilli tells it, that is engulfing and devouring, a body that "poses an immanent threat to Arendtian plurality" (1995: 171), an instrumental body defined through its purpose, and another sense of the body that desires and pluralizes.[8]

Though I certainly see a disparaging of women's work, biology, and private lives as formative for Arendt's critique, I still understand the private sphere to be more contradictory for Arendt's philosophical project, where the private sphere also shapes the experience of thinking that leads towards freedom, the I-will: "Thinking," Arendt asserts in *The Human Condition*, ". . . is a solitary and lonely business" (185). At the beginning of *The Human Condition,* the private divides between *animal laborans*—the pre-political work-life defined mostly through women's isolation from the public world of action and her connection to mere life—and *homo faber*—the fabricator, who reproduces things again and again "in order to remain in the human world" (1958: 139) (just as the law, in Benjamin, divides between natural and positive law). Like labor, or the tending of biological life, "work" is also connected to necessity because it is concerned with survival. Arendt treats labor, like work, with disdain because it reduces history to process and reduces action to violent action. "That violence is the midwife of history," she cites Engels, "means that the hidden forces of development of human productivity, insofar as they depend upon free and conscious human action, come to light only through the violence of wars and revolutions. Only in those violent periods does history show its true face and dispel the fog of mere ideological, hypocritical talk" (*Between Past and Future,* 22). Or, "But neither freedom nor any other meaning can ever be the product of human activity in the sense in which the table is clearly the end-product of the carpenter's activity" (*Between Past and Future,* 78). Work is governed by necessity, predictability, and repetition, where the ends are already decided before the means.

Even though critics like Honig and Pitkin privilege women's work as the target of Arendt's vindictive on the private sphere, Arendt is equally reproachful

102 A Critique of Violence

of the private as a site of work or making, where, again, the outcome is predetermined, circular, and predictable. "The actual work of fabrication," Arendt writes in *The Human Condition,* "is performed under the guidance of a model in accordance with which the object is constructed. This model can be an image beheld by the eye of the mind or a blueprint in which the image has already found a tentative materialization through work. In either case, what guides the work of fabrication is outside the fabricator and precedes the actual work process in much the same way as the urgencies of life process within the laborer precede the actual labor process" (140–141). As well, Arendt is very clear that work is equal to labor in concentrating its energies on the maintenance of life: "Aristotle distinguished three ways of life (*bioi*) which men might choose in freedom, that is, in full independence of the necessities of life and the relationships they originated. This prerequisite of freedom ruled out all ways of life chiefly devoted to keeping one's self alive—not only labor, which was the way of life of the slave, who was coerced by the necessity to stay live and by the rule of his master, but also the working life of the free craftsman and the acquisitive life of the merchant" (12).

Critics have also remarked on another feminist side of Arendtian privacy where privacy offers a separation from the administered world in a space of "disinterested" judgment that leads to politics. Arendt, says Linda Zerilli, for example, derives her politics from the "radical imagination" that can be constructed through Kant's "reflective judgment," where the private, the particular, the contingent, and the singular are not mediated through general concepts (like the understanding is) and so are "not bound to the law of causality"; they are "productive and spontaneous, not merely reproductive of what is already known" (2005: 163). Zerilli attributes this non-attributable newness to Arendt's avoidance of considering the gendered body as either concrete or fixed; Arendt, says Zerilli, does not fit the body inside a general concept like gender because she sees it as "the locus of radical heterogeneity and vitality" (1995: 180), a plurality similar to Julia Kristeva's "semiotic" body, that "transgresses all human borders, including those between public and private, nature and culture" (1995: 177). For Arendt, the private stands at times for a pre-modern type of work determined by nature but at other times for "the soundless dialogue we carry on with ourselves" (1971, "Thinking": 6) that frees us from the "growing inability to move" (1971, "Thinking": 12) imposed by modern administrative systems. In other words, accepting that Arendt's private sphere is stuck in a pre-modern foothold that locks in women according to predetermined rules—like Benjamin's mythic structure does to Niobe—means, also, attributing it solely to the kind of repetitive thought-action of historical necessity from which Arendt also thinks it promises relief.

Critics like Pitkin and Honig are responding to the dark currents that course through Arendt's descriptions of necessity as underlying historical causality, ascribing the private sphere as bound to repeat the past infinitely. Yet, this is exactly what Arendt critiques, and she does so not by relegating women to that sphere but rather by attributing that sphere to mythology or antiquity so that modern women are released from it as the private thought is released from repeating the general concept. For Arendt, the dangerous elision between power and violence parallels Benjamin's version of a mythical violence to be overcome, a type of violence defined through "historical necessity," most powerfully evident in

> the life process which permeates our bodies and keeps them in a constant state of change whose movements are automatic, independent of our own activities, and irresistible—i.e., of an overwhelming urgency. The less we are doing ourselves, the less active we are, the more forcefully will this biological process assert itself, impose its inherent necessity upon us, and overawe us with the fateful automatism of sheer happening that underlies all human history.
>
> *(1963: 49)*

Like Niobe, the figure of necessity here is bound to an eternal repetition imposed by nature (or biology), guilt, history, and "women's work"—or an apoliticized version of history—, retrospective; seeped in mourning, nostalgia, and loss; governed by a logic of revenge and retaliation; and weighted down in mimetic relationships that cancel out autonomous activity, newness, and will. In the retaliatory logic of antiquity, biological cycles trap women in the private sphere just as historical necessity traps contingency inside its administrative repetitions.[9] Arendt sees a way out, a new autonomy, in the political gathering.

The private sphere of domesticity and, traditionally, "women's work" also houses the condition for a break from necessity: that is, natality. As Arendt notes in *The Human Condition,* "natality . . . may be the central category of political, as distinguished from metaphysical, thought" (9). The introduction into the world of this indeterminate life guarantees the plurality that, for Arendt, undergirds politics: "No doubt every man, by virtue of his birth, is a new beginning" (1971, "Willing": 6). Examining in *The Life of the Mind* how Duns Scotus leads philosophy out of the chain of causality, Arendt recognizes "procreation, where two independent substances, male and female, must come together to bring forth the child," as underscoring "the theory that all change occurs because a plurality of causes happen to coincide, and the coincidence engenders the texture of reality in human affairs" (137). No child is the same as its parents; the child's life will not repeat history in a predictable way but, rather, is a new beginning that might not have been. Because of the fact of natality, "the human world is constantly invaded by strangers, newcomers whose actions and reactions cannot be foreseen by those who are already there and are going to leave in a short while" (*Between Past and Future,* 61). Even as the child comes into a world that pre-exists it and learns a language that is already in use, the child guarantees that history can begin again each time, because the child who has never existed before has the capacity to speak and act.

Arendt's "natality" transcribes Benjamin's formulation of "origin" from *The Origin of German Tragic Drama*; in turn, "origin" leads to "aura": authentic

104 A Critique of Violence

experience, proximity, and direct presence prior to the technological repetitions that distance gives to objects and experience. As an "authentic" phenomenon that is both "singular" and "eccentric" (46), the "origin" is never only revealed, says Benjamin, "in the naked and manifest existence of the factual" (*The Origin,* 45). It is neither solely a restoration of what was nor exclusively an individual instance under the aegis and form of a concept, but rather, as "something imperfect and incomplete," it will "constantly confront the historical world," as "a totality" (45). Benjamin calls this "natural history" (47): an "invalidation of the rule" (44). As Susan Buck-Morss reads it, "natural history" for Benjamin refers to "the use of archaic images to identify what is historically new about the 'nature' of commodities," making visible what "remains unreconciled" while interrupting "the context into which it [the image] is inserted" (1989: 67). As such, the image breaks through the mythic world, that is, a "meaning-filled world," the world under the sway of an "inescapable fate" laying claim to eternity, as in "the myth of automatic historical progress" (1989: 78–9). With "natality," Arendt envisions an interruption of historical causality much like Benjamin's "origin," where the object is pried from its historical shell and appears anew, as something that has "never existed at all" (1971, "Willing": 13). The plurality brought into the world with natality is, like Benjamin's "origin," a bursting forth into the present of a political engagement in the public sphere.[10]

Arendt twists her use of the private sphere to characterize, first, the dark weightiness of historical necessity, repetition, biological cyclicality, automation, command, force, and mechanism and, then, at the same time, this other version of history, a break, an "origin" outside of the imperatives of the causal chain, history starting anew.[11] Mary Dietz's analysis of Arendt might be helpful here. Dietz notes that feminist criticism's emphasis on the scorn that Arendt seemingly piles onto the idea of labor—"the biological process of the human body" or "life itself" (7) (*animal laborans*) in *The Human Condition*—is one-sided. She does see "the reproductive-birthing-consuming fertility of the female *animal laborans*" (130) as a woman, and "the productive-violating-fabricating artifice of the male *homo faber*" (131) as a man, with *animal laborans* defeating her adversary in modernity. Yet, instead of celebrating this as a victory for "woman-centered" viewpoints or as an attack on woman-centered social spheres, says Dietz, Arendt wants us to think beyond the categories of labor and work that rule our self-conceptions and our assumptions about the social, and consider the human capacity for action in other terms. She wants to disengage work and bodies from pre-scripted, mechanical meanings. For Arendt, freedom is outside of both labor and work.

> In Arendt's terms, the mentalities of *animal laborans* and *homo faber* dominate our self-understandings. Thus the answer to the question "And who are we?" is more frequently expressed in terms of "what" we are—what we own, what we want, what identity we wish to claim, to what social or cultural groups we belong—answers that reflect the dead end of "the last stage

of laboring society"... . Our ability to grasp political association as public happiness has diminished: "mere" life overrules everything else, the body eclipses the body politic.

(112)

According to Dietz, Arendt is asking us to think outside of instrumentalized general concepts like gender that determine work roles as necessary, as a means to an end. "Arendtian theory," elaborates Dietz, "distances freedom from the static language . . . of gender identity and locates it instead in acts of personal speech-revelation . . . that resolutely resist the control of predetermined, descriptive, bifurcated signifiers" (131). Rather than privileging gender, Arendt wants us to think about social organization as divided between a technological logic on the one hand—which sees social roles, including gendered ones, compelled by biological or productive forces, processes, violence, and cyclicalities—and, on the other, a logic of social power, where social meanings follow on human judgments.

As both determined by necessity and freed with plurality, the private sphere functions for Arendt in much the same way that, say, technology in Heidegger is both "a means to an end" and "a human activity" (4). The private sphere is tied to "mere" or "sacred life" which, for Arendt, "is not bound up with freedom but follows its own inherent necessity" (*Between Past and Future,* 149). Because of its connection to necessity, sacred or mere life is for Arendt "the politically most pernicious doctrine of the modern age, namely that life is the highest good, and that the life process of society is the very centre of human endeavour" (*On Revolution,* 54). However, a turning-away from human affairs, for the sake of attaining immortality or securing self-interest,[12] also "unconceals"—in Heidegger's terminology—"human action" that "like all strictly political phenomenon is bound up with human plurality" (*Between Past and Future,* 61).

The formulation of "mere life" here follows Benjamin's, who laments Niobe's plight as being consigned by the (sacred) law to a condition of "mere life." "Mythic power," for Benjamin as he accounts for Niobe's situation, "is bloody power over mere life for its own sake" (250).[13] But this life, he continues, "cannot at any price be said to coincide with the mere life in him, any more than it can be said to coincide with any other conditions and qualities" (251): life exceeds its conditions, its causes, and the laws that bind it. Benjamin names this redemptive excess "divine violence"—"pure power over all life for the sake of the living" (250)—that destroys the (mythic or sovereign state) law along with its bloody consignments of guilt and condemnation. What Benjamin means here by "the living" is rather opaque,[14] but Arendt understands what occurs in the place of "divine violence" as a "living together" in "the presence of others" (*The Human Condition,* 49)—countering the necessity of biology or the compulsion of mechanism like Benjamin's redemptive catastrophe counters the law.[15]

After the myth of Niobe, Benjamin next invokes the story of Korah, who rebelled against Moses and the law he brought down from the mountain. God

106 A Critique of Violence

punished Korah with a fire that consumed him and all his followers, burying them alive, a destruction of the state and "mere life," a violence whose outcome is uncertain. "Mere life" points here to life within the law, motivated by fate, like Arendt's necessity. Benjamin's is a disturbing image of redemption, a messianic annihilation that brings about a non-determining and non-sovereign power.[16] Arendt does not accept Benjamin's elision of violence into politics. Instead, the excess, for Arendt, is the gathering of indeterminate life in the exercise of action and judgment outside of administrative repetitions and command. In de-spiritualizing Benjamin's messianic moment, what Arendt offers is a story that releases bodies caught up in guilt over life and bound to its law, in order to reveal a politics of gender where "not life but the world is at stake" (*Between Past and Future,* 154).

Thinking, or a World beyond Appearances

The private sphere of labor and work is not the only place where Arendt considers privacy as a separation from the violent, administrative world of modernity. In Arendt's view, the seclusion of the private sphere is for thinking, separated from the external, empirical world of modernity's appearances. Yet, outside of a world to be shared with others, thinking is prone to repetition and compulsion. Thinking, like action, must be judged in a public arena.

In her coverage of the Eichmann trial, Arendt declared Eichmann's most pernicious crime to be not his role in corralling up Jews and organizing their transport to the camps, nor his administering of mass deportation and extermination, but rather his inability to think. The urgency for Arendt in countering the tendencies of historical causality was that she understood it as motivating administrative characters like Eichmann who were the masters of the Holocaust. What she meant by Eichmann's inability to think was that—in a Heideggerian sense—he was "inauthentic. He followed orders—like Niobe, his mental capacities were in complete alignment with his bureaucratic function: "every line of these scribblings," she notes in connection with the report, "shows his utter ignorance of everything that was not directly, technically and bureaucratically, connected with his job" (1963: 27). Thinking, for Arendt, should rather be a type of critical judgment that is removed from administrative causality, a separation from total identification with the "idle chatter" of the social mechanism.[17]

Like the private sphere, the thinking subject is both born as new, as a stranger, and born into a pre-existing world as one of its own. Plato's philosopher, who turned away from the sensory world of appearances, tradition, and human affairs in his exposure to truth outside the cave, furnishes Arendt with a parable for the thinker's life of contemplation. Because thinking is outside of appearances, it cannot be consumed in the spectacle of modernity, in its images and bureaucratic speech patterns, into which the public power of speech and action is disappearing. As Seyla Benhabib remarked in a recent article in *The New York Times* (where she defends Arendt against Richard Wolin's allegations of her anti-Semitism), Arendt concluded that "Eichmann could not 'think'—not because he was incapable of rational intelligence but because he could not think for himself beyond clichés" (2014). To think, she continues, "means to think for oneself and to think consistently, but also from the standpoint of everyone else" (2014).[18]

Arendt's main historical reference points include not only the Holocaust but also totalitarianism, nuclear proliferation,[19] the arms race, and the Vietnam War and could extend to our neoliberal moment. What concerns her is that technological rationality—total militarization—could take over all rationality, thinking, and education, with politics as the casualty. In a world of appearances like the one we live in, Arendt says, the thinking ego shielded inside its private refuge, impotent, triggers skepticism, distrust of sensory knowledge, doubt. Yet, thinking also triggers politics because it needs a public arena in which to be judged. As in Kant's aesthetic (or reflective) judgment, where "only the particular is given" and where "the universal is to be found" (67), thinking is a private, contemplative activity which, seeking objective value without a general concept, demands and expects potential universal assent. In contrast to "[w]hen everybody is swept away unthinkingly by what everybody else does and believes in"—, thinking turns to judgment, which is "political by implication" or even "which one might call with some reason the most political of man's mental abilities" (1971, "Thinking": 192). Arendt here returns to Ernst Bloch, who construes the private interiority of the soul as enabling the "intuition of the We" that, "absolutely eccentrically to time," feeds the "revolutionary mission absolutely inscribed in utopia" (237). For Arendt, likewise, the thinking happens in the presence of an internal witness, in conversation with a friend or a judge called conscience ("the two-in-one of the soundless dialogue"; 1971, "Thinking": 193) that is not determined by appearances but by a mixing of point-of-view. In a time of emergency, "the opposition of thought and reality can be reversed, so that only thought seems to be real" (1971, "Thinking": 198); then, thinking is the condition for sharing the world with others—interruptive, pluralizing like natality—as political action.

Spectatorship, or Judgment

Whereas some feminist critics, then, have understood Arendt's disparaging of necessity and the private sphere as a disparaging of the women who work in it, Arendt has interpreted the industrial private sphere as a model of historical materialism whose logic confines women to a retaliatory logic. In this model, activity is caught in a biological cyclicality where every occurrence seems like it had to have happened, fated, without accident. For Arendt, however, only if technological rationality overcomes the politics of thinking and action can women be reduced to the biological cycle, the retaliation of guilt, or the blueprint-model. Arendt challenges us not to accept production and reproduction as determinations of our historical action but rather to understand that action as what makes

108 A Critique of Violence

the world as free from determinants because it gives rise to a plurality that might not have happened. In contrast to the historical materialist mode of interpreting our historical existence, Arendt sees our bodies as the singular site of communication between ourselves and the world we share with others, something that, each time, has never happened before. Instead of disparaging women in their private sphere confinement, Arendt sees bodies as unconfinable in that they come into existence by bringing into simultaneous existence a politics whose future is radically undetermined.

"Nothing and nobody exists whose very being does not presuppose a spectator" ("Thinking": 19), Arendt begins the first article of her uncompleted manuscript for *Life of the Mind*. Spectatorship for Arendt recovers how we share the world with others. In spectatorship, the subject becomes the object of someone else's private contemplation, confirming that subject's sensory experience of the world as that subject confirms his own. Not bound by the means–ends revenge logic of modern law, the actions of spectatorship do not accede to a purpose anticipated consciously by an actor, a mental image that gets formed into a thing: fated, settled, directed, calculated, or inevitable. As "pure means,"[20] spectatorship stands at the crux of the relationship between the private individual and the potential public that judges—the irreconcilable appearance of private persons in action before the judgment of others.

Arendt borrows this correlating of "pure means" with spectatorship not only from Kant but also from Benjamin's famous essay "The Work of Art in the Age of Mechanical Reproduction," which she published in her collection of his work, *Illuminations.* In this essay, Benjamin introduces the cinematic apparatus as a means without ends, inspiring contemplation and distraction, where "the spectator can abandon himself to his associations" (238), becoming absorbed in the experience and in collective viewing, distracted.[21] Where the technological apparatus (or instrument) progresses through various stages of historical development, each made necessary by the last, the instrument expressive of the needs of the historical constellation, the cinematic spectator, in contrast, produces "a change in the mode of participation" (239) as a collective, revolutionary subject.

For Arendt, modernity has endangered the separation from appearances that thinking brings about in much the same way that the "aura" is endangered for Benjamin. A type of philosophical orientation that began with Plato's "turning away" ended with Marx, when science assumed that doing could make all things appear: everywhere the thinker turned, he could only see his own technical fabrications and biological systems; thinking could no longer leave the world of human affairs behind. Judgment, based on Kant's *Critique of Judgment,* demands that the spectator free himself from physical need and private, bodily desire in order to share with the viewpoints of others, to incorporate disembodied perspectives from elsewhere, and so to consider thought in common. A judgment "presupposes the presence of others" (1971, "Willing": 270), a "public quality" (*Beyond Past and Future,* 218) where thinking brings into being a community of thinking men with different points of view, or spectators. In thinking, what is most private, withdrawn, and removed is a crowd of public spectators whose judgment—without preconceptions and unguided by intention—makes the world-in-common appear, undetermined, where it did not appear before.[22]

Drones

> No government exclusively based on the means of violence has ever existed. Even the totalitarian ruler, whose chief instrument of rule is torture, needs a power basis—the secret police and its net of informers. Only the development of robot soldiers, which, as previously mentioned, would eliminate the human factor completely and, conceivably, permit one man with a push button to destroy whomever he pleased, could change this fundamental ascendency of power over violence.
>
> (Crises of the Republic, "On Violence," 149)

Drone warfare is seemingly bodiless. One might argue that this is its point. As Grégoire Chamayou has contended in his philosophy of drones, drones make it "a priori impossible to die as one kills" (13). Ushering in "crises in intelligibility" (14) for a social consciousness he calls "necro-ethics" (17), drones, as Chamayou defines them, are "flying, high-resolution video cameras armed with missiles" that "allow you to project power without projecting vulnerability" (12). As pure means that are their own ends, drone warfare is the ascendance of a means-ends logic of violence whose implications, says Chamayou, have yet to be discovered but that certainly have already changed the political landscape. Drones are the instrument of a sovereign power that is, as Benjamin's divine violence, removed from human affairs, destroying their law.

Because of drone warfare's bodilessness, states engaging in it, Chamayou continues, can disengage from liberalism's politics of warfare, no longer needing to convince citizens that the ideological causes of the war are worth the effects and the sacrifice. Chamayou called this "*democratic militarization*": "Once warfare became ghostly and teleguided, citizens, who no longer risked their lives, would no longer have a say in it" (188). In Arendt's terms, violence has ascended over power, and the ends and means are indistinguishable, leading to the automation of violent means that are justified by their own recurrence, a foreign policy steeped in the logic of retaliation and effectivity. Instead of the state acknowledging and confirming the thinking of its citizens, the military state can stand outside of the social life of the nation and reduce the lives of its citizens and enemies alike to predictable patterns on a panoptical screen and deviations from those patterns. Subject to scrutiny, these patterns can be turned into calculations and probabilities and "objectively" catalogued as degrees of suspicious activity. People's lives become automatic processes, administered as mechanical inferences.

The 2013 film *Drones* is about the militarization of gender, or the seizure of gender inside the means-ends logic of this new military apparatus. Earlier films

110 A Critique of Violence

were made about drones, of course, before drones had entered quite so resoundingly into political dialogue. One such film, Rob Cohen's 2005 film *Stealth,* introduces the idea that the instrumentalization or automation of state violence in the drone is a gender-defining issue. Unlike *Drones, Stealth* presents the drone as self-operating, making its own decisions in human expressions of personality and will. Three expert Navy pilots—a white man, a black man, and a white woman—are joined in their flying missions by an "Unmanned Combat Aerial Vehicle," or UCAV, named EDI (Extreme Deep Invader, and yes, there are sex jokes). When the weapon first arrives and is being displayed for the three pilots, Captain George Cummings informs them that "EDI flies all by himself." The first pilot, Lieutenant Ben Gannon, rejoins, "You mean 'itself,' don't you, sir?" Later on, after the first mission, Ben corrects the mechanic, who also refers to the plane's hearing and "voice recog" as "he": "You know what? I'll call it a 'he' when it gets out of its cockpit and takes a piss, how's that?" Though attributing a gender to the machine seems to raise the question of its humanness—since the machine evolves intelligently, and its mechanical insides are referenced with organic terminology like "blood," "veins," "nerves," and "skeleton," alongside allusions to its digestive excretions—, the woman pilot, Lieutenant Cara Wade, understands the gender of the machine as a question of, well, gender. When she asks Ben if the UCAV will replace them and take their jobs, he answers, "No way. War's about tools. Think about it . . . The best guy with the best weapon wins." "Or girl," she quips. Cara later raises the war tool's gender difference by worrying about ethical decisions—the human casualties and collateral damage in a bomb attack—while Ben is worrying about the impact and precision of the weapon. After the black pilot, Lieutenant Henry Purcell, crashes his plane, the UCAV ends up sacrificing itself (himself?) in a mass slaughter of the enemy while rescuing Ben and Cara from North Korea, suggesting that it combines male efficiencies with female empathies, or romance. EDI becomes human in death as it (he?) defends the happy white couple. The war tool is about effectiveness, yes, but only to uphold moral feeling.

Eight years later, *Drones* envisions gender, all gender, within a means-ends logic of the apparatus, where the command to do your gender right—to use your gender like an instrument—replaces judgment, moral feeling, or politics. "We're not getting paid to bake oatmeal cookies and make babies," Airman Jack Bowles informs his commanding officer, Lieutenant Sue Lawson, on her first day on the job. The statement brings out many qualities that Jack sees in his job: first, that it is a job (not a conviction nor a vocation, nor an act of patriotism, nor a moral duty); second, that it is not work that "real" girls do; and third, that having a job means that "the colonel tells you who to take out and you do it." To do the job of fighting the war right, one should follow the command to do his gender right, and to become a man means total obedience to command. The point returns in a later scene when Sue is resisting following orders to drop hellfire on the Iraqi suspects, including twelve civilians and two children; the colonel tells her, "I understand you're feeling emotional. There's nothing wrong with that, but it means you're not equipped to make cold, calculated, strategic decisions. Fortunately, that's not your job. That's for men like your father." Being a woman means standing apart, blocking command from execution or from reaching its target mechanically, like a weapon, by posing moral objections. Blood relations insert the soldier into the military apparatus: even parenting feeds the machine.

Though the film's title suggests that the film is about a new machine of war that ushers in a new way of waging war without bodies, the filmmaking itself does emphasize the gendered body as the film's focus, the secret the film will reveal. *Drones* begins at daybreak in a small empty town, a train crashing through the frame of the film, first with its booming sound even before the image appears. The camera then creeps up the street, following the ensuing silence towards the only noise, heavy breathing and rhythmic thumping coming from the gym at the end of the street. The camera advances through the window with its lighted red lettering, and displays, from behind, a solitary trainee in a hooded sweatshirt at the punching bag. The camera pans around the figure and then advances forward towards its first shot of Sue's face, partly concealed by the hood, making sentimental cause—even pausing in emphatic shock—over the fact of her womanness. Here at the gym, bodies matter, and Sue is soon displayed in the shower, steaming and wet, in full makeup (which, miraculously, does not run), face turned upward in post-workout bliss, eyes closed, water dripping. The post-workout cleaning ritual is interrupted by a boom of airpower as an aerial formation flies over the desert, and the film cuts out of the gym.

What astonishes later is that this film is not about bodies; it is, rather, a film about a historical situation that moves bodies out of the frame. In fact, the problem that bodies do not appear in the theater of war becomes a topic of conversation for Jack and Sue, as together they debate the meaning of what they are doing. Jack claims pride in doing a service for his country without putting himself at risk, of projecting power without vulnerability: "I'm only twenty-two," he says, "I don't want to die before I've had a threesome," and specifies nervously that it should only be with girls. Sue, meanwhile, wistfully remembers stories her father told her about flying over Hanoi, with his friend Tommy going down in flames, and then answers Jack's frustrations about their target Mahmoud by pronouncing angrily, "At least he's willing to die for what he believes in." Jack reminds her, "This isn't about being a hero like him [her father] and his pal [Tommy]. It's about winning the fucking war, doing our job." The problem for Sue is that all the wars she has read about have heroes, and heroism requires the exposure and risking of bodies in all their vulnerability, but in this war all she can do is watch from outside the action and mechanically follow command. The body is outside the job of war.

Drones runs parallel visually to Samuel Maoz's debut 2009 Israeli film *Lebanon*. As in *Drones* where the drone *is* the film apparatus, *Lebanon*'s *mise-en-scène* is an industrial tank moving into the war zone on the first day of the 1982 Israeli invasion. Most of the action takes place in the claustrophobic dark, hot inside as the soldiers, in terror, lose their reason, trying to make the weapon work—amidst

112 A Critique of Violence

leaks, loose wires, and electrical failures—, while the weapon's crosshairs, like a stalker, frame fragments of the war outside: destruction, confusion, civilian murders, animal torture, atrocities, betrayals, and threats. In *Drones,* the drone replaces the tank as the inside-camera space: the *mise-en-scène* registers disembodied voice and command in window-like openings, not to the immediate outside as in *Lebanon* but to half a world away—video-frames revealing action elsewhere. Jack and Sue are stationed in a trailer in the Nevada desert whose air conditioner is broken (the body that the new technology is supposed to make obsolete is constantly being recalled in its sweat). Nobody else enters except, briefly, somebody from the outside delivers a pizza, half onion (for her), half pepperoni (for him), that is never eaten. There are only three brief moments when the film moves outside, once for Sue to go to the outhouse, also a box, and twice more to see the military police sent to arrest them if they disobey command (the missiles will be dropped anyway, by the next team). The box contains nearly the entire action of the film, as though we were watching a play rather than a film, with a single set, and only dialogue directly represented. Most of the filming is accomplished through shot-reverse-shot sequences, with the camera occasionally dropping to show their fingers typing on the keyboards. To interrupt the banality of the closed, dull, dank, and gritty space, sometimes the shot-reverse-shot sequences are broken by interspersed moments when one of the characters throws a glance at the grainy terminal screen, and we see kids playing soccer in the sun, grown-ups dancing or cleaning, barbecuing, everyday domestic Iraq framed inside a Nevada trailer.

Unlike the U.S. forces, the Iraqis do have bodies, and those bodies do appear, as targets on the screen. Sue's appeal to an older age of heroic action is counterposed to what she imagines she will tell her own kids about the war: that "I pushed a button and watched a dead man's family pick his arms and legs off the road." Sue can identify with the actions on the screen from a distance, as she herself used to wait for her father's return from war. The screen allows her to experience her own history and emotions and her family history, as well as the history of the war. Sue experiences her own body only through distance, as a spectator, experiencing feeling by seeing the bodies on the screen living the stories of her own past or the stories her father told her. Her body is out there, on the screen.

Something similar happens with sex. The first scene Jack and Sue see when they turn on the image-console is the Iraqi couple having sex on the roof. This creates a *frisson* between Sue and Jack, only augmented by the heat in the trailer as the air conditioner continues to malfunction, and they sweat and disrobe (to a point). The flirtation between them threatens to destabilize her class position as the next generation of a family of military officers, and the possibility that she might *not* repeat the line of her inheritance disrupts, as well, the effectiveness of military command over its instruments; she becomes a girl by suggesting she might step out of her military family class, through the suggestion of sexual enticement between the Airman and herself. The debate between Jack and Sue over whether or not to follow command and fire on the Iraqis escalates when the colonel pits them against each other, holding Jack responsible, threatening court-martial, until they begin to box; yet, their discussion is about how to fake the fight, creating physical signs and bruises with minimal pain, staging the body's actualization only as a screen. Both Jack and the colonel obsess about what their actions will look like on TV. Only through distant identifications with the image on a screen can Sue or Jack experience physical sensations and action. The main action of the film is not in the line of the camera whose view is stuck inside a closed box, removed, or with the main characters that we, the filmgoers, see. The image-console as screen is what acts, in the distance, outside on the edge of the camera-eye; the trailer is empty of everything but language.

Arendt would say that being outside of appearances, the trailer would be outside of history's commands and its compulsive narrative of progress—a space representing contemplation, a "turning away," pure thought. The trailer is not controlled by the body's needs, by mechanical process or fabrication. The isolation of the trailer and the way the camera is mostly trapped inside of it make the film itself into a visualization of something invisible: citizens thinking about engaging in war. Yet, Jack continually warns Sue that the biggest danger they face here is thinking. Time and again, he cautions her: "Don't think too much," "We do what we gotta do"; "The colonel tells you who to take out and you do it. Some people are good at that and some people aren't because they think too much"; "I can tell that you're obviously a smart individual. It's kind of what I'm worried about"; "We need to focus on our mission"; "Don't think about it"; "We just gotta blast the terrorist son of a bitch and fly away"; "Obey orders from and trust the chain of command like they're god." Thinking, Jack informs her, distracts; it cannot be absorbed in the mechanism; it is what killed her predecessor, as he succeeded in taking out a Highly Valued Target, drank ten shots, and drove off a cliff.

Sue does think too much. Thinking, we learn, is what girls do, and it endangers the whole command structure. The first time Sue thinks, she is able to take an action and base a story on it, judging the action through multiple points of view. The Iraqis hang a banner on their roof, and she notices that the banner is similar to one she and her brother David hung for her father on his birthday, when he was expected home; she concludes that the terror suspect, Mahmoud Kahlil, is on his way home for his birthday party, and they confirm this by getting a translation of the words on the sign. Sue can interpret visual signs by not relying on just what appears on the screen but by moving between multiple perspectives. Though the colonel tells her he wants "indisputable visual confirmation"—signs on the screen that give direct and transparent reference to things in the world—, this is clearly *not* what the military command wants, as the colonel continues throughout the film to yell at and threaten her when she disputes the meaning the military command itself has given to the visuals. Military command next tells her to fire on the car driving towards the house, but again, instead of just accepting the interpretation of the visual sign as self-evident, she steps back, compares the photographic capture to an older file photo and rejects the identification, refusing to kill and

114 A Critique of Violence

incurring the wrath of her higher-ups. The military commands viewing as the work of war, but spectatorship does not get stuck in the singular viewpoint of command. Sue's ability to change perspectives is a metaphoric rendition of her physical ailment: she has a partially detached retina, due to a boxing accident while at flight school. She has, literally, taken her eye out of her eye-socket and moved its position. So the boxing scene that begins the film, situating her under the gaze as an object of desire, naked and steaming, now is treated as the spring of the subjective detachment that allows thinking, that does not accept the body of appearance as evidence or cause.

Through her detached viewing, Sue begins to suspect command as lying. A quick Internet search teaches her that Mahmoud Kahlil could actually be a pro-democracy activist who was organizing a protest movement against the Pakistani general Woleed Zehawi, and the U.S. forces could be targeting him and his family as a personal favor to their Pakistani ally. This alternative story gains credibility as she watches his image on the screen: he drinks alcohol, he dances in public—activities strictly prohibited in Al-Qaeda's fundamentalist Islamic codes, she reasons. Her conflict with Jack intensifies along with her opposition to the colonel's directives. The movie suggests that Sue's actions could be decided through her own autonomous thinking and witnessing, that she might mutiny even at the cost of court-martial and humiliation. We know that this will not happen, because the weapon has become the film's protagonist and motivational force, but the film still underlines this alternative resolution, this unreconciliation, as an obstacle to the means-ends logic of command.

Finally, the colonel flashes off the screen and, like a god, the face and voice of her father, the four-star general, come on. General Lawson tells Sue that Mahmoud Kahlil was one of the masterminds of 9/11 and thus responsible for killing her mother and her brother David in the attack, and that he is planning another chemical attack that would have an even more devastating effect. She has the opportunity and the duty now of stopping him from causing such pain to others. The general supports the allegation by showing her a photograph of Kahlil in a bar in Hamburg with one of the men who flew the planes into the towers on 9/11. "I love you, Susan," General Lawson signs off as the console goes dark.

This time, Jack is the one who thinks. He begins to see things through multiple perspectives that dislodge the authority of command. He remarks that General Lawson is lying because his own father, pushing him on a swingset, lied to him with the same words. Jack then finds on the Internet that the image that General Lawson identified with 9/11 plotters does not match up with the military's own posters. Yet, it is too late: no longer thinking or detached from the historical process, Sue has been turned by her father into a stone-cold master of revenge. Back in the family circle, her actions are predictable, automatic responses to the guilt she now feels: even if she insisted at the beginning of the film that "I do not play the daddy card," she now reacts to historical fate—like the classical Antigone—as her father's daughter, transformed into an arm of state violence and its retaliatory, angry law, unable to respond in any other way despite her acknowledgement of the counter-evidence. Thought turns into an instrument, a means to an end. As Arendt might have interpreted it: "Once man-made historical processes have become automatic, they are no less ruinous than the natural life process that drives our organism and which in its own terms, that is, biologically, leads from being to non-being, from birth to death" (*Between Past and Future,* 167).

At this point, Sue knocks Jack out of the way; she seizes the controls, the light in the trailer turns red (as in the gym), and a strange symphonic religious screeching sound crescendos. The film cuts to the screen she is watching, which is now marked with a red target, and, oddly, the grainy image bathed in red light of Kahlil pushing his kids on a swingset gives way to direct bright sunlight, as our observation follows the path of the missile crashing into this world of appearances. The sound turns off and ten seconds pass with Kahlil and his kids playing happily, mostly in silence, until the bomb hits, and the film cuts back to watching the flames and the dry bloodless landscape, with Sue and Jack, through the videoscreen in the Nevada trailer. Another cut puts us back directly onto the site of the explosion in the Iraqi sunlight, amidst the drifting rubble, as the happy birthday banner floats down on the debris and burns, the bodies buried in desert dust. The film ends with a close-up moving in on Sue's face, devilish in the red glow of the launch but victorious.

Conclusion

The military appropriation of women for war builds a structure of belief where gender is increasingly understood as a violent technology: as a means to an end, an extension of state sovereignty and its law. Arendt offers a diagnosis of how turning gender into an instrument for getting the job of war done is coterminous with a disempowering of judgment, thinking, and politics. Whereas Benjamin envisions a revolutionary spirit that will free itself from sovereign state law, Arendt's philosophy of freedom isolates politics from the instrumentalization of economics and human decision that she calls violence, or historical necessity. As Habermas articulates it,

> Arendt can reduce political power exclusively to praxis, the mutual speech and mutual action of individuals with one another, because she sets off praxis against the apolitical activities of production and labor. . . . In contrast with the production of objects . . ., communicative knowledge has to appear as the single political category. The basic conceptual narrowing of the political . . . permits . . . elimination of essentially practical contents from the political process so visible today. For this, however, Arendt pays the price of screening all strategic elements out of politics as "violence," severing politics from its ties to the economic and social environment in which it is embedded via the administrative system. . . .

(179)

116 A Critique of Violence

For Arendt, modern life increasingly and dangerously embeds gender in a division of labor that ties work to repetitive cycles of necessity and causality, or administration. Yet, "women's work" introduces a division from the world of things and appearances imposed by necessity, revealing that outside the world of instruments exists a plurality of points of view in mutual interaction and care, a history made by the people who live it, that she calls "thinking."

As Habermas warns, to consider gender as disconnected from the politics of work today is as impossible as considering it as outside the work of politics. Neoliberalism has claimed gender as one of its instruments. It implements its economic and political policy often with the command of doing gender right. What Habermas criticizes Arendt for is what neoliberalism does: she, he says, reduces reason to instrumental reason and then cannot find a way to formulate reason *inside* the world in any other way. The same can equally apply to gender: when gender is made into an instrument, just as when "thinking" appears in the world, it appears as a means to an end, under the command of equipment, economics, and law that sear its meaning and purpose into the earth. The body as thought is disappearing. In a neoliberal age, the spread of markets and the voiding of politics accomplished through endless war have brought us to a point of emergency.

Habermas' conception of politics is too narrow. Arendt does not so much set off praxis against production and labor as she demands that production and labor be assimilable to the lives of the people who live it, as politics. "Thinking" should find a way back within the world of things, senses, bodies, actions, and appearances, without becoming their tool; to speak as a plurality, to begin afresh. What Habermas misses is that the body, for Arendt, is not reduced to a fabrication made from a predetermined model and put into rationalized service—it comes into the world it brings into being, the world it shares with others as not having been thought before, as the radical work of imagination.

Notes

1 Richard J. Bernstein writes, "Arendt was responsible for introducing the writings of Benjamin to an American public when she published *Illuminations* in 1968—a collection of some of his most famous essays. Her introduction to this collection—a portrait of Benjamin as a person and as a writer—is one of the most beautiful and loving essays she wrote. She did not, however, include Benjamin's 'Critique of Violence' in *Illuminations.* The essay appeared in a second collection of Benjamin essays, *Reflections,* published after Arendt's death. Arendt never discusses or even mentions Benjamin's 'Critique of Violence' in any of her published writings. To the best of my knowledge, she never even refers to it in any of her unpublished manuscripts or private correspondence. When she reviews the discussions of violence in her essay *On Violence,* she refers to Sorel, Sartre, Pareto, and Fanon (among others), but there is no mention of Benjamin. Nor does she ever explicitly discuss 'mythical violence' or 'divine violence'" (164–165).

2 With "divine violence" as a messianic manifestation without concrete, recognizable historical content, Derrida can read "A Critique of Violence" as denying politics,

A Critique of Violence **117**

exhibiting rather the "temptation to think the holocaust as an uninterpretable mani-festation of divine violence . . . at the same time annihilating, expiatory and bloodless" (1992: 62).

3 Winfried Menninghaus: "This cyclical structure of guilt (offending of a valid order) and expiation (retribution, punishment) reveals for Benjamin the fundamental rela-tionship of mythical fate and law. The mythical retribution, however, produces, as in the case of the revenge of the spouse's murder by matricide, a new guilt; and in this way the fateful cycle of guilt and expiation virtually eternalizes itself" (318–319).

4 As Bloch embellishes, "[W]e drew from it [a godless Judgment Day], even *on the other side of* this one life, the idea of a recurrent beginning" (264) where "every subject [is] simultaneously present" (266).

5 James R. Martel interprets this as Arendt's inability to think of an alternative to sover-eignty as radically as Benjamin does in his focus on a "flash" of resisting power: "Unlike Arendt, Benjamin seeks to render politics visible in its distinction from sovereignty, even while allowing sovereignty itself to remain. By avoiding the dream of getting rid of sovereignty once and for all, he also avoids contaminating that 'non-sovereign space' with just more of the same" (36).

6 On the other hand, Jean Elshtain reads the depoliticization of the private sphere in Arendt as hopeful. She recognizes in Arendt a "discourse [that] constitutes its subjects as citizens: neither victims nor warriors" (1986: 109) through its "female images and female-linked imperatives" (1986: 105). Elshtain's interpretations are unconventional: she relies on an essential figure of femininity in Arendt's concept of natality, where women are defined by their biology, and then revalues that biology as redemptive. This oversimplifies Arendt.

7 "[P]overty is abject," Arendt remarks, "because it puts men under the absolute dictate of their bodies, that is, under the absolute dictate of necessity as all men know it from their most intimate experience" (*On Revolution,* 50). Necessity's capture of the political stage in the French Revolution is what makes the Revolution "fail" in Arendt's eyes, and the American Revolution's disregard of necessity, matters of life and the body, is what makes that Revolution "succeed." For Antonio Negri, this is where Arendt loses her argument. Instead of following the course of a revolutionary spirit that is always starting itself anew, the correlation of this constant founding with the American Revo-lution turns it into just another form of liberalism: "The choice of taking the American Revolution as an exemplary model not only blocks the ontological process but also cheapens the analysis of the political apparatus. For Arendt the *Constitutio libertatis* is simply and merely identified with the historical events of the American Constitution. All the theoretical problems that the definition of constituent power has raised are resolved by seeking rational alternatives and a political decision founded not on them but on the basis of the solutions imposed on them by the American Constitution . . . [She] proposes a 'positive sum' political exchange, polite and consensual, [that] has very little to do with [her] intuition of the absolute foundation" (1999: 17–18). I find this an imprecise reading of Arendt's use of Kantian aesthetic judgment, which does not assume resolution, decision, or consensus in the exercise of political power.

8 Some feminist critics—Benhabib (1995) and Joan Landes come to mind—counter allegations that Arendt confines women as *animal laborans* to the drudgery of the apo-litical by demonstrating the presence of women in various public spheres that Arendt references, like the salons in the former and the barricades in the later. Such readings still leave in place the cultural divide between public and private spheres, even as some women do not get relegated to the private sphere so severely or so permanently.

9 In *On Violence,* Arendt sees that Hegel's idea of the continuity of progress—borrowed by Marx—rests on a mechanical process, where each stage of history is produced to reflect the configuration that came before. The description of history as a machine

118 A Critique of Violence

relies on a birth metaphor caught in mechanical cycles: "Every old society harbors the seeds of its successors in the same way every living organism harbors the seeds of its offspring" (*Crises,* 128). In *Between Past and Future,* Arendt calls necessity "emasculated . . . reasoning and cognitive faculties": "The necessity which prevents me from doing what I know and will may arise from the world, or from my body" (158).

10 As with thinking (as we shall see), Arendt models politics on the idea of the Greek αγορα, a life of speech that makes action appear in the presence of others. Ephemeral and inconsequential, heroic action would disappear from memory if it did not get told as a story which is heard by others and endures, even in the absence of the particular event.

11 Joan Cocks, for example, sees Arendt's emphasis on freedom defined through speech and action as a denial of "the ascription of fixed characteristic to individuals" or the allegation that lives are "chained entirely to the repetitive cycles of the biological life process" (41).

12 "The Christian reversal is based . . . upon the . . . teachings of the Hebrews, who always held that life itself is sacred, more sacred than anything else in the world, and that man is the supreme being on earth. Connected with this inner conviction of the sacredness of life as such, which has remained with us even after the security of the Christian faith in life after death has passed away, is the stress on the all-importance of self-interest, still so prominent in all modern political philosophy . . . Since we have made life our supreme and foremost concern, we have no room left for an activity based on contempt for one's own life-interest" (*Between Past and Future,* 52–53).

13 Miriam Hansen has already observed the signs of the maternal in Benjamin's conception of myth and memory. Reading Benjamin's essay on "The Work of Art in the Age of Mechanical Reproduction" through the Freudian "uncanny," Hansen reads Benjamin's "natural history" as a type of reificiation, where history hides its connection to nature. "His theory of experience," says Hansen, "hovers over and around the body of the mother—as a memory of an intensity that becomes the measure of all cognition" (214). Karyn Ball agrees, highlighting, in the libidinal impulses behind Benjamin's "history" and "aura," the "transfer of erotic affect to nature" and the "recourse to physiognomy to transcribe the aura" (74).

14 Judith Butler interprets Benjamin's reference to "the living" here as a recognition of a "soul" that is sufficient grounds for opposing the law. She reads Benjamin as introducing a kind of solitude for ethical contemplation against the law. "In a rather peculiar twist, Benjamin appears to be reading the commandment not to kill as a commandment not to murder the soul of the living and therefore a commandment to do violence against the positive law that is responsible for such a murder" (2012: 81–82).

15 Jacques Derrida, on "divine violence": "For the decision . . . on the subject, the determinant decision, the one that permits us to know or to recognize such a pure and revolutionary violence *as* such, is a *decision not accessible to man.* Here we must deal with a whole other undecidability . . . [D]ivine violence, which is the most just, the most historic, the most revolutionary, the most decidable, or the most deciding does not lend itself to any human determination, to any knowledge or decidable 'certainty' on our part. It is never known in itself" (55–56). Richard Bernstein: "There are further reasons to be uneasy about Benjamin's enigmatic essay. There are many relevant issues that Benjamin leaves open—or, at the very least, fails to provide sufficient guidance for us to answer" (73).

16 Judith Butler tries to work around it, finding in it a parable that justifies the commandment "Thou shalt not kill" and its centrality to Jewish ethics. Ultimately, she asks, "But is this violence truly bloodless if it can involve the annihilation of people, as in the Korah story, or if it relies on a questionable distinction between a natural life and the soul of the living? Is there a tacit Platonism at work in the notion of the 'soul' of the living'?" (2012: 82). Disagreeing with Butler, who wants to read Benjamin's

A Critique of Violence **119**

"non-violent" divine violence as an invitation to engage a Jewish tradition of ethical contemplation rather than violent violence, Richard Bernstein notes the difficulty of reading Benjamin as appealing to ethics in his solicitation of the Korah story: "And we should not forget," he writes, "—although Benjamin doesn't mention it—that when the surviving people protest, when they murmur against Moses, the Lord—as the Hebrew Bible tells us—sends a plague that kills 14,700 of them. There is a further irony in the story of Korah when we realize what his offense was. It was an act of rebellion—a revolutionary act—against the authority of Moses and his law . . . The point of contrasting mythic and divine violence is to distinguish sharply two very different types of violence, but there is no *direct* basis in Benjamin's text for claiming that divine violence is nonviolent" (62–63).

17 "[T]he thinking ego," Arendt explains, ". . . has no urge to appear in the world of appearances. It is a slippery fellow, not only invisible to others but also, for the self, impalpable, impossible to grasp . . . In any case, seen from the world of appearances, from the marketplace, the thinking ego always lives in hiding" (1971, "Thinking": 167). Thinking—a separation from external coercion or worldly determinations— underlies alienation, an "inner feeling," an estrangement from the world that constitutes an "absolute freedom within one's own self" (*Between Past and Future,* 145).

18 As Judith Butler adds, Arendt's stress on thinking as justice's calling is her way of insisting on "legal innovation, something that demands the exercise of judgment when existing legal precedents cannot fathom the crime" (159), particularly when judging the vital question of "with whom to share the earth" (162).

19 Jonathan Schell writes that "the atomic bomb appears to have been a starting point for her political thinking" (250). He notes that much of this focus has gone unremarked, even by Arendt herself, until Jerome Kohn published some of her unpublished works posthumously, making public pieces of a volume called "An Introduction into Politics" that Arendt herself gave up on finishing. In these pieces, Arendt makes clear the connections between totalitarianism and total nuclear annihilation as both threats to her version of politics: "To put simply, totalitarianism, the form of politics that relies on violence more than any other, kills politics at its root by using 'systematic terror to destroy all inter-human relationships.'. . . The atomic bomb . . . threatens the common world from another angle—not destroying all freedom directly, but simply by destroying all life" (254). Climate change may have been analogous.

20 Arendt's articulation of thinking as "pure means" takes various forms, each one a scene of judgment. Coinciding with the "the discovery of the 'interior man'" (1971, "Willing": 150), Will comes to exist at the same time as evil. Evil would be incompatible with its divine origin (just as "the new" might seem incompatible with a subject who is born into a pre-existing world). In order for Will to be exercised, it must give birth to an internal contrarian that it can Nil for Will, as Arendt expresses it, borrowing from Augustine and his followers: "The will, addressing itself to itself, arouses the counter-will because the exchange is entirely mental. . . . Since it is in the nature of the will to command and demand obedience, it is also in the nature of the will to be resisted" (1971, "Willing": 95–96). In other words, Willing is an internal, unreconciled, private world, composed of a plurality—where deliberative power makes judgments that do not fall into a means-ends logic or correspond with the factual world of necessity but can, therefore, bring forth something not thought before.

21 Beatrice Hanssen: "[T]he early politics of pure means re-emerged in the 1930s, notably in his celebrated 'The Work of Art in the Age of Mechanical Reproduction,' a text that, I would suggest, can also be read as an extended reflection on the relations between means, the mediality of the (film) medium, and political ends. In this Marxist attempt to reappropriate the means of (re)production, Benjamin hoped to separate the pure, unalloyed use of technological means, that is, film as a revolutionary medium, from its exploitation in fascist propaganda" (24).

120   A Critique of Violence

22 Bryan Garsten concludes that Arendtian judgment, like Kantian judgment, is completely subjective as it requires the presence of imagined others rather than real others. He sees her intersubjective community formed through the very subjective task of deciding who the other judges are: "My judgment is, in the end, *my* judgment" (330), he insists. My reading is different: I do not read Arendt as ever posing a subjective moment where the subject is ever unpopulated or isolated. The subject is born into a human world that preexists the subject and is part of that human world; the world is the subject. For Arendt, this is never about the subject selecting certain communities with which to judge—in fact, she is adamantly opposed to such a selection.

4

KILLERS AND SPIES

The Postcolonial Legacy in Real Estate

Elizabeth Bowen's 1948 novel *The Heat of the Day* has two simultaneous plotlines: one, a "romance," where the woman tries to help her spy-lover escape in defiance of British legal, military, and diplomatic authorities, and the other, a "spy novel"—less evident—, where she kills him.[1] The novel uses the conventions of both genres, but incompletely—Stella and Robert Kelway contemplate marriage but never marry, while the content and intrigue of Robert's secret negotiations with the Nazis are quite marginal to the text, more philosophical teaser than narratologically committed.

Critics have not remarked on the possibility that Stella kills Robert, almost as though the logic of Stella's violence would defy the logic of a text where violence is erupting everywhere else, yet such a reading is, in fact, possible. Though Stella shows Robert the secret exit to her apartment building through the roof, urging that the agents who will apprehend him are waiting in the street, Stella also knows that Robert's war injuries are particularly disabling when he is under stress, when he would be prone to imbalance and accident, and in the end we learn that nobody is stationed in the street. Stella could have very well led Robert to the roof because she knew such an attempted escape would end fatally.

This possibility that Stella participates in war violence as a soldier for the British state is certainly not outside of the thematic purview of the text, not only because of Stella's job working for British intelligence (like Bowen's at the time; she was tasked with spying on the Irish) and not only because the novel alludes to her possible collusion with the British agent Harrison. Also, Stella's role as combatant is taken up in relation to the question of Irish neutrality[2] and the specter of the colonial legacy: would Ireland support England by participating in its side of the war, or would a newly independent Ireland stay free of the violence? The question of whether Stella commits violence for the sake of Britain or does not, relates to

122 Killers and Spies

the question of her Irish national allegiance the British side of the war reflects the novel's position of whether Ireland should support Britain or stay independent.

As this book has observed, the literature of women in combat has served a variety of ideological purposes, for the most part revealing the effects of depoliticizing the relation between the soft, protective arm of the state and the citizens it promises to protect. As an effect of such depoliticization, such citizens are dispossessed of control over the conditions of cultural and political belonging and responsibility. Dismantling even the ideological work of social contract theory, this apoliticizing trend is connected to an administrative and technological reorganization of work that serves to introduce the non-representational politics of imperial governance into the liberal social contract's promise to govern by consent. Chapter One focused on how the female combatant has appeared in contemporary literature as a seeming aberration in a moment of urgency even as she is, rather, a reflection of an ongoing crisis in care. Chapter Two, meanwhile, presented the case that female combatants were known both in literature and global armed conflict and civil wars previously to the present moment, particularly in twentieth-century wars of decolonization, where the combatant forces sought to integrate a new social, communal vision. Following this, Chapter Three then argues that the female combatant has served as a politicizing influence in philosophy, disappearing in the face of war's instrumentalizing compulsions and celebrations of technology. All of these chapters show that war turns the woman's body into a tool, where the ends are embedded in the means, as opposed to a political culture of thought, judgment, and care for those who people the earth together.

Despite pervasive contemporary claims that women's combat is either a new and transformative concept for a broader democratic inclusion or a dangerous new threat to national defense, the female combatant has had a significant historical literary and cultural presence across time and geographical space. This chapter and the next discuss the female combatant's literary predecessors from the mid-twentieth century. In these chapters, the female protagonist appears to be adopting the soldier's character in the tradition of nationalist literature, taking on the soldier's particular historical place and symbolic resonance. Feminizing aspects of nationalist struggle that are meant, as explored in Chapter Two, to integrate new ideas more fully, deeply, and thoroughly into social structures, she still brings to the surface many contradictions and imbalances in the social relations and political expectations imposed first through imperialism and then through neoliberalism. Reading *The Heat of the Day* against Bowen's earlier treatments of Ireland, this chapter argues that the female combatant represents a particular conjuncture for a type of feminist independence modeled on the struggle for Irish independence, where late modernist form "stands in" for postcolonial politics and alienation inside the construction of the feminist character. *The Heat of the Day* is an instance where the woman combatant embodies the liberal possibility of new social relations and political openness as they are threatened by an imposition on

Killers and Spies **123**

civil society of authoritarian war-command in the form of a Nazi victory and administration. In the novel, the character of the emancipated woman evolves out of the character developed as a fighter for the postcolonial emancipation of Ireland in other of Bowen's works. In the perspective offered by Bowen, feminism adopts the character of property liberalization that Irish independence made part of its historical momentum. In order to make this link, the novel attempts to construct politics through relations of commodities, of objects and bodies that uproot and circulate, so that instead of responding to need, politics appears reduced as a response to changes in property due to modern forms of commodification. This move prepares the literary arrival of the female combatant as an image that— embodying the contradictions of liberalism's notions of care through inheritance and acquisition—works to redefine politics in the guise of property management, or bureaucracy.

The Heat of the Day's division of allegiance between Irish nationalism and British lineage becomes evident as the text employs a modernist aesthetic as the visible stand-in for a postcolonial politics of emancipation. *The Heat of the Day* is a classic of modernism, with its subjective focus, its confusion of identities, its critique of nations, its broken temporalities, its representational skepticism, and its cosmopolitan detachment. Instead of Irish independence being taken on directly, *The Heat of the Day* shows the effects of postcolonial nationalism by foregrounding a change in the relationship between names and ownership that the *blitz* brings out in the open. Bowen depicts the wreckage of the *blitz* as resulting in an alienation of property, where newly-mobilized citizens live in buildings torn from their foundational histories, ancestral significance, and names. In an odd reversal, England—or London, specifically—stands in for Ireland under British occupation, with the Nazis as its occupiers. As in the fight for Irish independence, violence, like the free market, frees up houses from an older order based in the caretaking of property inherited by name, ancestry, and nation (especially caretaking by women) and puts such properties, instead, in the hands of transients.

The question of Stella's hand in the violence, then, introduces, as well, not only a plotline about Irish involvement but also a post-independence vision of a future governed by free market administration and best represented in broken storyline, disassociated language, fractured temporalities, and split and circulating identities. The character's relation to the houses she inhabits, by marginalizing the "care" of "tradition," foregrounds an indifferent, administrative-like circuit of exchange that looks prototypical in today's wars. Certainly, my aim *is not in any way* to blame the violent and systematic dispossession happening in the cultures of our current wars on Irish independence and its legacies. The suggestion would be offensive that what Bowen depicts as an older, quasi-aristocratic order of inheritance and class prerogative is in any way preferable to what replaces it as that order breaks down. Rather, I read Bowen as understanding Irish independence as a battle over who owns what and how, an understanding that frames the female combatant as

124 Killers and Spies

constellating a new social order, privileging markets, as freedom, over politics, as care for sharing the world with others.

The Heat of the Day takes place in London during the *blitz,* and the plotline that leads to Ireland is not the central one: Stella attends a funeral of her former husband's Irish cousin, Francis Morris, and learns that her son Roderick, though never having met him, has inherited his family house and land in the south of Ireland—"'in the hope,' it was written, 'that he may care in his own way to carry on the old tradition'" (77). Cousin Francis had kept the house "almost, in its original state," (83) in the same manner as his grandfather; though "a salesman would find him as easy to 'interest'" (83), he chose to reject air-conditioning, mechanization, modern lighting, and domestic appliances in favor of maintaining the old social relations. Cousin Francis had died in England where he went "to offer that country his services in war" (74), impatient that Ireland was hesitating in supporting Britain's war effort and that Ireland saw its interests as independent of Britain's. Though seemingly marginal, this subtext about Ireland plays out in Roderick's eventual decision, after having completed his military service, to take residence of the old house and "care" for its "tradition," even though Roderick had had no prior experience of the Anglo-Irish tradition. The idea of Irish independence also enters the narrative in Stella's hesitation over whether to side with British authorities in capturing Robert, who would be her enemy as much as theirs, or, on the other hand, to break with Britain and marry Robert. This decision, which Bowen uses to develop Stella's character, also develops as the symbolic space of Stella's feminist autonomy. *The Heat of the Day* stages no Irish opposition or a rebel contingent, yet uses the potential demise of ancestral lines in landed property to showcase Irish autonomy as the threat faced by English occupation in Irish territory.

By displacing the struggle over Irish territory onto the central plotline in London, Bowen imagines an alternative to British rule in Ireland but equates that alternative not to Irish self-rule but rather to historical forces that have weakened British land-holding authority and traditional care. The idea that the subjectivity of the Irish insurgent could not be imagined except as a depersonalized historical force works to shut down some of the political possibilities that might have surfaced otherwise. The construction of feminist subjectivity might have spotlighted the limitations of a technological rationality for feminist emancipation that the novel also makes visible, but instead the combatant woman inherits such depersonalized power as feminist subjectivity. *The Heat of the Day* offers commercial property markets as the promise of universal equality that opposes hierarchies based in ancestral ownership and colonial privilege. Unable or unwilling to sketch characters or formulate subjective positions resistant to British authority, Bowen folds ideas of freedom, equality, and sovereign independence into the resistant subjectivity of the non-sovereign market and symbolic exchange. Instead of showing independence as an Irish nationalist project, Bowen constructs her struggle for independence as a conflict between the modern woman in urban space, on the one hand, and, on the other, women in traditional domestic space.

Real Estate and Violence

The Heat of the Day is a novel about the city of London during the war, about how its population negotiates its daily movements between moments when the sky lights up with fiery bursts from invisible enemy air power. It begins in a scene in a park, a free concert that Bowen portrays as a peaceful hiatus when free people freely intermingle and appreciate the languid beauty of a sunny Sunday afternoon at the brink of dusk. Soon afterwards, Stella is approached by Harrison who works for British intelligence and tells her that the British have collected incontrovertible evidence that her lover Robert has been selling secrets to the Nazis. Harrison solicits her to end her romance with Robert. Much of the novel takes place as Stella tries to decide her allegiance: whether Harrison is convincing, whether she should marry Robert, and whether she should sleep with Harrison in exchange for Robert's exoneration.

Stella's war story is counterposed to the story of a working-class young woman, Louie Lewis, whose Seale-on-Sea home has been destroyed in the Battle of Britain, along with her parents. Louie's husband Tom is away serving as a British soldier. Before she has told him that she is pregnant by one of many soldiers on leave in London for a night, he dies in combat. Louie's story begins *The Heat of the Day* when she is in a London park, looking for companionship, and meets Harrison, and then ends it, when she moves out of London with her baby, though her connection to Stella's main plotline remains obtuse: they meet only once.

Whereas Virginia Woolf' *Three Guineas* concludes that there is a disarticulation between women and war,[3] *The Heat of the Day* shows this disarticulation as unsustainable. Much of the "action" in the novel is relayed through conversations inside of detached domestic residences, and the violent events of the war are external to the plot's unfolding. As Allan Hepburn notes, citing Bowen's own blurb, "Within the view of the reader there is no violent act" (134). "[T]he violence of warfare," he continues, "while felt as an external pressure, does not enter representation" (133). Yet, even with the bordering off of the novel's own descriptive domestic "women's space" from the war, the war is quite evidently pushing in from everywhere that the plot is not currently spotlighting, just on the other side of the fragile walls. For example, contemplating from her window during an air barrage:

> To her [Stella], tonight, "outside" meant the harmless world: the mischief was in her own and in other rooms. The grind and scream of battles, mechanized advances excoriating flesh and country, tearing through nerves and tearing up trees, were indoor-plotted; this was a war of dry cerebration inside windowless walls.
>
> *(157)*

The war hits outside targets like trees but also indoor plants and inner walls. In as much as women mark an "inside" space that is outside to war and history and

126 Killers and Spies

devoid of violence, the war has limits, but the domestic space is not kept outside of the war's reach. The buildings themselves echo and purvey the violence, absorbing it, protracting it, escalating it, and extending it in turn.

The bridging of modernist forms and postcolonial concerns in *The Heat of the Day* affects the characterization of houses as the social spaces shaped in reference to the female subjectivities that inhabit them. Though it would be overly simplistic to claim that Louie plays postcolonialism against Stella's modernist sensibility (especially since Stella is the one with Irish roots, the one closest to Bowen's own biography, and Louie is distinctively English working class), it would not be outrageous to say that Louie's presence in the text helps to define Stella as situated between a postcolonial politics of nationalist dispossession and a modernist cosmopolitan orientation of sexual freedom. Louis' dispossession from home and belonging by the Nazi bombings mirrors and emphasizes Stella's, who loses her brothers in World War I. Louis' loss of her husband Tom parallels Stella's loss of her husband Victor, who was injured in the First World War, and dies, of ill health sustained as a result of the injury, three weeks after she divorces him, before the novel's start. Both Stella and Robert have families that are established socially through inheriting houses with names attached, but the regime of social stability in old houses is receding before the detachment from names and houses that Louie's war story foregrounds by ending the novel with her fatherless child, a child without name. Louie *wants to* position Stella as stabilizing and defending a nationalist tradition of belonging but, in *blitz*-time London, real estate is constantly changing hands because of its exposure to war, left bereft of the names and lineages that give them identity and value. The violence of postcolonial dispossession, then, underlies the war's production of a market culture, while the violence of market culture creates the disorientations and disassociations linking female sexualities to modernist aesthetics.

The Heat of the Day locates this relationship between postcolonial violence and market dispossession within the changing historical connection between women, their sexuality, and houses. War violence in the novel exposes what is most private; that is, it forces what belongs inside, the stability of identity, into circulation, offering its possession to the unnameable many. In *The Heat of the Day,* the war splits things from the names they are supposed to belong to, giving a sense—sensible in a spy novel—that everything is exposed because of the porousness of barriers, the shattering of enclosures, and nothing means what it seems it should mean. As Maud Ellmann reads it, "This is a novel about leaks, about the porousness of architectural and psychic space, about the failure to keep secrets in, intruders out. Bowen herself remembers living 'with every pore open' during the War: 'Sometimes I hardly knew where I stopped and somebody else began'" (153). Returning home one Sunday, Stella has the feeling that "she should instantaneously know herself to be on the return to a watched house" (140). By dispossessing Stella of what should belong to her by name, the watching state, like the stalker that Harrison is, eroticizes Stella.

Wartime surveillance opens closed domestic spaces. Harrison, spying, appears at Stella's elbow as she turns the key to her flat, enters the dark stairway with her, announces that this type of being together makes him feel "quite at home" (141) even as Stella admits to herself that she likes this being watched, though she finds it "grotesque" (141). Ashley Maher construes this violation of private space in *The Heat of the Day* to be a presaging of the welfare state that Britain was on the verge of constructing and to which London was central. Sounding a lot like the post-war housing reformers, Bowen, according to Maher, envisioned the home as an opening to a new social organization in the mode of architectural planners of the time, that is, as part of a social drama around the penetration of public powers into private lives, "the breakdown between interiority and exteriority" of the welfare state, suggested in that "the Blitz can easily turn the home inside out" (256). If Harrison is a representative of the state, however, the state is pure punitive surveillance and police enforcement rather than, as Maher indicates, a mechanism of benevolence and nurturing redistribution: the promise of improved housing and social insurance like health care, national rebuilding, and child allowances.

Nevertheless, the entry of Harrison as surveillance state into Stella's home, and his comfort there, normalizes violence. Violence becomes everyday, even cozy; it appears as part of the furniture, in a particular style of smoking, a way of listening to a ringing phone, glancing at his watch, or touching her things; as Stella herself observes, "a deadening acclimatization to it began to set in" (100). The surveillance state is staged within a familiar domestic scene as a threat. Instead of care-giving, Stella works for the war state, becoming its agent as she watches Robert for clues and proofs, and reports back, finally enforcing his sentence.

Throughout the novel, houses are never secure from such violations from the outside. The inability of walls, windows, doors, and stairways to separate the outside from the inside means that the violence of the war enters private space as enterprise. As Stella mis-recognizes Harrison for a traveling salesman, the surveillance state arrives in Stella's living room seemingly as a representative of commercialism that leaves a trace, casting suspicions on objects and making them seem unreal: Stella's son Roderick, on leave from military training, inspects the furniture "like a detective" (54) to see if they gave signs of unexpected use. Roderick sees Harrison's Chinese cigarette stubs left on the mantle and wonders who had stood there previously. But Roderick cannot really guess from the remaining stubs the smoker's story. In effect, these objects are unanchored, repossessed by Harrison's use, making narrative meaning indeterminable.

In Bowen's work, such objects get separated from the names that shaped their narrative meaning. Elizabeth Inglesby also notices the disjunction between characters, on the one hand, and, on the other, their surrounding objects and settings in Bowen's work: "houses and their furnishings are more than the sum of human projections onto them; they sit in silent judgment, secretly animated and seemingly fully capable of living alongside their occupants" (313).[4] Inglesby,

128 Killers and Spies

though, attributes these tendencies in Bowen's work to vitalism, or a spiritualized materiality—a "love of the tangible world" (326)—that inspired modernist ideas of creativity, not, as I do here, to alienation.[5] As an aesthetic choice, the separation of objects from the personalities they mark, for Ingelsby, is proof that Bowen "saw more than economic value, and more than crass materialist fervor for riches and possessions" (326), whereas I am, rather, reading this separation in the increased mobility of things in commercial culture. This cut between the object and the name of its possessor applies not only to objects, houses, and properties but also to countries: as Robert says when he confesses his spying to Stella: "there are no more countries left; nothing but names. What country have you and I outside this room? Exhausted shadows . . ." (301). Robert gives away secrets because, he says, the country "sold itself out already" (302). For Robert, strength and lawlessness prevail over freedom and loyalty because ideals are content-less, naming nothing, belonging nowhere, and conjuring, as Robert himself notes, "the hangover from the word" (301). "Don't you understand," Robert berates Stella, "that all that language is dead currency?" (301). A commercial circulation replaces both the home and the nation that had been previously stabilized through name and inheritance. *The Heat of the Day* suggests that knowledge of identities at one time was transparent in the objects and symbols that surrounded them, and now war and other historical forces are putting an end to that absolute readability and certainty. By contextualizing, in London of the *blitz,* the modernist demise of naming as certainty and a consequent distrust of symbolic footing, Bowen changes a story about the re-appropriation of Irish lands by the Irish into a story about questionable inheritance introduced by female promiscuity. I will return to this point in the last section.

Interior spaces in *The Heat of the Day* absorb the war rather than offering escape from it, to the point of producing a paranoic text (as any spy novel ought to be) mostly around women and private space. The war penetrates these insides with reflections and shadows, flaring up in light showers on walls, beaming against curtains during blackouts, bursting through in vibrations of shooting sound, augmenting anxiety: "War at present worked as a thinning of the membrane between the this and the that" (218). The interiors where the characters interact and converse in semi-isolation from the effects of the war do not grant them a sense of belonging, of protection, or of self-definition. "There are always two or three places where I can turn in" (155), responds Harrison when Stella asks him where he lives. "Privacy" belongs to other people, often to the dead or to refugees, while the population remaining in London moves through abandoned space, alienated, using other people's furniture, feeding their pets, wearing their clothes. "'It's not mine,'" admits Stella, referring to an ashtray on the chimneypiece, "'Nothing in this flat is'" (27). Stella is in exile always, never really part of the scene: "Stella woke next morning not knowing where she was or when. Her place in time had been lost" (196), evincing her "unearthly disassociation from everything" (196). Like the objects lying around in her flat, Stella is mis-placed. While, as I explore below, women of a prior generation are associated with a more stable form of property, where walled-in spaces provide a protective privacy for personalized objects and habits of belonging, war turns Stella into a ghost, alienated, time out of place.

On a narrative level, wartime violence instantiates not just the destruction of property but the destruction of inheritance, the mobility of possession, in particular through redefining women's roles. War violence may seem historical or even spiritual—a kind of atmospheric pressure that permeates social interactions though does not seem to be controlled by a source, an agent, or an intention. Yet, it also bears a remarkable resemblance to a postcolonial rupture. In shaking architectural foundations, the bombardment also jolts and shatters the idea of Britain upheld in property estate ownership and the establishment of the family names onto which such ownership passes. This sense that the old idea of the nation is splintering under the German attack, in fact, mirrors descriptions that Bowen herself is simultaneously writing about the loss of her family home and Anglo-Irish power against rebel opposition, as I explain below (Bowen's own family home was destroyed in 1959). But here, the implosion of the old order takes the form of female sexuality that, like the new property order, escapes the certainty of the inheritance of the paternal name. As in the postcolonial situation that Rey Chow recounts, female sexuality insinuates "the potential destruction of the group" (39), a potential "that could break down all boundaries and thus disrupt social order in the most fundamental fashion" (39) as it destabilizes and opens to question the lines of belonging and identity that establish power and community. As sexual beings, women's elision into a new market culture in Britain is what allies them to the destruction of the old Britain.

Because *The Heat of the Day* displays the process of replacing the old Britain with a new—of destroying the old order of old family names with a new order of circulating identities—, much history appears in the text as ghosts, appearing only as disappearing. Gothic like the old houses, the city of London is populated by the walking war dead from this war and others.

> Most of all the dead, from mortuaries, from under cataracts of rubble, made their anonymous presence—not as today's dead but as yesterday's living—felt through London. Uncounted, they continued to move in shoals through the city day, pervading everything to be seen or heard or felt with their torn-off senses, drawing on this tomorrow they had expected—for death cannot be so sudden as all that. Absent from the routine which had been life, they stamped upon that routine their absence—not knowing who the dead were, you could not know which might be the staircase somebody for the first time was not mounting this morning, or at which street corner the newsvendor missed a face, or which trains and buses in the homegoing rush were this evening lighter by at least one passenger.

> *(99)*

130 Killers and Spies

As Stella arrives in Euston train station, the dead coming out of history take the guise of travelers, roaming ghosts like the crowds in transit into and out of London—at hospitals, refugee centers, and train stations—acting on "some inhuman resolution" (201) like an "[a]rrival of shades in Hades" (201). Envisioning the war dead as antagonistic to the divisions of individuated space reminiscent of house-property through lineage, Bowen continues, "The wall between the living and the living became less solid as the wall between the living and the dead thinned" (99–100). Mattison reads this "timelessness" (400)—where images of the past endure into the present—as characteristic of Bowen's objects transforming and deteriorating as they refuse the present expression of the human subject. Yet, such persistence of ghostly after-images also applies to living people in *The Heat of the Day,* particularly to women alienated from lines of ancestral property-ownership, and, as well, it introduces a gothic aesthetic that connects the national experience of war to the tradition of "Big House" literature in Ireland.

In effect, ghosts indicate that residences and the names attached to residences are deteriorating and disappearing; that is, that the foundations of an old society and power structure are under attack by historical forces. Commodification thus operates like an army of insurgents challenging hereditary authority. Bowen traces out the difference between a commodified present and an older accumulation of power held in houses. The demise of the old authority occurs as women's sexuality becomes unowned like things. The past generation of house matrons visibly passes away, and with them the stability of the old order. An older generation of women (Stella's cousin Nellie; Robert's mother Mrs. Kelway) who seemed architecturally bound to staid, enduring physical interiors, like furnishings, is replaced by a wartime generation of women, like Stella (and Louie), who have no family ties and no place of lineage and who circulate. "[T]he lady of the house" (193), Stella's cousin Nettie—the former mistress of the house in Ireland, Mount Morris, her son Roderick is to inherit—, is a ghosting of a memory (having escaped into an insane asylum),[6] part of an array of "fancies, fantasies only so to be called because circumstance outlawed them from reality" (52): "old things would be pushed into a new position" (195). The ghosting of the woman of the house serves not only as an atmospheric effect, where the language of war explodes into a gothic imagery reminiscent of an Irish literary past. Also, her fading suggests a sense, even a danger, that family identity is being wrenched away from houses, properties, authority, and things, now ambulatory, ephemeral, and transitional.

The ghostliness of Robert's mother Mrs. Kelway parallels the loss of solidity and substance of objects and the family house Holme Dene itself, a house which could be witnessed from the walkway, like a "peaceful scene" in an era of war, murky, disappearing, "as it were through glass" (114). Holme Dene is up for sale, and Robert wants to sell. Representing "one kind of pattern of English life at its most incoherent and reassuring" (113), Holme Dene takes on the name if not the content of Robert's "abandoned past" (125) with teapots, mahogany furniture, and antique oak; the family had designed its interiors to appear as old and established property: "the grandfather clock . . . must have stood there always—time had clogged its ticking" (117).Yet, the effect is fake: Robert's father had purchased the house in order to appear as part of a landed class that was in the process of losing its hold. For Robert, the English past, like his own, is already alienated.

Property and Colonization

In *The Heat of the Day,* "habitat"—a word also used to describe Stella and Robert's relationship[7]—has become temporal and tradable, as against a provincial countryside, outside of London, where ancestry decides property through generations of inheritance in names. Property markets in London erupt against property inheritance, turning them into ghosts. They underlie Stella's non-belonging: her family-lessness, her possessions interchangeable, always in migration among similarly abandoned objects up-for-grabs.[8]

The violence of the London war zone in *The Heat of the Day* shares these historical features with the frontline of the Irish Civil War in an autobiographical work that Bowen was simultaneously writing: *Bowen's Court* (1942). A biography of her family house in County Cork, *Bowen's Court* ends just before the outbreak of the Irish Civil War, but then picks up the author's present again in a 1963 "Afterward," suggesting that the years of British withdrawal and the establishing of Irish independence sit somewhere invisibly outside its representation. *The Heat of the Day* fills this gap. Through the ghostly descriptions of London, Bowen is, in fact, transposing other historical fronts onto the London scene of the *blitz*, particularly other ghostly fronts in moments of occupation: "She began to feel it was not the country but occupied Europe that was occupying London—suspicious listening, surreptitious movement and leaden hearts. The weather-quarter tonight was the conquered lands" (139). With Stella's two brothers killed during the first war (overlapping with the Irish one), London's wandering dead can be seen as begging this war to be their second chance, that is, their redemption.

In *Bowen's Court,* like in *The Heat of the Day,* real estate plays the protagonist. *Bowen's Court* is like a "bio-pic": it tells of the ascendance of a budding original talent (a house, like a young girl), its maturing and beautifying and prospering under the caring hands of an inherited ancestral line, until it reaches overindulgence, then its descent into a sinful "rock bottom" that comes close to annihilation, and finally its reconciliation and recovery as the resting-place of a famous novelist, Elizabeth Bowen herself. The book tells the story of the British conquest and colonization of Ireland as a real estate deal. As Bowen explains, "For these people—my family and their associates—the idea of power was mostly vested in property (property having been acquired by use or misuse of power in the first place" (455). The first Bowens' settlement and then the colonial transfer

132 Killers and Spies

of sovereignty take place as a seizure of property, an occupation, and then through housing construction in County Cork. The establishment of British authority (through the "Bowen" name) occurs in an attribution and titling of property in the family line: "Colonel Bowen, going to Ireland with the Cromwellian army, took with him from Gower his pair of hawks . . . He [Cromwell] then proposed to give Bowen as much Irish land as the second hawk could fly over before it came down, Bowen to choose the spot from which to let off the bird" (68). Like Harrison in *The Heat of the Day,* Britain comfortably settles into Ireland by settling into its interiors. Colonization continues through the many phases of building, repairing, decorating, keeping, litigating, caring for, and improving Bowen's Court.

The British hold on names and titles, however, was not fully secure and gradually became less so: "By English reform as well as by Irish feeling hereditary position had been assailed. Henry [VI, Elizabeth Bowen's father] by, at this juncture [in the 1880s], turning from his position [of full-time landlord, to become a lawyer] must have appeared to slight it. . . . He was not content to say, 'I have, therefore I am.'" (375). Such was Henry VI's betrayal of the Anglo-Irish: the house and property were the concrete, sedimented form of the hereditary line in the king's name, each ancestor having made a mark, left behind a residue of character, taste, vision, and life story in the house's construction and reconstruction: "The dead do not need to visit Bowen's Court rooms," Bowen concludes, "as I said, we had no ghosts in that house—because they already permeated them" (451). The house itself, registering the family's and the colonizer's ghostly history, would be up for sale eventually, as the surrounding property would be divided up, subject to various claims, caught in various legal battles over title, possession, and rights. As Bowen concludes, "I was writing (as though it were everlasting) about a home during a time when all homes were threatened and hundreds and thousands of them were wiped out" (454). Though referring to Irish independence here, this scene could just as well be used to describe the *blitz* in *The Heat of the Day.*

In the absence of Irish characters in *Bowen's Court*, the upsurge of non-British claims and legal battles shows Irish resistance pushing at the holes in the authority of British landholding: "One may say that while property lasted the dangerous power-idea stayed, like a sword in a scabbard, fairly safe at rest . . . I have shown how their [her family's] natures shifted direction—or the nature of the *débordement* that occurred—when property could no longer be guaranteed" (455). When Henry VI decides to enter the law profession, arguing "for free will, as against predestination" (376), the Bowens' hold on the property was threatened by Land Purchase, where the British government, in order to propitiate the unionists in the Irish parliament, would buy out the landlords and give the land to the tenants. "The most aggressive act," (400) says Bowen, of the Irish defenders of Land Purchase, was to develop a domestic Irish market: "the instigation of a 'Buy Irish' campaign" (400). The frontline is drawn between inherited property, on the one hand, and, on the other, the violence that develops in the form of domestic markets.

"[H]ereditary position had been assailed" (375), Bowen highlights as an outcome of the Irish challenge in *Bowen's Court*, as "the headlong decline of Bowen's Court seems to have been implicit" (376). This same frontline that divides the Anglo-Irish landholding class from the rise of an Irish decolonizing movement in *Bowen's Court* is reflected in *The Heat of the* Day: the woman custodian of the house is fading before the opening up of privacy, names, and property to the circulation of the historical, the sexual, and the political.

In *Bowen's Court,* Bowen uses "the sale" as the dispossession of a sovereign royal interest, an upsetting of its consolidation of property in the names of a ruling class as it loses its hold on female sexuality, its name and its care. *Bowen's Court* is *The Heat of the Day*'s ghost text: one indication of this being that "Robert"—the first name of Kelway and then, as we learn at the end, of Harrison as well—is also the name of Elizabeth Bowen's grandfather and the last owner to be a full-time resident of Bowen's court. Stella considers joining with Robert, who will help to orchestrate the conquest of territory, as did the first Bowens in *Bowen's Court*: the Nazis, in the role of Britain, might conquer London, in the role of Ireland.

Modernism, the Big House, and Sex

Criticism of *The Heat of the Day* and of Bowen's work more generally has been split between tracing her place within Irish literary history on the one hand and, on the other, interpreting her as modernist and so thoroughly cosmopolitan. Though Anna Teekell claims that *The Heat of the Day* "is rarely read as an Irish novel" (63), critics such as Kreilkamp, Yoshino, and Backus have indeed all placed Bowen within an Anglo-Irish tradition, in the genre of the "Big House."[9] Such readings have understood the house in this tradition as historically divided, that is, as, arguably, reflecting an "equation of political stability with the architectural image of the great house" (Kreilkamp, 19) in the ascendency of the British land-owning aristocracy, or, on the other hand, in its later forms, "fraught with the question of legitimacy" (Yoshino, 48) of this class and "the decline of the landed class" (Yoshino, 50) while acknowledging "the historical culpability of the settler colonial system" (Backus, 147). Though Ashley Maher, interpreting Bowen as within a late modernist or post-experimental generation, lists Bowen among three post-War British writers who, she declares, "seldom appear in accounts of modernism" (253),[10] other critics, such as Sinéad Mooney (for example), have noticed the aspects of stylization[11] that Bowen shares with Beckett (or modernism generally), attributing such similarities to "their shared [Irish] vision of the second half of the twentieth century as dislocated, dispossessed, and denatured" (246). Bowen exhibits modernism as formative in Irish history and Irish culture as immanent in modernism.

For Bowen, modernist style is the expression of how Irish modern experience settles uncomfortably into Anglo-Irish houses. Names break from things; dispossessed, identities circulate. As Bowen takes it up in *Bowen's Court* and then in *The*

134 Killers and Spies

Heat of the Day, the Big House tradition in Irish literature traces how the properties on which British domination and authority depended became speculative, opened to outside influence, commercial and state interest, and legal conflicts. Bowen makes visible this sense of the speculative in her ghosting of women who preside over such houses, aligning the gothic of the Irish Big House with a modernist stylistic conveying the evanescence of property, names, and things.

Whereas *Bowen's Court* depicts Irish history through the viewpoint of a house, its life and times, to the point where the house itself seems to speak—and then to live and lament and, finally, to lose its parentage—, *The Heat of the Day* is framed through the perspective of the orphan, Louie. This is not the first or the last time that Bowen centers on a young woman, specifically a young woman coming to terms with mature sexuality, without parentage or clear social place, and paired with a more mature and seemingly more sexually experienced or sexually unconventional female character in a house that becomes character-like in solidifying the partnership.[12] As Maud Ellmann notes, "Bowen persistently pairs off girls with women" where "the older woman [strives] to be the author of the younger" (165). For example, in *The Last September* (1929)—about the start of the Irish Civil War—, Lois moves in with her aunt and uncle when her parents die, and there, as the British garrison runs its first encounters with an incipient Irish uprising, makes the acquaintance of Myra, a more continental, artistic, and sexually experimental woman. The novel begins with a scene where the girl's budding sexuality animates her family house: "In those days, girls wore crisp white skirts and transparent blouses clotted with white flowers; ribbons threaded through with a view to appearance, appeared over the shoulders. So that Lois stood at the top of the steps looking cool and fresh . . . [A]bove, the large façade of the house stared coldly over its mounting lawns" (3–4). Other houses are being sold, and families that were once solidly established become transnationally migrant. In the end, Lois' family house is destroyed in flames by the rebellions, and Lois, whose British soldier fiancé had died guarding the region (like Louie's husband Tom dies fighting for the British against the European occupiers), leaves for the continent to study art. With the violent loss of Anglo-Irish property stability, Irish history—its moment of independence—follows the girl's sexual passage to maturity, when she abandons the Anglo-Irish tradition.

The Heat of the Day is Bowen's only such novel where the young woman and the older one do not belong to the same family or live in the same house or frequent the same sections of the city or even really know each other except for one brief, accidental encounter in a bar. Louie, also, is not sexually inexperienced but both married and sexually rambunctious, reversing the pedagogical partnership. Nevertheless, as Neil Corcoran has pointed out, "The novel establishes an elaborate parallelism between Louie and Stella" (173): both have lost their families, for example, and Louie's husband Tom dies in the war at approximately the same moment as Robert does. Unlike in the other novels, the women do not live in houses symbolically doubling the maturing body of the young woman living

Killers and Spies **135**

there—Louie's house having been leveled and Stella's family house yet to be taken possession of by her son or her potential conjugal house to be sold by Robert's family. Instead, the houses are ghosts, made plot elements through their absence and alienation, reflective of the disassociation between objects, their names, and their expression. Whereas, in the other novels, the house is the material form of the girl's attachments, in *The Heat of the Day* the absent house connotes the girl's detachment. The words in the newspaper, for example, make Louie feel distant from her surroundings and from the recognizable newspaper categories naming British national identity, categories like wife, mother, sufferer, and sweetheart: while reading the newspaper, "[s]he felt she did not make sense, and still worse felt that the others knew it" (165). After Robert falls from the roof, Louie becomes a witness to Stella's sexual unconventionality as reported in newspaper accounts that are just as arbitrary: whereas Louie wanted Stella to be the stalwart of English names and values that she thought the war was fought for, the stability of the old order, she learns that, instead, "Stella [was] not to be virtuous" (345)—the man fallen from the roof was not the same one Louie had seen with her at the bar, and maybe, Louie concludes, Stella killed him in a melodramatic episode.

Like Bowen's other young women characters, Louie's world is put in conflict by the revelations of what she thinks of as the older woman's sexual biography. Louie serves as Stella's foil: in Louie's imagination, Stella cements an old order—like the house in *Bowen's Court*—against the historical forces of violent change, and Stella's breaking of that expectation makes Louie aware of a crisis that had been forming within national culture, a dispossession that makes Stella too much like Louie for Louie's liking. Stella's sex—in Louie's imagination, like the words in the newspaper—had circulated without possession, without name, like a ghost, against the inherited order. Stella's confession, as printed in the newspaper, leaves "blanks in Louie's vocabulary which operated inwardly on her soul; most strongly she felt the undertow of what she could not name" (345). Women here threaten British property and rule as Irish Land Purchase does in *Bowen's Court*: whereas in *Bowen's Court,* the house loses its name through purchase, and purchase is the political form of a sovereign representation that counters British occupation, in *The Heat of the Day*, Stella may be selling herself, sleeping with Harrison; the name loses its national bearings.

The adaption of Bowen's story of her house in Ireland into a cultural mapping of London during World War II, though, changes its meanings. Without Irish resistance underpinning and fueling a decolonizing momentum, the market in *The Heat of the Day* does not provide the same ethical content: it is no longer the representation of the landless, the afflicted, the needy, and the righteously dispossessed in their desire for democracy. Whereas in *Bowen's Court,* Bowen (though lukewarm in her position on Anglo-Irish rights) is tracing a moral history around a sovereign claim, in *The Heat of the Day,* the maturing of markets underneath the protection of the surveillance security state leads to a different type of sovereign vision. Here Britain stakes its moral claim by fully adopting and freely becoming

136 Killers and Spies

the post-war future of Europe. *The future of Britain conquers Britain*, taking over the hegemonic power structure once dominated by the inheritance of name, class, and property. Stella's post-war, national realities normalize the post-national vision for which Robert dies: a type of quasi-Nietzschian violent action *for peace* where laws, boundaries, and regulations are circumspect.

By constructing a version of post-war liberalism that inherits the Irish narrative of postcolonial violence and its quest for sovereignty, Bowen acknowledges violence at the very heart of liberalism's administering projects. Bowen's mistake was in seeing the solutions to liberalism's contradictions in a more thorough and extended liberalism. In her vision, a post-nationalized culture of free exchange and circulation would end the violence that colonialism introduced in its inheritance of conquered territories passed down through the name. She did not foresee what Robert might have learned from his Nazi partners and what David Harvey observes: "that the liberal (and by extension the neoliberal) utopian project could only ultimately by sustained by a resort to authoritarianism" (70). "Freedom to be what?" Robert defends his decision against Stella's accusations. "[T]he muddled, mediocre, damned . . . who could want to be free when he could be strong? . . . We must have law—if necessary let it break us" (302).

Bowen condemns the imperial state for its "primitive accumulation" in titling Irish lands to British subjects even as she nostalgically laments the loss of her ancestral property seized in imperial wars in Ireland. She despairs of a violent ghosting of populations as a result of imperial land-grabs even as she herself feels dispossessed of those unfairly captured lands. As well, the shifting of Bowen's ethical sympathies creates an irresolution in her national identifications and allegiances that builds her modernist aesthetic. This irresolution translates into a divide in her main character's political character as a British cosmopolitan modeled on an Irish combatant. Instead of imagining Stella as a willing participant in Irish resistance, Bowen balances Stella's option to marry, continuing the ancestral line in the connection of the property to the name, against an ethical (feminist) claim not to marry, to circulate in order to disinvest the names that authorized sovereign imperial power, and the latter wins. Bowen keeps alive the militancy of Irish Purchase inside the incipient but problematic construction of a feminist as late modernist, her independent sexuality—by destabilizing names and lineages— shaking the property foundations of imperial power.

The idea of feminism in *The Heat of the Day* is, then, influenced by its connection to Irish independence in *Bowen's Court*. Stella's power inherits the power of the combatant in her refusal to marry, the possibility that her sexuality would threaten the inheritance of Robert's name, Bowen's own with its colonial legacy. In *Bowen's Court,* Bowen frames the Irish insurgency as a property claim: Parnell rises to leadership as he takes the side of troubled tenants, demanding compensation and land-handovers: "For the land trouble Parnell saw one remedy: he did *not* suggest confiscation; he suggested, rather, the buying out of the landlords at a price to be fixed by the State, then the setting up of the peasant proprietary"

Killers and Spies **137**

(359). The settlement on property—that Bowen calls "revolutionary" for striking at "property's moral prerogative" (359–360)—translates into parliamentary representation. A phrase like "violence broke out again throughout Ireland" (360) describes the Irish position as without agency, riding history without anyone in control. "We have everything to dread from the dispossessed" (455), writes Bowen, deferring the Irish ascendance indefinitely: the Irish are acted on rather than acting, waiting for their historical role to present itself. Property, on the other hand, acts as the character driving the historical forward, at the helm, making the decisions: "At least, property gave my people and people like them the means to exercise power" (455). Property steps in as depersonalized power, a mechanical propulsion or physical force, a political maturation.

The representation of the house as historical force fails to repress the appearances of the human ghosts, the bodies and their needs, whose characters the house absorbs. The body of the independent, modern woman makes the name of authority questionable in much the same way as the Irish independence fighter. The body of Irish resistance in *Bowen's Court* survives inside the incipient feminist body in action in *The Heat of the Day* as a symbolic challenge and a continual political demand.

Notes

1   The woman who commits murder is not a foreign theme to Bowen's opus. For example, in her 1932 novel *To the North,* Emmeline drives her ex-lover Markie off of the side of the road in a fatal speeding frenzy. Markie, at least, saw this as purposeful: "He watched the next lights dawn like doom, make a harsh aurora, bite into the road's hard horizon and, widening, flood the Great North Road from bank to bank. His fingers an inch from the wheel, wondering if he dared stun her, he said hopelessly: '*Emmeline . . .*' with the last calm of impotence. As though hearing her name on his lips for the first time, dazzled, she turned to smile" (306). In *Eva Trout* (1968), it is not unreasonable to read Eva's murder by her adopted child Jeremy as instigated by her former teacher and stand-in guardian Iseult, who supplied Jeremy with both the weapon and possibly the idea when she kidnapped him on an afternoon. Iseult's intentions during the final murderous scene are not clearly marked: "Jeremy, at sight of Eva, had twisted free from Iseult—who had not succeeded in disarming him" (302).
2   Bowen herself exhibited ambivalence on the subject of Irish neutrality. In an article Bowen wrote for the *New Statesman* in 1941, she advocated neutrality as "Eire's first major independent act" (as cited in *The Mulberry Tree,* 31), having not only political but also moral, religious, and symbolic significance. Defining the newly independent nation by taking a neutral stand, however, produces, according to Bowen, an odd sort of identity, on the one hand an "abnormal isolation" that refuses "to go back to the old" (as cited in *The Mulberry Tree,* 32), but, on the other, a separate identity that can only be produced by a watchful ban on incoming news of the war. Scholars such as Ellmann, Corcoran, and McCormack have also pointed to the importance of Ireland's particular stance of neutrality during World War II in *Heat of the Day*'s plotlines and characters, McCormack even going as far to say that Robert's Nazi sympathies framed an Irish point of view, as Bowen, in her own researches for the British Home Office, "could gauge the extent of Irish sympathies with the Axis powers" (213).

138 Killers and Spies

3 In 1938, Virginia Woolf famously contemplated how women could help to stop the impending war and the commercialism that the propagation of the war required: "As it is a fact that she cannot understand what instinct compels him, what glory, what interest, what manly satisfaction fighting provides for him . . . as fighting thus is a sex characteristic which she cannot share, the counterpart some claim of the maternal instinct which he cannot share, so is it an instinct which she cannot judge . . . The outsider [she] therefore must leave him free to deal with this instinct by himself . . . an instinct which is as foreign to her as centuries of tradition and education can make it" (*Three Guineas,* 107).

4 Ingelsby also remarks on how this severance of things from the way they define character in the realist tradition influences the appearance of ghosts in Bowen's work, where objects are "inhabitants of another dimension of reality not dependent on humanity to lend it significance" (310).

5 Following Inglesby, as well as Rose Braidotti, Henri Bergson, and Gilles Deleuze, Laci Mattison also sees the disassociation of objects from subjective expression, but attributes this tendency to Bowen's interest in posthumanism: "In their appearance in parlors, tearooms, and boutiques, these things can be read not as supporting social relations, but as markers of a type of existence beyond the human" (394). Objects, she continues, "no longer signify the expected meaning projected onto them by the human world" (397). Though I find compelling the careful historicization Mattison applies to Bowen's thinking on objects and their broken relation to subjectivity, I would say, rather, that objects are haunted according to an Irish gothic. The haunting therefore references a tradition that sets itself against the scientism of European hegemony rather than against the human per se.

6 Kristine Miller observes, "[M]iddle-class English culture had conceived of the house as a private haven from the economic and political aggression of the public sphere" (140). For Miller, the *blitz* in the *Heat of the Day* explodes the insularity of bourgeois domestic space, offering women opportunities by increasing the possibilities of mobility: "It is not surprising that Bowen felt exhilarated by the wartime emergence of women out of domestic space" (151). It is hard to see, however, how *The Heat of the Day* could be read as celebrating the war for its feminist potential. Cousin Nettie ends up in an insane asylum; Stella plans to enter a seemingly loveless marriage after Robert's death; Louie is a widow left to bring up her child on her own; London itself is left in rubble, misery, and despair.

7 "What the inheritance came to be for Roderick, Robert was for Stella—a habitat" (97).

8 Critics have noticed Bowen's interest in the connection between markets and aesthetics, but mostly in relation to art markets. Brook Miller, for example, has positioned Elizabeth Bowen as a "late modernist" particularly in her considerations of building a bridge between a modernist high aesthetic and a popular literature mass market. Bowen, says Miller, "conscious of the inextricability of art from its conditions of production" (354) sees high modernist detachment from mass culture—its contesting of norms—giving way to a late modernist connection to markets—modernism's normalization.

9 Such critics have her read as appropriating pre-modernist literary conventions: a revival of late Victorian gothic (Backus, 148), a "political novel" (McCormack, 210), a "social novel" (Kreilkamp, 5), a "domestic novel" (Yoshino, 53), or a "romance" (McCormack, 240).

10 Interest in Bowen among scholars of modernism privilege modernism's cosmopolitanism and experimentalism identifying her modernist aesthetic. Ample critical attention to such notably modernist features of Bowen's work as "the uncertain 'I'" (Corcoran, 170), "destabilizations or erosions of identity" (Corcoran, 168), the "wry exposure of its own fictionality" (Corcoran, 171), its "rootlessness" (Ellmann, 158), and its "breaking of narrative form" (Ellmann, 165).

11 Such as: "dramatization of impasse, paralysis and lack of presence, deliberative narrative and unpicking, actions repeatedly arrested or aborted" (239).

Killers and Spies **139**

12 In *The Death of the Heart* (1938), for example, teenage orphan Portia moves in with her half-brother and his wife Anna to the house on Regent's Park they bought with their inheritance; in *To the North* (1932), Emmeline moves in—to a house they buy in St. John's Wood—with her brother's widow Cecilia, from whom she hides her affair with a non-committal cosmopolitan playboy whom Cecilia had met on a train; in *The House in Paris* (1935), orphaned Henrietta visits the Parisian house where a young woman started an affair with a man who was engaged to her friend; and in *A World of Love* (1955), Jane finds, in the attic of the Irish country mansion Montefort where she lives, her mother's love letters from her now-dead-in-the-war betrothed (who bequeathed the house) and starts, hauntingly, to emulate the beloved.

5

THE WOMAN, THE WORKER, THE WARRIOR, AND THE WRITER

The Military Nation and the Making of Female Neoliberal Subjectivity

An argument that the female protagonist in Brazilian novelist Clarice Lispector's 1977 work *The Hour of the Star* is a combatant would be counter-intuitive, if not downright ridiculous. After all, the character is obviously pathetic. Phrases like "quivering thinness" (11) and "calcium deficiency" (20) litter the narrator's descriptions of her; she is compared to a "weed" (20) with a "drooping head" (21) or "the form of grass in the sewer" (71) and has trouble holding down her own food. As Hélène Cixous summarizes, "the 'protagonist' is so infinitely small that she is not even noticeable" (1990: 149). In addition, the plot is not replete with heroic exploits, hair-splitting action, cruel intrigue, or physical contest but rather with, well, nothing, or nearly so. "[T]his story is almost nothing" (16), the narrator admits, and then talks about beginning but can only continue with a dash. The main character lives, works (but badly), tries not to throw up, listens to the radio, nearly falls in love, visits a doctor who does not help her, and then, exiting from an appointment with a fortune-teller, gets crushed by a yellow Mercedes Benz in a hit-and-run and bleeds out on the sidewalk.

In other words, the protagonist in *The Hour of the Star* is an eerie example of a human subject broken off from social bonding and completely alienated. Without friends or family, Macabéa's very body exhibits all signs that it is lacking in social care and connection: undernourished, unhygienic, unloved, ugly, "mute" (21), lackluster, asexual, fatigued, "gratuitous" (24), alone, covered in skin defects and filth. Socially unsustained, even her body resists life. As she lies dying on the sidewalk, "Some people sprouted in the alleyway out of nowhere and gathered around Macabéa without doing anything just as people had always done nothing for her" (71–72). This total indifference directed at her throughout her life means, for her, that she lacks "existence" (72). Though critics have mostly focused on Macabéa as suffering from an existential angst related to gender, migrant status, expression, spiritualism, poverty, and modern life, Macabéa's total solitude is also the upshot of her inability to present herself in the symbolic terms of new economic modes of exchange. By modeling Macabéa's character on a tradition of Brazilian nationalism that celebrates the soldier in national formation, Lispector illustrates that Macabéa has no place in the narratives the nation is producing for the nation-formers in a new economy of reproductive service. Macabéa's "nothing" is a calculation, a statement of "no" economic worth, that translates into a representational deficiency making her hard to be noticed.

The "non"-representation of her as completely outside of human connection, I argue, results from a new economic context where Macabéa does not fit into the symbolic mechanisms for producing profit, circulation, and exchange through administrative repetition. Even as much as the economy depends on workers like her, she is impossible to instrumentalize because she stands outside of the possibility of representation and identity within these new economic modes. Macabéa's invisible existence makes visible the necessary inequality embedded inside these economic relations, an inequality defined by its outsidedness to human care or connection, its dispossession and political disinvestment. Showing the breakage in a social system reliant totally on the reproduction of the productive apparatus, Macabéa's situation on the edge exposes a politics of need on the tragic edge of the new economy.

Lispector is most often read, however, as focused on spirit, subjectivity, and thought movements rather than on physical action, political conflict, or critique. Reading the alienation as predominantly a reflection on art or existential crises, critics have mostly noticed how, in place of a plot, *The Hour of the Star* chronicles each slight shifting of thought and mental imagery as an event of some magnitude. In one of her self-reflections on writing in her 1964 collection *The Foreign Legion,* Lispector herself notes that her work "assume[s] a note of hermeticism" (121), and her critics mostly agree that Lispector narrates through abstraction and interiority. The celebrated translator Gregory Rabassa observes that Lispector is concerned with "original thought patterns" (*Apple,* xii) that are "interior and hermetic" (x), and Assis Brasil remarks that she is "[t]racing a subjective world, in which interior action is more important than the simple external episode" (26; my translation). As Cynthia Sloan has lamented, "Throughout her career, Lispector's work was criticized for being too ephemeral and unconcerned with contemporary social and political problems" (100), and her biographer and translator Benjamin Moser also concludes that Lispector's stylistic innovations, introspectiveness, and literary excellence somehow would lay to waste an "offensive" and obstructive politics: "As her early writing suggests, and the whole of her life would prove, her interests were spiritual rather than material. Whatever material or ideological strains her early writing betrays—the rather strident feminism, for example—would soon disappear" (105). Her novels and stories generally slow the movement of time down to the point where, for example, a hesitation in walking reaches a similar intensity of turmoil and change as an act of war, what Lispector describes as

142 Woman, Worker, Warrior, and Writer

"a kind of intimate violence" (*The Apple,* 17) or a "spasm of this blind totality" (*The Apple,* 49). In particular, *The Hour of the Star* obsessively plots the subjective moments that move between objective events, turning story-time and history inside-out.

The interpretive history of *The Hour of the Star* does not, however, interrogate how the extreme isolation of the subject is an effect of the extreme alienation induced by a political dispossession and economic disposability, an irreconcilability whose politics are left submerged within the frame. As Lispector's work in general has been understood as adapting modernist style and technique, often seemingly unassimilable to what would be considered "authentic" Brazilian experience, the extreme isolation of her characters might be said to be a borrowing of modernist form in Brazilian terms and, in that way, putting into play a politics through its very subjective intensity. In the words of Theodor Adorno, "The *monologue intérieur,* the worldlessness of modern art . . . is both the truth and the appearance of a free-floating subjectivity—it is truth, because in the universal state of the world, alienation rules over men, turning them into mere shadows of themselves" (160). The "solitary consciousness" of the modernist subject in art and literature, says Adorno, "potentially destroys and transcends itself by revealing itself in works of art as the hidden truth common to all men" (166). Extreme loneliness in modernism is destructive of the world it inhabits by not fitting into that world, not being able to sustain it or be sustained by it. Modernist alienation, for Adorno, opens itself up to a politics that responds to modernity's inability to produce the conditions of a social life amenable to living; it is a politics of social rejection, a rejection that, ironically, binds us to others. "Art," concludes Adorno, "is the negative knowledge of the actual world" (160).

Indeed, Macabéa's patheticness demands some response. The more disgust her descriptions elicit and the more Lispector seems to be testing the boundaries of empathy and care, the more *The Hour of the Star* insists on a politics of care that would extend to the impossible edges, outside of representation: "I am going to do everything to keep her from dying," laments the narrator who does nothing to keep her from dying. "But what an urge to put her to sleep and to go off to bed myself" (71). The contradiction between Macabéa's total isolation and the need for care that her very presence persistently pleads (a care that is just as persistently absent) seems to induce a sense that everything is on the verge of an explosive convergence whose origin, like Macabéa, is inexpressible. The violence that underlies everything seems as a condition of the lonely subject, a sense of non-compliance within a world reliant on the production of inequality for its existence.

Lispector foregrounds the perennial presence of violence in almost every encounter, and not only for this character in this work. Lispector locates violence, for example, in everyday objects: "The egg for the present is always revolutionary" (*Foreign,* 49). Even her most introspective constructions of intimacy and love and the simplest, most basic, acts of living and sensing are saturated in violence: she

Woman, Worker, Warrior, and Writer **143**

writes, for instance, in her 1964 novel *The Passion According to G. H.*, "[T]his present world of mine, I would have called it violent before. For water's tastelessness is violence, the colorlessness of a piece of glass is violent" (150). The escalation of violence in this novel occurs when the middle-class narrator enters her maid's room and, for the first time, only in the maid's absence, confronts signs of the maid's presence.

As in *The Passion According to G. H.*, in *The Hour of the Star*, violence sizzles up between the self-reflections on narrative construction and the objects of that construction that are unequal to it, in the failures of representation. *The Hour of the Star* addresses problems of fictional construction and literary form *as though* they were problems brought into play by a new global corporate reliance on female labor, particularly in fields relating to the reproduction of the capital's narratives. In *The Hour of the Star*, the construction of the main character's passivity and pathos references a violent literary/folkloric romantic tradition of a savage hypermasculine warrior anti-hero. Though rooted in a nationalist heritage, such constructions of subjectivity allude as well to Brazil's military dictatorship between 1964 and 1985 when Lispector is writing her fictions: "I forgot to say," admits *The Hour of the Star*'s narrator (or the author), "that everything I'm now writing is accompanied by the emphatic ruffle of a drum being beaten by a soldier" (14) with the main character suffering from "[w]ar neurosis" (27) and, Lispector adds in the introduction, this "story takes place in a state of emergency" (xiv). The military imagery which resounds throughout *The Hour of the Star* is not just a background metaphor to give texture to emotional intensity and psychological conflict. It ushers in a gap in representation that grants a non-representational sense of the violence in the production of Macabéa as inequality as well as to her implicit demand for a response.

The military regime instituted economic change in Brazil as it responded to a growth period that led, in turn, to a downturn with the oil crisis in the early 1970s. As in most of Latin America, the regime managed the growth with increased industrialization, import substitution, and export diversification, debt-financed by U.S. commercial banks. The expansion of foreign finance capital throughout Latin America, as Ernesto Laclau has argued, meant that areas previously outside of industrial production and accumulation shifted, "from its traditional patterns into the production of either strategic materials—the typical case is oil—or industrial output" (185). This happened because "pre-capitalist super-exploitation of labour power," or regions that were still involved in crafts production within medieval-like localized relations of production, came to seem "anti-economic" (185). This shift corresponded with a significant increase in migration to the cities and employment in the service sector, from 33.3 percent of the economically active population in 1970, to 40.8 percent in 1980 and 57.4 percent in 1992.[1] Communicating within a period of downturn where the reproductive spheres are expanding, when the production of texts is coming to dominate over the production of

144 Woman, Worker, Warrior, and Writer

objects, *The Hour of the Star* shows that the capitalization of hitherto uncapitalized forms demands violent, often military, imposition.[2]

Even as Macabéa's character inherits the heroic form of the soldier in Brazil's national foundation, Macabéa's very existence disputes the terms of a national reality set by this inheritance. Through the feminization of the soldier, the novel brings out as a thematic and stylistic point what Antonio Negri addresses as a crisis in the socialization of capital—where the social relations of the new economy cannot be reproduced in subjectivity, at least not within the narratives of identity developed for standardized object production and ideological conformity. That is, neoliberalism seeks to turn all aspects of social life and subjectivity into forms of universal exchange that can be compared and repeated, like money. Macabéa reveals its failure, a failure in neoliberalism's self-legitimating self-representations. Indeed, the military presence always bordering on Macabéa's consciousness and bursting through the narrative line crowds all other social relations, leaving Macabéa bereft, unsustained and unsustainable, disconnected from any emotional reflection that could share in the life of others. The soldiering of Macabéa's consciousness reveals that changes in economic organization take on literary form as literature is the non-convergence of social reality with itself. In Adorno's terms, literature, like art, "remains the antithesis of that which is the case" (159). This "antithesis," in the case of *The Hour of the Star,* is social reality's incapacity to seize hold of Macabéa as what makes sense of itself in a reproductive economy.

The Hour of the Star is a story about reproduction as crisis. Clarice Lispector brings into focus the reproduction of subjectivity and language as part of a production process formerly organized in reference to objects. As such, the text obsesses over the mechanisms of textual/subjective reproduction, including its own, allowing thoughts and descriptions about its own production to overcome the plot. *The Hour of the Star* makes the production of female subjectivity its center: the male narrator, reflecting on his processes of creative production, reproduces the female protagonist in his image, and she, in turn, becomes a producer of texts, but failed texts. The texts and other creations are supposed to produce continuity in universal exchange, as one period of production repeats in another; yet, the military imagery of Brazil's nationalist history can never sit comfortably within its reproduction as the nationalist form of the new working-class subjectivity. The representation can never be equal to the thing for which it is exchanged.

Equivalence and Exchangeability

Critics have read the violence in *The Hour of the Star* as a symbolic problem. Luciana Namorato, for example, summarizes, "Macabéa is . . . the personification of the combat [*embate*] of the writer with language" (52; my translation).[3] While

Woman, Worker, Warrior, and Writer **145**

noting an irresolvable tension in *The Hour of the Star* in its treatment of gender, the predominant feminist interpretation of *The Hour of the Star* does not generally understand gender as standing for a violent inequality in new reproductive economies. For example, Cixous identifies with Lispector's interest in these subjective moments as a "general equivalence" (1990: 156) in excess to the economy: "I can situate myself at the paradoxical limits . . . of all markets," she explains. "We deal with economies said to be human . . . with libidinal economies, our own personal economies of affective and psychic investment" (1990: 156). For Cixous, the "openness to the other"—the possibility of a chain of substitutions and metaphoric displacements on which Cixous' *écriture* depends—needs to be, says Cixous, without tension.[4] Following Cixous, many critics have attributed the social importance of violence and inequality in *The Hour of the Star* to a critique of metaphysics, an overcoming of difference. Anna Klobucka, for example, remarks that "Hélène fell in love with Clarice" (41), and this love entailed "a faithful recognition" (42) and acceptance where Lispector's foreignness "disappears *without a trace,* leaving behind only such a pale reflection of itself as can, in effect, be labeled 'Cixousian'" (46), or total assimilation. Marta Peixoto agrees that Cixous' reading of Lispector "allows no outside voices" (42). Following Cixous' reading of desire as an equalizer, a perfect equation, critics have generally understood the appearances of violence in Lispector as a problem of narrative and the symbolic rather than as a problem of social reproduction and a fundamental transformation in the social relations of production and work. Very few have read the symbolic reflection in *The Hour of the Star* not as assimilable difference but rather as failure to assimilate.[5]

In effect, *The Hour of the Star* makes impossible such a balanced economy of exchange based on reproducing general equivalences of affect, partly because of its recourse to violence.[6] Peixoto, for example, understands Lispector's fictions to be "fraught with violence" (82).[7] In *The Hour of the Star,* Peixoto observes, violence is representational. Representational coherence is broken and the possibility of mimesis is disrupted, owing to "the class differences between the narrator and the characters" (92). Yet, she goes on to interpret Macabéa's "improbable job as a typist" as farcical (90) because Macabéa cannot spell correctly. Peixoto does not recognize the violent disruption of mimesis in the narrative as doubled in Macabéa's typing mistakes. She does not see that *The Hour of the Star* formulates failures of narrative and representational coherence through Macabéa's placement in the reproductive economy. The text seems purposefully "inadequate," calling attention to its construction by its emphatic commentary on process. Such commentary shows the narrative making mistakes, changing its mind and changing direction, foregrounding its disequilibrium. Crisis, then, is not just in the content of this story ostensibly about the poverty of a woman migrant service worker, and not just in the experimental or linguistically dissonant style. *The Hour of the Star* stages an antagonism or crisis between the narrative and the narrative material whose thought-life it creates.

146 Woman, Worker, Warrior, and Writer

Military Narrative

Tropes of the worker and of the combatant are not obvious facsimiles. For one, as the worker transfers his/her subjectivity onto objects, the combatant is usually imagined as pure physicality, coercion, and force. Whereas a worker might be an extension of systemic rationality and everyday repetition, the combatant erupts in the spontaneity of an irregular, conflictual, irreversible encounter or event, a disruption of time. Liberalism's worker is the barrier against violence: under contract, the worker willingly relinquishes violence to the state in exchange for the promises of productivity and security in civil peace.[8] To become a liberal citizen, as I discuss in Chapter One, the warrior surrenders her liberties and rights of violent acquisition to a state body that acts in combative mode in order to protect her, her rights, and her property from the violent acquisition of other warriors. This surrendering separates the acquisition of objects through war from a peaceful co-existence with others, the possibility of social life and of fair, contractual, and equal exchange. *The Hour of the Star* does not allow for these resolutions. The difference between the woman worker and the warrior makes visible a fundamental, non-compliant inequality between the nation as a narrative of productive militarism, on the one hand, and, on the other, a nation composed of its working citizens, especially the poor and the uncared for.

Not only does *The Hour of the Star*'s protagonist take her name out of the lore of legendary combatants—named after Judah Maccabee, the fabled Jewish warrior who saved the Hanukkah oil—, but also her literary forbearers are drawn from early twentieth century Brazilian social realism with its focus on the rugged savagery and backland romantic heroism of the northeastern *sertanejo*. These conquering figures appeared, as Cynthia Sloan describes, "before anything, as a fortress" (93; my translation). Euclides da Cunha's 1902 classic journalistic-like documentation of Antonio Conselheiro's 1888 stand-off in Canudos, *Rebellion in the Backlands,* for example, describes the cowboy of the northeast as organically arising—an object to be feared—from the natural violence of the landscape and of history:

> Working hand in hand with the meteorological elements, with the northeast wind, the suction of the air strata, the dog-days, the Aeolian erosion, the sudden tempests—collaborating with all these, man became an unholy accomplice to the forces of demolition in this climate. If he did not create the climate, he transformed it, made it worse. He was an auxiliary to the work of soil erosion accomplished by the tempests, and to the ax of the *catingueiro*; he supplemented the effects of the parching suns. He, it may be, made the desert.
>
> *(45)*

This warrior produces the nation by bringing natural objects—the desert—under his control, in his image. Though seemingly primitive and pre-rational, the northeastern warrior is actually embodying the force of nature to control nature in the name of its rationalization. In fact, battle is a form of writing: it converts the uncontrollable movements of nature into recognizable symbols and usable categories of controllable territory.[9] Nature grants power when its violence is converted into useable objects.

> His clothes are a suit of armor. Clad in his tanned leather doublet, made of goatskin or cowhide, in a leather vest, and in skintight leggings of the same material that come up to his crotch and which are fitted with knee pads, and with his hands and feet protected by calfskin gloves and shinguards, he presents the crude aspect of some medieval knight who has strayed into modern times.
>
> *(92)*

Such *sertanejos* were able to hold off the newly-formed Brazilian Republic's army for a year.[10]

Da Cunha's sensationalized report turns national conquest into the conquest of nature by a primitive masculinity turning nature into things. Whereas Da Cunha envisions violence as the physicality of productive masculinity in the northeastern backlands, Lispector situates violence, rather, in productive urban femininity that cannot reproduce or mimic nature.[11] For example, from the beginning, the character of Joana in Lispector's first book, *Near to the Wild Heart* (1943), like the character of the northeastern *sertanejo,* develops as nature's violence but is unable to find a correspondence with social, symbolic, and conceptual systems: "What else was that feeling of contained force," an undetermined voice says, seeming as Joana's thought, "ready to burst forth in violence, that longing to apply it with her eyes closed, all of it, with the rash confidence of a wild beast? . . . She felt a perfect animal inside her" (9). For the nationality and territory that da Cunha's masculine hero constructs as an object to be conquered, tamed, and made productive, Lispector's feminine hero substitutes a nationality figured as an untamable subjective force.

The violence that characterized the Brazilian tradition of the romantic warrior in the northeast's past inhabits Macabéa's modern character too: "born with rickets," she is "a legacy of the backlands" (19): "Macabéa was actually a medieval figure" (38); she "sprouted from the soil of the Alagoas backlands like an instantly molded mushroom" (21). However, Macabéa's insufficiencies do not relate to a primitive return, nostalgia, or custom—a rural residue, ritual, or village life. Like da Cunha's rebellion, Macabéa's subjectivity operates through erosions, tempests, and heat as fluctuations and dissonances that move the landscape violently. By feminizing the soldier-figure and treating it as the working girl's subjectivity, Lispector translates the violence of the battle—a temporally situated event that imposes controls—into a linguistic but violent disruption of capital's programmatic but

148 Woman, Worker, Warrior, and Writer

extensive control. Displayed in the breaking of narrative sequence and floating referentiality, Macabéa's subjectivity cannot completely comply with the rules of work nor does she shape all her actions and intentions into property-form; instead, her thoughts reveal an unequal but violent remainder beyond symbolic exchange.

Macabéa's position in relation to capital is therefore twofold. Macabéa's subjectivity is formed by capital as part of its machine, with her desire for rote repetition and her assigned task of copying text, exchanging one for its equal. Macabéa, though, appears as excess, a remainder outside the control of things. Macabéa is an effect of capital's current demands for soldiers: "she lived in a technological society in which she was a dispensable cog" (21). She is part of the machine, even in her backwardness, or especially because of it. Yet, as well, modern technology interrupts, violently, bursting out in splitting atoms and explosions that break apart sentences (both the ones she utters and the ones that describe her). These technological explosions strip apart the coherence of a capitalist narrative based on repetition, showing nature's disruptive violence inside capital's functionality, technologies, and militarism. When Macabéa gets interrupted by a "small explosion" while putting on lipstick to look like Marilyn Monroe, "instead of lipstick it looked like thick blood had spurted from her lips from a tooth-breaking flesh-busting sock in the mouth" (53). "You look," responds her co-worker Glória, reflectively, "like the kind of girl who goes with soldiers" (53). She cannot look like a girl or celebrity star because she is, like a soldier, dusted by the earth of the backlands. Macabéa cannot look like Marilyn, says Olímpico, her sometimes boyfriend, because "you're all dirt. You don't have the face or the body to be a movie star" (45). The commodity cannot absorb its other in infinite substitutions.

Lispector's characters enact, through thinking and daily encounters, the territorial struggles of the northeast's regional ancestry. Throughout her works, the social geographies of the violent backland landscapes filter into enclosed domestic spaces and modern workspaces where her plots take place. In *The Passion According to G. H.*, the principle narrative event occurs through the main character's reaction to a cockroach she finds in the absent maid's closet, the principle narrative event of the novel: "At that time there were beginning to take place in me— and still I didn't know it—the first signs of collapse of subterranean limestone caves that were falling in under the weight of stratified archaeological layers—and the force of the first collapse lowered the corners of my mouth, made my arms fall" (36–37). This empty bedroom brings to existential and geological furor the absence of the maid from the northeast who had just quit work and likely quit the city to go back to northeast (the northeast is just a place of absence within the city), but the absence is full of natural, evolutionary, and divine violence: "Cockroaches gnaw each other and kill each other and penetrate each other in procreation and eat each other in an eternal summer that falls into night" (116). The northeastern landscape has been sucked into the bedroom, the thinking, the evolutionary development, and the digestive track of the narrator's warrior subjectivity, making identification and repetition in the object impossible. "I spit myself out, never reaching the point of feeling that I had finally spit out my whole soul . . . I spat and spat and it kept on being me" (160). The maid, the main character of *The World According to G. H.*, like the main character in *The Hour of the Star* (Macabéa), never really enters the text, its codes, or its symbols. The narrative cannot hold her—she is outside its terms of reference, impossible to pin down. Unable to tame the violent spiritual forces that are invading her urban modern living room, the narrator in *The World According to G.H.* eats the cockroach—the symbol that the maid leaves behind—in a display of communion, disgust, dismemberment, and gory murder: the revenge of the dirt. The narrator's crisis—here a philosophical crisis—is in her inability to come to terms with the missing maid even by imagining her, in her absence, through symbols and murals, as she cannot turn the cockroach into body by eating it. Despite the narrator's efforts, there is yet no balance, communion, resolution, or assimilation of the object into a recognizable form or national purpose.

Social Factory

Critics attribute Lispector's allusions towards northeastern legendary figures to autobiographical influence, citing the parallel between Macabéa's origins and Lispector's childhood in the northeast (although Macabéa, unlike Lispector, is an orphan, and Lispector, unlike Macabéa, is a Jewish Ukrainian refugee rather than a Brazilian native) and her later move to Rio, or retrospectively claiming that Lispector is coming to terms with death (she dies of cancer in the same year that *The Hour of the Star* is published). Violence within Lispector's formations of subjectivity often is read by the critics as an upshot of personal and psychological crises: disappointments in her career and marriage, family traumas, personal hardship, the critical dismissal of some of her books, the illness of her son, and the early loss of her mother, with an intimation of Lispector's own possible mental illness. Others have understood the violence as underlining Lispector's intention of drawing her roots and connections to Brazilian literature by referencing its popular figures and traditions, even as her writings seem, on the surface, mostly devoid of context, outside of history, and drawing on European antecedents from modernist, existentialist, and phenomenological literary practices. Paulo de Medieros, for example, reads *The Hour of the Star* as a "revisionist allegory of the nation" (149), where Lispector rewrites Alencar's "love story" *Iracema* (1865) without the indigenous princess heroine getting to marry the conquering Portuguese soldier or having his mixed-race, nationally-regenerative child. Still others have read Lispector's use of violence as stemming from her existential or deconstructive critique of essentialism.[12]

What such criticism fails to recognize is that this odd and uncomfortable doubling—between the physically and spiritually wretched Macabéa, on the one hand, and, on the other, tropes of the northeastern warrior's courageous and

150 Woman, Worker, Warrior, and Writer

violent persona—is not solely an allusion to the biography of the author as it appears within the text or to the nation in its literature. Instead, violence bursts forth stylistically within an explicit though unresolvable interrogation of the relationships between textualization (narrative, subjective ideas) and materialization (objects): "I juggle with intonation and force another breathing to accompany my text" (14), the narrator reflects on the process, and maybe the author too. The violence erupts between the idea and the object: "[t]he action of this story," the narrator confesses, "will end up with . . . my materialization finally as an object" (12).[13] The novel is concerned with violence as it plays a part in the production of subjectivity, that is, in the failures of language as it forces correspondence with the essences of things and commodity objects. *The Hour of the Star* sees the violence of the commodity as expressing an irresolvable rift between the subject that creates the world through creative work and the world she creates in objects. This rift appears in the text as a problem of gender.

Macabéa's connections to the northeastern warrior foreground this investigation of gender as wrapped up in a pervasive social crisis. The socialization of this violence tells of a change in the status of the warrior and the worker conforming to an economic shift away from industrialization and a concomitant new form of alienation. As Georges Sorel makes clear from his standpoint in early twentieth century industrial society: "When we are studying the modern economy, we should always bear in mind this similarity between the capitalist type and the warrior type" (75). For Sorel, the warrior ethic saturates productive social relations under industrial capitalism; spontaneous violence makes evident class interests and positions not only in law and order but also in ideas and the imagination, at the specific times of its occurrence. The proletariat understands itself as existing in a field of battle "when the slightest incidents of daily life become symptoms of the state of struggle between the classes" (124). The criticisms of Sorel are legion: for example, there can be no resolution—"no longer any place for the reconciliation of opposites" (113), no end to the periodic eruptions of battle as long as needs still exist, and the violence appears, in the general strike, as a most muscular form of physical contact and brute strength that Sorel himself identifies as "virile" (275). Sorel's brutally physical conception of violence is defined at the level of the body, restricted within the engaged times of production. In *The Hour of the Star,* instead, the warrior type signals crisis as integral to every social instance and every use of language.

The Hour of the Star is registering a crisis in *social reproduction* at the level of the global economy. Lispector describes this crisis in reproduction taking place as process: the invention of a female subjectivity that repeats *and* interrupts the symbolic production of the national warrior-hero. Certainly, Macabéa is not only a worker but a bad worker, and, like a soldier, not easily assimilable into the norms of the category. The entry of the northeastern girl into the urban workforce forces traditional forms of life on the margins of technological innovation and capitalization to redefine themselves within universally exchangeable and technological forms.

Macabéa is not skillful at this. She violates the symbolic of universal exchange, the form of comparative value on which exchange depends, and the technological turn; she blocks the return on the exchange. Macabéa cannot be compared or equated; she cannot be made similar. She cannot be positioned as capital's outside or capitalism's pre-story that can be abstracted into capital's forms through an appeal to similarity—a hailing. She is not capital's eventuality or potentiality. Instead, she represents inequality. As such, she is unsymbolizable, unassimilable: a "vague existence" (9), "sparse" (15), "an emptiness of soul" (6), "the flavorlessness of the word" (11), the "invisible in the mud itself" (11), "almost erased" (11): "don't you have a face?" (56), asks her co-worker Glória; "[c]ould her physical existence have vanished?" (17).

According to Antonio Negri, the late seventies, when Lispector is writing *The Hour of the Star,* witnesses the advent of the "social factory" (or real subsumption), where the reproductive capacities that industrial capitalism had separated out into a "separate sphere" were absorbed into the productive matrix, and capital infiltrated every aspect of social life.[14] Unlike for Sorel's industrialism, the body and its exertions do not set temporal or spatial limits to production's violent outbursts. Like *The Hour of the Star,* Negri highlights the central violence of inequality in capital's production of subjects. For Negri, because capital can only expand by expanding inequality, capital contains its own internal antagonism that cannot be overcome: "[I]f money is an equivalent, if it has the nature of an equivalent, it is above all *the equivalence of social inequality.* Crisis, then, does not come from the imperfection of circulation in a regime of equivalence, and it cannot be corrected by a reform of circulation in a regime of equivalence. Crisis derives from the inequality of the relations of production" (Negri's emphasis; 1991: 26). As the character that thematizes the reproduction of subjectivity as a failure, Macabéa cannot be equal to the symbolic repetition of the same that exchangeability requires. In addition, this capitalist production of subjects is caught up in what Negri has called "feminization": capital markets in care, affective, and biopolitical functions and a selling off of state socialization management agencies—education, health care, retirement, priorly under-capitalized—to private interests. Subjectivities and social relations everywhere are objectified in the money form as care is transformed into uncare. This led, says Negri, to permanent crisis.

This marks a transitional moment. In the early twentieth century, Sorel, for example, distinguishes a "mysterious region" (137), which is the family, outside of exchange, where individuality is practiced, personal opinion can flourish, and the moral rule will not and cannot be diverted into mere exploitation (235). Violence does not happen there. Sorel chastises those who believe that this indeterminate region "must disappear with the progress of enlightenment" (136). On the other hand, for Negri, social relations everywhere are objectified in the money form. Exceeding its boundaries, capital wants as much surplus as it can squeeze, in everything.

For Negri, money is *crisis as the social.* Surplus value seeks to claim socially necessary labor, which is antagonistic to it. Surplus value needs to expand the wage

152 Woman, Worker, Warrior, and Writer

relation in order to increase, but in so doing also expands wage labor (inequality), the oppositional social force of socially necessary labor embedded in reproduction: "the formation of *opposed subjectivities*," says Negri, "opposed wills and intellects, opposed processes of valorization; in short, an antagonistic dynamism" (1991: 93; Negri's emphasis). Money-value is the form taken by this struggle between the worker's needs and reproduction (subjectivity), on the one hand, and, on the other, the capitalist's desire to reduce worker needs in order to increase surplus (calculation). Surplus expands and can only do so by expanding the antagonism. "[H]ostile to the point of destroying each other reciprocally" (145), these two forms increasingly separate; the equality of exchange is destroyed.[15]

Whereas, according to Negri, Marx's theory of value leads towards an evening out of productive differences, a balancing and equalizing, where value and price can reach equilibrium, it has, says Negri, left unconsidered reproduction— Sorel's "mysterious region"—as an outside, resistant to calculation. A theory of money, however, also includes reproduction (the time transpired between productive events) as what is constantly tearing value away from prices, making them incongruous, imbalanced, and contradictory: price cannot be equal to value in exchange. The new productive cycle does not exactly replicate the last one because of changes in technology, delays in delivery and transportation, hoardings, unpredictable consumption, and points of ill-convergence, so reproduction does not meet up adequately with production's needs in the next cycle. Similarly, even though exchange value replaces use value by transforming things and people into abstract calculable equivalents, reproduction makes clear that exchange value is never free of the use value (or subjectivity, the social) that antagonizes it from inside. Though liberal and Marxist theorists alike, says Negri, have understood imbalances in productive processes to smooth out in the circulation phase, the dominance of money—as the form creating values that look similar for universal exchange—allows for the constant restructuring of inequality as antagonism. "Socially necessary labor time" (or reproduction) is constantly oscillating, and so the "real" value of a commodity never equates to its symbolic exchange value, its reproduction of the same. "Value, in the figure of money," says Negri, "is given as contradiction, as the 'possibility that these two separated forms in which the commodity exists are not convertible into one another' (*Grundrisse*)" (30). This—capital's reach into the social to force a symbolic equivalence that can never be—intensifies antagonism to the point of violence.

Lispector foregrounds this violent non-convergence of the reproductive cycle as a problem specifically attributable to the increasing number of waged women workers in service industries. The money form of capital, Negri cites in the *Grundrisse,* "appears as a necessary phase [universal prostitution]" (33), where even regulations of the body and mind are offered up to the vicissitudes of sale, abstracted for exchange. In *Hour of the Star,* however, Macabéa is a physical and conceptual impossibility, the body that cannot be appropriated or capitalized, the

Woman, Worker, Warrior, and Writer **153**

non-signifiable within the abstract representational forms of global capital's violent and universal demand for subjects. She "scarcely," announces Lispector's narrator, "has a body to sell" (5); "[s]he belongs to no one" (59). An early scene in the novel relates, in fact, how Macabéa gets fired for making too many typing mistakes, but her boss keeps her on out of pity. Unable to be capitalized and unable to respond to her boss, she notes that her incompetence is a "kind of absence" (16) when the "tarnished mirror [in the bathroom] didn't reflect any image" (17). Not only is Macabéa's body devoid of physical reproductive capacities, reflection, and symbolic or organic coherence, but also, as a service worker in the role of reproducing text-copy for the bureaucracy (a typist), she fails: "she made too many typing mistakes, besides invariably dirtying the pages" (16). Here, the violence of the northeast—as the dirt in its landscapes—interrupts the process of capital's textual reproduction: as a natural insurgence that falls out of the symbolic controls, dirt is inappropriable to form; it is a disturbance. Because she is pathetic or because she is so singular, marking the pages with her grimy singularity—because her patheticness makes her so singular—, Macabéa cannot repeat, embody, mime or make visible the symbolic codes and commands through which capital reproduces itself in her.

Macabéa's physical and performative inappropriatenesses link her to money in Negri's sense: she is the irreducibility of violence, what does not fit, an autonomy produced in the name of capital as its opposite, the imbalance, antagonism, or inequality (produced by capital's expansion) that remains in money's definition as a self-repeating system of producing equivalents. What money claims but cannot objectively represent appears grossly impoverished, ignorant, sick, and in need of treatment, as is Macabéa with her skin ailments, her possible pulmonary tuberculosis, her neuroses, and her "cavity-ridden body" (52). The "doctor of the poor" (58), however, cannot treat her. The doctor's problem, explains the narrator (or the author), is that he wants to be included in high society but treating the poor is not getting him there. He wants to turn her sickness into money and cannot: "But it was more comfortable to keep insisting that she shouldn't diet to lose weight . . . That's what he said while prescribing a tonic that she afterwards didn't even bother to buy" (58). As much as he desires her to be money so he can have money, she cannot be converted. He tells her to eat pasta and drink no alcohol, but she does not know what pasta and alcohol are. For him, she is an irritant.

For Negri, as surplus value expands and becomes more socialized, it takes on the form of the state, leading Negri "from the critique of money to the critique of power" (1991: 40). Negri conceives these inequalities as a political force that has no prior representational grounding, divided between the struggle of need and the system of profit. This violence is what Negri calls "constituent" violence, the clash of inequality with prior representation.[16] "Constituent" violence is mobile; it antagonizes and differentiates from its prior narrative form or from any prior representation of law or politics, from what is already constituted—its constitution. "[T]he paradigm of constituent power is that of a force that bursts apart,

154 Woman, Worker, Warrior, and Writer

breaks, interrupts, unhinges any preexisting equilibrium and any possible continuity" (1999: 11). This violence cannot be abstracted as a repetition or recurrence of a prior identity or as a pre-constituted will.[17]

Macabéa—like the northeastern warrior of yore—instantiates the transition from an unprecedented violence of original national appropriation to the established, constituted violence of national law. Whereas the *sertanejos* of Canudos wage a battle to make the products of the natural landscape into the future commodity productivity of the nation, Macabéa, unassimilable to the profit-generation constituted in the state, is crushed to death by a foreign commodity. Macabéa collides in the meeting of the national form of money that she never quite could be and the acceleration of an international commerce that eludes her.

The Problem of Reproduction and the Creative Economy

The Hour of the Star is a tale about the failures of reproduction, about crisis. These failures structure not just the content but also the form. The narrative breaks linearity and causality, while words deviate from meaning. Repetition does not succeed for characters trying to conform to their social setting by repeating given, standardized scripts: the repeated element does not match up to the original statement. The textual form seems purposefully "inadequate" to describing, controlling, and holding in place the social relations necessary for its own sense-making. The text calls attention to this digression from convention by its emphatic commentary on process, constantly foregrounding that the narratives through which capital reproduces itself are in disequilibrium. "I'm invading you with such an exterior and explicit narrative," the narrator admits. As female reproductive labor from the northeast, Macabéa falls away from the established forms of representation; her character is nothing but a rupture in the representational process, a block to its repetition: "I see the northeastern girl looking in the mirror and—ruffle of the drum—in the mirror appears my weary and shaven face" (14). Interrupted by external sound, parade, and fanfare, the established forms of representation that can only be expected to reproduce themselves in a universal exchange of sameness cannot accommodate the crisis: Macabéa is lost for her image.

Crisis, then, is not just in the content of this story ostensibly about the poverty of a woman migrant service worker, and not just in the experimental or linguistically dissonant style. Crisis is fundamentally a problem of production, of the text's own production of meaning. *The Hour of the Star* is a self-reflective novel about the production of commodity objects within the creative economy. For Negri, creativity leads to innovation and expansion, but also to excess. As he says about creative, immaterial, biopolitical, and affective labor and the labor of socialization (often labor, like Macabéa's, that *makes* language as its product), "The extension of the concept of the reality of productive labor, to circulation, to reproduction, forces the appearance not only of the historical character but also of the multiple variety of the constituting process of . . . historical individuality" (1991: 183). As capital's productivity through the wage generates inequality in the circuits of reproduction, the creative economy arises inside those circuits, as something inexpressible in constituted terms. Though many critics have been wary of Negri's overestimation of the creative economy's potential to violently disorganize and degrade capital while re-humanizing the subject,[18] for Negri, the need that capital has to augment and appropriate the creative process for profit is what, in turn, produces the creativity that exceeds the controls of capital's self-reproduction.[19] Likewise, *The Hour of the Star* models capital's grasp at the creative process through staging a relation of force between the narrative and the narrative material whose thought-life it creates and appropriates and which eventually exceeds, violently, its categorical controls.

The narrative in *The Hour of the Star* unwinds as a series of narrations about repetitive creative processes. Each narrative box has a producer that produces an object, or a god that gives life to its image.[20] Each layer of the story creates another layer that is supposed to be its reproduction. The last layer is Macabéa's where production, in a sense, ends, "a virgin" (12) with her "tiny ova so shriveled" (25) and her "ovaries shriveled as a cooked mushroom" (50). The form seems to aspire to a line of repetition, where a subject produces an object that in turn becomes a subject that produces an object, mirroring the original production. Each layer should be in balance, equal with the one that initiated it and the one that comes after, but the production process itself upsets the balance.

The narrative of *The Hour of the Star* is, then, itself a project of reproduction, even at the level of language. In the initial scene, when the author reproduces herself as the narrator, the two are conjoined, similar and balanced, difficult even to differentiate because of the exchangeability of the grammatical form: the statement "as I am" references both the author and the narrator. The authorial content often overlaps with the contents of the narrator's speech. Seemingly before the story-novel marks out its start, the "Dedication," for example, is written "actually" by Clarice Lispector, and leads (in the English reproduction) into the multi-title page with Lispector's signature sprawled across it interrupting the list of thirteen titles that replace and reproduce each other. The multiple titles reinforce the sense of the scattering and confusion of parenting origins, the identity that ought to belong to a name. On the first page that follows the title page, without number or heading, before the narrator has introduced itself, there is a first-person character who describes the beginning of writing, and there is no distinguishing mark that would tell that the "I" of the beginning story content is the same or different from the "I" (the "actual" author's) that came before in the introductory remarks and dedication with its name scrawled over the title page. The "I" that governs as subject now that the novel-section seems to have begun might or might not divide its references from what has come before in the lead-in or from what comes next as the novel's start (in the Portuguese, the "I" has no separate articulation but appears in the verb "consigo" and then "continuarei a escrever" (11), the continual present

156 Woman, Worker, Warrior, and Writer

and the future tenses running into each other, while the "actual" author's "Dedicatória" comes after the title page).

The ambiguity of the continuity (or the break)—between the prior "I" (which might be "actually" authorial, and therefore past) and the "I" of what could be the narrator, on the cusp of a hesitation with the story-as-present-about-to-begin—surfaces in this discussion of whether time is divided, that is, whether the beginning of the story divides or continues time between the before of its creation, the time of the "actual" author, and the story's time, the time of the narrator: "the universe," notes Lispector, or the narrator, or both, "never began" (3). The text is asking if time is repeating a prior time (if the narrator reproduces the "actual" author), or if something is starting anew. Parallel to the questioning of origins in the subjective ambiguity, a birthing metaphor begins the story-part: "All the world began with a yes. One molecule said yes to another molecule and life was born" (3), but the naturalized coming-to-be of the narrative subject immediately loses credibility in the narrative skepticism: "How do you start at the beginning . . .?" (3).

The process of reproducing equivalencies becomes increasingly complicated leading into the story's start. Is the moment of the narrator's appearance—the "I"—something new or something that repeats what came before, in the author's dedication? Whoever is writing here ("Actual" author? Narrator? The Portuguese has no distinguishing pronoun at all) stresses beginning as a question, beginning by not beginning, that is, beginning by following or not following out the sequence, the developing, or the chain of consecutive events where molecules say "yes" to each other and reproduce. The plight of the molecules is not mentioned again until halfway down page three, and then sparingly. Instead, there is a hesitation filled with self-interruptions, half-sentences, doubt ("How do I know everything that's about to happen?" (4)), and twists of logic, an interior rumination about thinking, song, and the narrator's, or author's, pain: the author's, or narrator's, giving birth, "[o]ut of which however blood so pantingly full of life might ooze and instantly congeal in cubes of trembling jelly" (4), but yet there cannot be a perfect conflation of narrator to author here—of the metaphoric to the literal—partly because gender splits them apart.[21] Lispector, the female author, writes through a male narrator, so the "I" has two genders: the narrator's and the author's. The narrator cannot then replicate himself adequately in the authorial pronoun.[22]

While the text progresses towards Macabéa's appearance, or invention, the possibility that creative production could produce equivalence (between a word and its reproduction in meaning, between an author and a first-person narrator) becomes increasingly troubling. As Lispector invents (or births?) her alter-authorial-persona (narrator), Rodrigo S. M., both separating from and inhabiting her invention, so this persona (narrator) shapes the life of a girl as her author, again assimilating his own personality and desire with the "object-thing" (9) of his crafting. Both the author and the narrator get referred to as God. The narrator

Woman, Worker, Warrior, and Writer **157**

is mirroring the work of the author; he is Her image. Could we then say that the narrator is also mirroring the work of his character, copying the "actual" author's making-of-him-as-text with a little bit of dirt and some typing errors? "I'm sure of one thing," the narrator confesses with a certainty that sounds so uncertain, "this narrative will deal with something delicate: the creation of a whole person who surely is alive as I am" (11). The certainty dissolves.

This creation narrative repeats. Like the author, the narrator invents; he invents a character with a story. Through him, the process of narrative invention is meant to be a sequencing, a continual production and reproduction of what is intended to be identical material forms, of objects: an endless repetition of the same. Yet, Macabéa is reproductive excess: as an incompetent copier of texts, she cannot equalize herself to the repetitions of the productive line. Though calling himself a "manual laborer" (11) doing a "carpenter's job" (6) as well as an "author of life" (32), the narrator is not part of a pre-industrial workforce, craft or artisanal trade. Instead, Rodrigo as creator, he admits, participates in the global production line, sponsored by "the most popular soft drink in the world even though it's not paying me a cent, a soft drink distributed in every country. Moreover it's the same soft drink that sponsored the last earthquake in Guatemala. Even though it tastes like nail polish, Aristolino soap and chewed plastic" (15). In fact, Macabéa is an extension of these global circuits.

She loves ads. She gets pleasure from them and becomes their spokesperson. She admires and memorizes the slogans from Clock Radio and replicates them. Clock Radio, as its name would imply, mostly broadcasts the time, repeating the sound of a drop as each minute passes. It is the time-announcement by which working-class girls like Macabéa regulate the working day. Clock Radio interrupts the regularity of its rhythms by running short ads that Macabéa mimics, always getting them wrong. "'Repent in Christ and He will give you happiness.' So she repented. Since she wasn't quite sure for what, she repented entirely" (29). Or, "'I just love hearing the drops of the minutes of time like this: tic-tac-tic-tac-tic-tac. Clock Radio says that it gives the correct time, culture and ads. What does culture mean? . . . What does 'per capita income' mean?" (41). Macabéa is so seduced by the call of the advertisements on Clock Radio that she tries to reinvent herself for the object the ad-language promises to become, but fails: "There was an ad," she notes, in her collection of ads pasted into an album,

> the most precious of all, that showed in full color the open pot of cream for the skin of women who simply were not her. Blinking furiously (a fatal tic she had recently acquired), she lay there imagining with delight: the cream was so appetizing that if she had the money to buy it she wouldn't be a fool. To hell with her skin, she'd eat it, that's right, in large spoonfuls straight from the jar.
>
> *(30)*

158 Woman, Worker, Warrior, and Writer

Macabéa has no use for the cream, as the dryness of her skin is so extreme as to elude remedy. She transforms the product from a useless commercial set of promises, healing, and narrative ideals to a fulfillment of a basic need, and in this shows that her needs are antagonistic to the commodity, unequal to it.

Macabéa's existence contradicts what capital, in its self-promotions, invents her to be. Macabéa nullifies the content of the texts on the circuit. "[S]he wrote so badly, she only had three years of school" (7). Does this make her similar to Rodrigo—whose text (the one we are reading) breaks apart linguistic and narrative conventions, splitting the meanings of words in multiple different directions at once, fragmenting the storyline with interruptions and hesitations—or dissimilar? Unlike when Rodrigo and the author are equalized in the exchange of their "I"—when the author calls Rodrigo into being in the articulation of a shared first-person continuous present—, Macabéa cannot continue the generation. She reproduces nothing but crisis.

Gender

As an embodied contradiction, the appearances of a soldier that flicker up and sometimes overtake Macabéa's characterization cannot be extricated from the doubts about language that fill large portions of the text. Just as Macabéa cannot quite adopt the character of national-founding whose literary legacy she is meant to continue, much of the plot is about words that just do not fit. As soldier, Macabéa is a figure of authority whose physicality is dissolving, or the figure of command whose language never meets its targets. *The Hour of the Star* is couched in a national narrative framework that traditionally referenced the protagonist on a military field but is unable to conform to the demand that such a framework poses. As the production of objects is delayed in the process of its reproduction, reproduction manifests as crisis. The literary project of reproducing the nation by reproducing its set of representational objects, militaristic and physical forms, is blocked by excesses and interventions inside the literary form itself.

The text's interest in women in service work coincides with what Negri identifies as an explosion in the reproductive, creative economy. The text reflects this explosion by showing an imbalance in its moments of production related to the feminization of its processes, when a self-reflexive language of reproductive processes crowd out the objective field. The explicit narrative about narrating is, indeed, glaring, eclipsing what could be seen as the "plot." "Sometimes," Rodrigo says, "I manage to get a word out of her but it slips through my fingers" (21). Inequality works as a stylistic motif, coming in between the productive narrator and the (female) objects of reproduction, between the narrative language and its objects. "I have a fidgety character on my hands and who escapes me at every turn expecting me to retrieve her" (13). The formation of narrative as a problem takes the place of the plot because the plot focuses on a female character who cannot be plotted.

Arising in response to an influx of migrant female labor, this crisis in reproduction obstructs production. Where "male language" ought to confer authority, "female" elusiveness constantly shreds that authority: "It's going to be hard to write this story," Rodrigo laments. "Even though I don't have anything to do with the girl, I'll have to write out all of myself through her amidst frights of my own. The facts are sonorous but between the facts there's a whispering. It's the whispering that astounds me" (16). "She's accusing me," Rodrigo complains, "and the way to defend myself is to write about her" (9). And, "[E]ven what I'm writing somebody else could write. A male writer, that is, because a woman would make it all weepy and maudlin" (6). Yet, Rodrigo himself is authored by Clarice, so that the male author becomes the object of another, female authority, and the origin of authority is unlocatable. Such reflections crowd, even overwhelm the text. The intensity and richness of this writing on writing as a problem of women's work is such that the "plot" and its "objective" moments appear marginal as superficial add-ons, as almost nothing.

Many have attributed the meta-fictional commentaries to Lispector's interest in subjective interiority over social injustices despite what seems on the novel's surface to be a protest against poverty. *The Hour of the Star,* Cynthia Sloan argues, for example, fails in its primary politics, doubling "Rodrigo's frustrated attempts to forget himself and to identify with the 'other'" (99). Lispector's translator Giovanni Pontiero also notes that "The social evils underlying Macabéa's privations are treated mainly as asides" (163). Namorato, on the other hand, sees these narrative disturbances around gender as an opening for a critique of power: "the account of the misunderstandings between Rodrigo and his protagonist incites the reader to suspect the ability of the narrator to speak *for* another and to attack the use of fictional discourses as an instrument for the elaboration and maintaining of diverse forms of power" (51; my translation). The narrative elisions, Namorato goes on to explain, demonstrate Macabéa's total alienation from a public symbolic that would allow her to formulate a denunciation. In this, *The Hour of the Star* constitutes a condemnation of the realist romance as conciliatory in the face of atrocity, marginalization, neglect, and social degradation.

What such criticism overlooks is the broader political-economic environment shared by *The Hour of the Star,* the one described by Negri. *The Hour of the Star* communicates within an economic realm where the reproductive spheres are expanding, being absorbed into a still-burgeoning productive system that has formerly not represented them. Instead of depicting young women recruited and moving from marginal regions to work in industrial centers, recounting the change of identity in terms of a developing form of economic involvement and capture, *The Hour of the Star* tells of a young woman urban migrant working in a service sector already formed and ubiquitous, and yet she still does not fit. The focus on the already-constituted service sector and its female employment involves a reorientation of capital's self-inscription to include the production of texts as coming to dominate over the production of objects. As such, the text

160 Woman, Worker, Warrior, and Writer

obsesses over the mechanisms of textual reproduction, including its own, allowing thoughts and descriptions about its own production to overcome the plot. Rejecting reconciliation, it demands a different politics.

As *The Hour of the Star* augurs a shift to a type of production newly performed by women workers because of the predominance of reproductive tasks, inequalities in class and gender become evident as blockages within the text's movement and development between one empty plot-space and another. "Like the northeastern girl," explains Rodrigo, "there are thousands of girls scattered throughout the tenement slums, vacancies in beds in a room, behind the shop counters working to the point of exhaustion. They don't even realize how easily substitutable they are and that they could just as soon drop off the face of the earth" (6). But the story contradicts this assertion, as Macabéa is unrepeatable in substitutes, not doubled in language, alienated from her reflection. "If she was dumb enough to ask herself 'who am I?'" Rodrigo continues, "she would fall on her face" (7). The mechanisms of reproduction and objectification fall short in this case.

The rise of this new emphasis in reproduction appears as violent throughout, citing the literary images of the wars of national foundation. Though fading, old conventions continue but without the new, circulating raw materials fitting comfortably the old productive needs. So, even though the main character is molded in response to the conventional frameworks of national figures, heroes, and fighters, she cannot reproduce such models and ideas or carry them into the future: she cannot repeat them. Instead of making objects, production always goes awry, often creating explosions, collisions, blockages, discontinuities, and misery. Macabéa is nothing and, as nothing, she is unbearable.

By introducing new forms of reproductive women's work as a problem of creative production, Lispector has created a literary style that develops as a potential for a future that does not reproduce the present in its money form. In *The Hour of the Star,* the woman reproductive worker is so disentangled from capital's narratives of itself that she dies painfully, alone and alienated, surrounded by spectators who do nothing. On a parallel level, as Negri might say, the impossibility of capitalism's subjective reproduction opens a glimpse of something that the narratives through which capital reproduces itself cannot capture. Capital's creation of a female reproductive workforce exceeds the boundaries of capital's own object-world, eliciting a story that cannot be told, at least not yet. *The Hour of the Star* wants to frame Macabéa's life as a recognizable object within the romantic storylines of its national form—as, for example, the soldier that drives narratives of national and literary founding, of life and death, by turning nature into commodifiable objects and instruments. Yet, capital's demand calls into being a symbol of femininity that cannot reproduce itself as such an object of value and so "felt inside of her a hope more violent than any despair she had ever felt" (70).

The Hour of the Star suggests a different story to be told about women's relationship to state violence than the stories being told about U.S. women in combat today. Unlike the women soldiers in Chapter One who have been instrumentalized

Woman, Worker, Warrior, and Writer **161**

in the process of war's increasing technologization, Lispector shows that the current stage of neoliberal capitalism has politicized women's bodies thoroughly in ways that cannot be captured in instrumentalization policies. The body as politics cannot be shut down by a new field of social relations governed by technology. For Lispector, the war story makes need evident, in particular, a need expressed in the vulnerability and isolation of bodies facing a terrifying violence. She sees such a war story as inside of a changing economic system that, in producing need, compels the terrifying exploitation of these vulnerable bodies. Riddled in need, women's working bodies, heretofore marginalized or left out by industrialization and bereft of care, reveal neoliberal capital's failures to turn all means into ends in an embracing universal liberal inclusion. As capital grasps at reproductive economies that used to fall outside of its productive circuits, women's work in these reproductive economies has made inequality more visible as central to capital's profit momentum. It demands "an answer" (xiv), a "right to scream," as Lispector stipulates in her titles, for a politics of life.

Notes

1 "Brazil—Economy Index." Sources: The Library of Congress Country Studies and the CIA World Factbook. www.photius.com/countries/brazil/economy/brazil_economy_the_services_sector.html. Accessed: 27 March 2016.

2 The Brazilian military dictatorship was run by technocrats, bureaucrats, and economic planners who were not democratically accountable to the population and who used up to $200 billion per year in debt to U.S. commercial banks on roads and other national projects that many critics agree were instances of overspending and inefficiency. Helio Beltrao, the Minister for Social Welfare, at the time in charge of "debureaucratization" (reduction in paperwork required of citizens), told Peter T. Kilborn of the *New York Times* that the regime had been "dominated by the fascinating exercise of abstract planning, by the optical illusion of centralized decisions and macroeconomic theories, by the rapture of important and sophisticated decisions, incompatible with our reality" (he does not call this "corruption").

3 Earl Fitz agrees that the novel centers on its own reflections on itself: "Clarice was a writer for whom the problem of meaning (how it is generated, how it is mentally processed and how it is reformulated as literary art) lies restively, at the very heart of the human condition" (1988: 34). Cixous, too, observes, "As soon as one opens the book one is suspended . . . The title . . . can barely hold on to a text" (1990: 157). Or later: "The text is full of parentheses . . . One can only make signs of what Clarice Lispector is, because they are so obviously false that they give off signs on the side of truth" (1990: 159).

4 Cixous says she speaks through Lispector, adopting her tenderness and nurturance of the other, her insights into "how to love the other, the strange, the unknown, the not-at-all-myself" (1989: 128). The "other," says Cixous, appears "l'égal à l'égal" (1989: 160). In the epic, for example, equal displays on the battlefield convert into equality in love, where armor disappears as "cette fausse peau d'homme" (1989:161). *The Hour of the Star,* says Cixous, is "a book about love" (1990: 143). Violence and inequality are defeated by love (or sublation in the chain of meaning): "Her [Macabéa's/Lispector's] force is in her invisibility, her inexistence, her negative force, her 'not' . . . Combat between presence and absence, between an undesirable absence, unverifiable, undecided, and a presence that is not only a presence" (my translation, 1989: 138). Combat

162 Woman, Worker, Warrior, and Writer

here is a symbolic space of difference between signifiers that can be equalized in desire, outside the world of objects. Difference itself is located between empty signifiers. In the end, they are equal because, as signifiers, they are each other's mirror. Class inequality for Cixous does not stand in the way of assimilation, exchange with the other. This does not contradict my reading of her work on Algeria in Chapter Two, where she also poses a radical equality between herself and the combatant.

5 As Luciana Namorato observes, "[T]he 'construction' fails repeated times in *The Hour of the Star.* The barriers that separate Macabéa from the discourse, and by extension, Macabéa from the reader, are reinforced by a boasted expressive inaptitude on the part of the narrator who, similarly to Lispector in many of her own statements, confesses and openly discusses her difficulty in managing words" (52; my translation). Renate Kroll agrees that "[t]here is no doubt that the work of the Brazilian author broke through the conventional structures of signification and undermined the fixed starting points of observation" (14–15; my translation).

6 As Zizek puts it, "The appearance of *égalité* is always discursively sustained by an asymmetric axis of master versus servant" (62).

7 Peixoto divides the construction of violence in Lispector's work between, on the one hand, the earlier stories, which naturalize and minimize violence against women (83) in discrete, impersonal acts and "specific incidents of aggression" (89) where women are victims (such as rape), and, on the other, the later works, exemplified by *The Hour of the Star,* where violence "involves . . . an unleashing of aggressive forces" (83) that cannot be constrained.

8 In contrast, Marxism (and Lispector is by no means a Marxist) makes the worker into a warrior, the subject of an eventual overturning whose interests in relation to production are always contrary to the *status quo* of class domination.

9 The idea that military technology gains some amount of symbolic power from allying with "primitivism"—like in the "Apache" or "Black Hawk" helicopters—has been a focus in the anthropological work of Michael Taussig. Taussig understands colonialism as attributing terror and power to the "primitive" and the "savage" in order to appropriate the power of their savagery. For example: "[I]t is worth inquiring . . . whether . . . those within the 'civilized' confines of that State find (magical) power in an image of the Indian forester. Certainly the army recruits from the interior valley of the Cauca River who marched down into the Putumayo in 1931 had strong beliefs in the magical power of the Indian healers to protect them, if the accounts of two old soldiers I talked to in the sugarcane town of Puerto Tejada decades later are any indication. Certainly most of the poor peasant colonists who daily make their way down into the Putumayo today express similar notions as to the power of the Indian, a power that derives from the mysteries that they, the colonists, attribute to the primevality accorded Indian rite and lore, which places the Indian healer of the forest as much in the supernatural capacity as in an infrahuman one."

10 Peruvian novelist Mario Vargas Llosa retold this story of the rebellion in Canudos in his 1981 novel *La guerra del fin del mundo.* Vargas Llosa repeats many of Da Cunha's gestures in making the warriors in Canudos out of the primitive fierceness and exoticism of the northeastern savage landscape. For example: "[E]l bandido es un rebelde en estado natural," or "The outlaw is a rebel in a natural state" (my translation; 59). Or, "No está hecho para la vida civilizada. Extraña el bosque," or "He is not made for civilized life. He misses the jungle" (my translation; 39), observes one of the characters about one of the rebels as a child. As the novel is told from multiple points of view rather than from Da Cunha's singular journalistic point of view, the defenders of Canudos in Vargas Llosa's novel have greater variety both in physical and emotional make-ups, some even feminized, and the rebellion itself is often gendered as feminine because of the difficulty of taming it and its need for strong-arm military controls and state control. Free sexuality—or the end of civil matrimony—was one of the demands of the rebels,

Woman, Worker, Warrior, and Writer 163

who were also demanding the end of taxation: "asegurarse que la revolución no sólo suprima la explotación del hombre por el hombre, sino, también, la de la mujer por el hombre y establezca, a la vez que la igualdad de clases, la de sexos," or "make sure that the revolution doesn't only suppress the exploitation of man by man but, as well, the exploitation of woman by man, and establishes sex equality at the same time as class equality" (my translation; 93). I have written about the gendering of Vargas Llosa's space of battle for his vision of neoliberal national construction in *Infertilities: Exploring Fictions of Barren Bodies* (University of Minnesota Press, 2001).

11 Speaking of Lispector's first book, *Near to the Wild at Heart,* for example, Benjamin Moser writes, "Over the course of the book Clarice compares her [the protagonist Joana] to a snake, a dog, a wildcat, a horse, and a bird . . . Like Joana, Nature has 'positive' attributes, freedom, for instance, alongside the 'negative': Joana is violent, thieving, aggressive" (122).

12 Tace Hedrick, for example, reads "what has been called by various critics negation, loss, violence, lack" (42) as pointing away from language and towards "a move toward an alinguistic essence" (42). This strategy by Lispector contributes, for Hedrick and others, to a critique of Western philosophic traditions that use the female body as a "'prop' for the playing-out of being" (42) and, therefore, as anti-materialist, where Lispector wants to restore materialism and physicality through a metaphysics of motherhood.

13 Many read this of course as Christian imagery.

14 For a more in-depth discussion of the ways in which the "feminization of work" is integrated into Negri's ideas about "real subsumption," see my analysis of this in the last chapter of *Gender Work: Feminism After Neoliberalism* (2013).

15 The wage, as the place of struggle between surplus and necessary labor (reproduction), allows a relative independence and mobility of the worker in exchange. Because of the crisis, socially necessary labor time becomes more autonomous: capital replaces direct labor with science, speculation, and technology, while living labor self-valorizes—in subjective collectivity, self-sufficiency, social force, the free development of individualities and disposable time—outside of the wage, and there no longer has to be exchange between them. Negri: "The path of subjectivity is an intensive path. It is a continual and coherent recomposition of successive negations. It raises labor to the point where it can destroy surplus labor" (1991: 149).

16 "Constituent" violence is revolutionary violence, linked to the history of revolutions but not prepared by them, never before experienced each time it is experienced, not tied to parties, property, or consensus.

17 Eventually, this constituent power is codified into law as the basis of juridical authority. When it enters such representation—"the effort of enclosing constituent power in a cage of spatiotemporal limitation" (1999: 13)—, it is then controlled, subjected to rules, to time calculation, losing its originality, congealed "in a static system" (1999: 4), its power diminished because "it is not possible to define its innovative singularity in advance" (13).

18 A particularly scathing example of such criticism is Nick Dyer-Witheford's: "The new circuits of capital looked a lot less 'phantom-like', 'immaterial' and 'intellectual' to the female and Southern workers doing the grueling physical toil demanded by a capitalist 'general intellect' whose headquarters remain preponderantly male and Northern" (149–150).

19 Hardt and Negri re-ignite this idea almost twenty years later in *Commonwealth*: "Living labor oriented toward producing immaterial goods, such as cognitive or intellectual labor, always exceeds the bounds set on it and poses forms of desire that are not consumed and forms of life that accumulate. When immaterial production becomes hegemonic, all the elements of the capitalist process have to be viewed in a new light, sometimes in terms completely inverted from the traditional analysis of historical materialism" (25). And again, "the biopolitical process is not limited to the reproduction of

164 Woman, Worker, Warrior, and Writer

capital as a social relation but also presents the potential for an autonomous process that could destroy capital and create something new" (136).

20 Lispector's final, uncompleted novel, *A Breath of Life*, replicates the Pygmalian aspect, where writing initiates life but also announces death: "I am a man who chose the great silence. Creating a being who stands in opposition to me is within the silence" (18). The combining of divine creation and artistic invention inspired Pedro Almodóvar to write an appreciative introduction to the novel in the wake of the popular reception of his 2011 film *The Skin that I Live In* (*La piel que habito*). In that film, the inventive act takes place as a revenge castration narrative that creates a woman out of a man. Similarly to much of Lispector's work, and particularly to *The Hour of the Star*, this film translates existential, creative violence into a crisis of gender.

21 Like Cixous and Namorato, Fitz treats the problem of narrative meaning in the text as a problem of gender: "Rodrigo, a writer, perceives of language as a fluid semiotic system that controls him and that both creates and undercuts his sense of being and his sense of authority . . . Rodrigo here presents himself . . . as a privileged male narrator whose old textual authority has been transformed, or undermined, by his new awareness of language, the inexorable force that, embodying poststructural ethos, ceaselessly births and rebirths us all" (2001: 114–115).

22 The confusion of who governs the "I" continues throughout the text. When Macabéa is preparing to go to the fortune-teller, there is an intervention which could either be a character's self reflection, a continuation of the text's own commentary of its process of narration, or, alternatively, a passage from the outside, from the author's life, that refers to something outside of the story—a kind of *deus ex machina* but without a direct connection to the storyline: "I am absolutely tired of literature . . . The search for the word in the dark. My small success invades me and exposes me to glances on the street . . . I have to interrupt this story for about three days" (61). And then, after a page break: "For the last three days, alone, without characters, I depersonalize myself and take myself off as if taking off clothes" (61). Are we supposed to think that the page break represents the narrator's three days (the narrator has confessed he has had a "meager success in literature" (9)), or that it was Lispector who came back and recommenced as "I" on the page where she left off? Who is speaking as "I"?

CONCLUSION

Gender for the Warfare State argues that military recruitment in the U.S. depends on neoliberal cuts to the caring arm of the state. Since the end of U.S. military conscription in 1972 and the advent of an all-volunteer army, women returning from war and telling their story almost always say they joined the military because of lack of educational opportunities, child care, health care, job supports, and other basic needs that should be and might have once been provided by state redistributive policies and public institutions with the mission of evening out some of the imbalances generated in economic expansion and growth. Equally, they most often expect access to help services on return: mental health counseling, tuition assistance, job placement, housing provisions, and the like. As neoliberalism has ushered in a redeployment of resources away from social supports, the military lures in citizens without other political or economic recourse to satisfy basic needs. What is more, in popular culture, literature, political reporting, commentary, rhetoric, and film, among other sites of popular address, militarism is shown as endless, moral, inclusive, empowering, and heroic, saturating social relations and ethical thinking alike. The military takes in volunteers who aspire to ethical participation in the affairs of the world, who desire to improve human existence through caring for others, and who see military careers as an opportunity for committed social connection, with goals towards improvement and action. The breakdown in the traditional institutions for caring for and attending to others has shifted expectations towards the military for carrying that role. In turn, the military's monopolization over practices of care has led to a redefinition of what constitutes care. This book has argued that the increased presence of women in the military is a consequence and an expression of such neoliberal transformations.

In addition, the increased entry of women into state combat roles in the U.S. from the 1970s till now has played a part in re-envisioning work in the neoliberal

166 Conclusion

present. The claim that anybody could fill the role of soldier dovetails with a contemporary characterization of workers as bundles of skills that can be combined and recombined like machines; it also feeds an increasing sense that human capital is infinitely interchangeable and can be reduced to the lowest common denominator of comparative equivalence for exchange. This leveling out of worker difference deepens neoliberalism by: 1) modeling work on administration, where work takes place as a series of repeated and repeatable tasks; and 2) understanding the working body as a piece of technology, an instrument or a tool, and focusing much work around the repetitive chore of mending or replacing broken equipment rather than improving the human world through intervening in it.

As Mady Wechsler Segal has noted, such a "greater emphasis on technology . . . [has] contributed to women's greater representation in wars" (90). As well, this technologization of war has had profound effects on the politics involved in waging war. The body's organic capacities matter less when confronting war's monumental and deathless machines, so that physical differences seem negligible. Human error and accident can be made as seemingly insignificant as physical prowess or contest. Such insinuations suggest that war's magnitude has become so incomprehensible as to render the human form helpless and inconsequential, as though in the face of God; as with the Kantian sublime, technology renders war limitless, formless, and "doing violence to our imagination" (129), the "wildest and most unruly disorder and devastation" (130). Jet aviator Amy "Krusty" McGrath's war experience illustrates war's marginalization of the body as war's power is increasingly technologized: "This may sound strange," she confesses in Kirsten Holmstedt's *Band of Sisters,* "but modern war is fought at the speed of sound from 17,000 feet above the earth, a fast-paced round-robin of missions that all run together" (87). Margot Norris describes the contemporary war scene as a Baudrillardian simulation, with technology becoming the organic and the real as bodies disappear, "transforming war into a seemingly virtual event . . . murderously destructive yet simultaneously corpseless" (236) as well, I would add, as increasingly riskless.

As a result, Grégoire Chamayou observes that the traditional avenues for making decisions about waging war are receding behind what he identifies as an apoliticized technological determinism: "Once warfare became ghostly and teleguided, citizens, who no longer risked their lives, would no longer have a say in it" (188). Command is centralized and taken out of human control as automatic feedback loops stand in the place of ethical determinations and requests for consent. If the state's war mobilizations no longer require putting citizens' bodies at risk, then decisions to go to war no longer have to be addressed to citizens, and citizens do not have to be convinced that the war is worth the sacrifice. Violence then becomes a much more acceptable "default option of foreign policy" (188) as the bonds of service, responsibility, protection, and rights that bind states to those it represents become less binding. Technologized warfare weakens the political understanding that underlies liberalism's sovereign obligation: "I protect, so I am obliged" (178). When bodies disappear with all their vulnerabilities, needs, and demands for care, politics also disappears.

Opponents of women's military inclusion generally cite their bodies as a site of vulnerability and demand for care. "Perhaps the most common concern male Marines have," writes Thomas James Brennan in the *New York Times*, "is about whether women can handle the physical rigors of being in the infantry." He goes on quoting Marine Lance Cpl. John Chun: "I feel that a woman's physical capabilities will diminish faster than a male's with all the long foot patrols, post and base force protection." Another line of reasoning positions women as lower in battle preparedness because men might rape them: "I think it's safe to say," Thom Shanker cites an unnamed first sergeant in the Marines, "there is going to be more sexual assault and harassment when females do go into these organizations" (even though more men are raped in the military than women[1]). Such arguments emphasize that rhetoric about war cannot avoid a political question about vulnerability and care that the very presence of (women's) bodies elicits.

Such arguments compel counter-arguments that project women's bodies as coterminous with new technology rather than defenseless in the face of the military apparatus. Rhetoric defending women's involvement affirms bodies as not vulnerable to war's violence but rather offer infinitely expandable strength and endurance like technology, always amenable to technological enhancements, fixes, improving capacities and functionalities. "Sarah Waldman, MP and former Girl Scout who loved sewing as much as survival training stood before a cluster of surveillance monitors at the operations center," Gayle Tzemach Lemmon describes one of her special-ops Rangers in *Ashley's War*. "All over Afghanistan the U.S. military's counterterrorism teams rely on technology to verify and amplify the intelligence gathered" (201–202). Instead of the body becoming small in the face of technological magnitude, the body becomes infinite in its technological extensions, a limitless technological mass as war machine. This perspective on the body suggests that the body as an organic form, too much mired in its empirical materiality, deficiencies, and vincibility, produces unnecessary conceptual limits to war's transformative powers that the body as technology is able to overcome. In order for women and others to insist on women's inclusion in combat forces, they have to reject that certain (male) bodies—i.e., with their internal strengths, sensibility, intelligence, affect, endurance, size, fortitude, aggressivity—guarantee success in the field because of what they are. That is, the (feminine) body can only mean one thing: vulnerability. The field of combat must be understood, then, as the clashing of technologies without bodies, and such combat technologies must be celebrated as the driving force of history.

Advocates for including women in combat dangerously deny the body's presence in war in order to celebrate war's transcendent instrumentality. This formulation imagines the organic body in war, in all its vulnerabilities, as a historical relic, a pre-technological bit of matter confined to its biological smallness and exposure to injury. The problem in imagining the body as a regressive biological

168 Conclusion

fact, as Toril Moi indicates, is that the body's situation or "lived experience"—politics—is made invisible. In referring to the body as a situation, Moi contends that the body is always politicized. The logic of the body as situation, continues Moi, "is that greater freedom will produce new ways of being a woman, new ways of experiencing the possibilities of a woman's body" (66). That is, the body's encounters with the world open possibilities for deciding how we live in and experience that world. Reducing the body to its empirical, scientific, or technological determinants marginalizes its solicitations of politics as care, its social connectedness as part of the world. Whereas in decolonizing movements, women are included in combat often with the intention of saturating the social field in new political ideas, the inclusion of women in combat in the contemporary U.S. military creates a new version of war as a war without bodies, their vulnerabilities, and the politics they elicit. If a new world comes into being as a response to technologies without bodies, then politics can be seemingly remade as a calculation or a command loop, unaccountable to those it touches.

In contrast, *Gender for the Warfare State* shows that including women in combat has, before now, intensified politics rather than eliciting the emptied-out form of liberal inclusion, sacrifice, technological triumph, and consent. In Hélène Cixous' Algerian narratives, combatant women invoke an ideal of a political association outside of sovereign state administration, countering dispossession. For Elizabeth Bowen in *The Heat of the Day,* the woman in combat models political independence against colonial property confiscation and inheritance. In Clarice Lispector's *The Hour of the Star,* the woman as soldier makes evident the politics of neoliberalism's inherent inequality, where neoliberalism is unable to reproduce its consciousness in its workers, to rationalize their creativity, or to abstract workers as empty signifiers of infinite exchangeability, like objects. These examples understand the woman in combat as a politicizing figure specifically, as Hannah Arendt's work implies, because she cannot be turned into an instrument or a preordained means to an end, because her presence conjures up thinking and the indeterminate fact of natality, bringing forth people to share the earth. Arendt recognizes that war engenders need, but understands that need as determining politics, even as she reads bodies as politicizing in ways that are impossible to reduce to determinism, while Lispector situates that need as political and demanding a response.

All this is not to say that we should return to an earlier moment when the body was exposed to mortal threat and massive destruction, or to when women's work opportunities were restricted because of ideological beliefs about where their bodies' potential should reside and how far it could extend. Political rhetoric should find strategies for maintaining a distinction between care and war not dependent on adopting a historically obsolete, gendered division of labor, while institutions of care should be built and defended that do not depend on the continuation of war. These current wars should end, and care should be restored in institutions other than military ones. As well, the social arrangements and articulations of the time of life and the time of care—the human condition—should not be left up to the exclusive decision of those with the violent means to profit from eliminating their urgent centrality to the meaning of a working democracy.

Note

1 Andrew Tilghman in the *Military Times* writes, "Across the military, men suffered more sexual assaults last year than women." "The majority of the victims are men," concludes Jennifer Koons in *CQ Researcher.* According to Hayes Brown in *Think Progress,* in 2012, 14,000 military men reported that they were sexually assaulted, as opposed to 12,000 women, as reported in the Associated Press.

WORKS CITED

Adorno, Theodor. "Reconciliation Under Duress." *Aesthetics and Politics: The Key Texts of the Classic Debate Within German Marxism.* Trans. Ronald Taylor. London and New York: Verso, 1977.

Althusser, Louis. "Ideology and Ideological State Apparatuses (Notes Towards an Investigation)." *Lenin and Philosophy and Other Essays.* Trans. Ben Brewster. London: New Left Books, 1971. Pp. 121–175.

Alvarez, L. "G. I. Jane Breaks the Combat Barrier as War Evolves." *The New York Times* (16 August 2009): www.nytimes.com/2009/08/16/us/16women.html. Accessed: 10 November 2014.

Andreas, Carol. "Women at War." *Report on the Americas* XXIV, 4 (January 1990/1991): 20–27.

Arendt, Hannah. *Between Past and Future.* New York: Penguin Books, 1954.

Arendt, Hannah. *Crises of the Republic.* San Diego, New York and London: Harcourt Brace & Company, 1972.

Arendt, Hannah. *Eichmann and the Holocaust.* New York: Penguin Books, 1963.

Arendt, Hannah. *The Human Condition.* Second Edition. Chicago, IL and London: University of Chicago Press, 1958.

Arendt, Hannah. *The Life of the Mind.* San Diego, New York, and London: Harcourt, Inc., 1971, 1978.

Arendt, Hannah. *On Revolution.* New York: Penguin Books, 1963, 1965.

Aretxaga, Begoña. *Shattering Silence: Women, Nationalism, and Political Subjectivity in Northern Ireland.* Princeton, NJ: Princeton University Press, 1997.

Asad, Talal. *On Suicide Bombing.* New York: Columbia University Press, 2007.

Backus, Margot Gayle. *The Gothic Family Romance: Heterosexuality, Child Sacrifice, and the Anglo-Irish Colonial Order.* Durham, NC and London: Duke University Press, 1999.

Bagnold, Enid. *A Diary Without Dates.* Boston, MA: John W. Luce and Company, 1918.

Ball, Karyn. "The Longing for Material." *differences* 17, 1 (2006): 47–87.

Bauman, Zygmunt. *In Search of Politics.* Stanford, CA: Stanford University Press, 1999.

Beauvoir, Simone de. *The Second Sex.* Trans. and Ed. H. M. Parshley. New York: Vintage Books, 1989.

172 Works Cited

Belli, Gioconda. *El país bajo mi piel: memorias de amor y guerra*. New York: Vintage Español, 2002.

Benedict, Helen. *The Lonely Soldier: The Private War of Women Serving in Iraq*. Boston: Beacon Press, 2009.

Benedict, Helen. *Sand Queen*. New York: Soho, 2011.

Benhabib, Seyla. "Arendt and Adorno: The Elusiveness of the Particular and the Benjaminian Moment." In *Arendt and Adorno: Political and Philosophical Investigations*. Eds. Lars Rensmann and Samir Gandesha. Stanford, CA: Stanford University Press, 2012. Pp. 31–55.

Benhabib, Seyla. "Feminist Theory and Hannah Arendt's Concept of Public Space." *History of the Human Sciences* 6, 2 (1993): 97–114.

Benhabib, Seyla. "The Pariah and Her Shadow: Hannah Arendt's Biography of Rahel Varnhagen." In *Feminist Interpretations of Hannah Arendt*. Ed. Bonnie Honig. University Park, PA: Pennsylvania State University Press, 1995. Pp. 83–104.

Benhabib, Seyla. "Who's on Trial, Eichmann or Arendt?" *The New York Times* (21 September 2014): http://opinionator.blogs.nytimes.com/2014/09/21/whos-on-trial-eichmann-or-anrendt/. Accessed: 20 May 2015.

Benjamin, Walter. "Critique of Violence." In *Selected Writings Volume I, 1913–1926*. Eds. Marcus Bullock and Michael W. Jennings. Cambridge, MA and London: Harvard University Press, 1996. Pp. 236–252.

Benjamin, Walter. *The Origin of German Tragic Drama*. Trans. John Osborne. New York: Verso, 1998.

Benjamin, Walter. "The Work of Art in the Age of Mechanical Reproduction." In *Illuminations*. Ed. Hannah Arendt. Trans. Harry Zohn. New York: Schocken Books, 1968. Pp. 217–251.

Bernstein, Richard J. *Violence: Thinking Without Banisters*. Cambridge, UK and Malden, MA: Polity, 2013.

Biank, Tanya. *Undaunted: The Real Story of America's Servicewomen in Today's Military*. New York: New American Library, 2013.

Blair, Jane. *Hesitation Kills: A Female Marine Officer's Combat Experience in Iraq*. Lanham, MD and Boulder, CO: Rowman & Littlefield, 2011.

Bloch, Ernst. *The Spirit of Utopia*. Trans. Anthony A. Nassar. Stanford, CA: Stanford University Press, 2000.

Bloom, Mia. *Bombshell: Women and Terrorism*. Philadelphia, PA: University of Pennsylvania Press, 2011.

Borden, Mary. *The Forbidden Zone*. Ed. Hazel Hutchison. London: Hesperus Press, 1929, 2008.

Bourdieu, Pierre. *Acts of Resistance: Against the Tyranny of the Market*. Trans. Richard Nice. New York: New Press, 1998.

Bowen, Elizabeth. *Bowen's Court & Seven Winters*. London: Vintage, 1942, 1964.

Bowen, Elizabeth. "Eire." In *The Mulberry Tree: Writings of Elizabeth Bowen*. Ed. Hermione Lee. London: Virago, 1986. Pp. 30–35.

Bowen, Elizabeth. *Eva Trout*. New York: Anchor Books, 1968, 1996.

Bowen, Elizabeth. *The Heat of the Day*. New York: Anchor Books, 1948.

Bowen, Elizabeth. *The Last September*. New York: Anchor Books, 1929, 2000.

Bowen, Elizabeth. *To the North*. New York: Anchor Books, 1932, 1933, 1961.

Boyle, Claire. "Writing Self-Estrangement: Possessive Knowledge and Loss in Cixous's Recent Autobiographical Work." *Dalhousie French Studies* 68 (Fall 2004): 69–77.

Works Cited **173**

Brant, George. *Grounded.* London: Oberon Books, 2013.

Brasil, Assis. *Clarice Lispector: Ensaio.* Rio de Janeiro: Organização Simões, 1969.

Brennan, Thomas James. "Women in Combat? Some Marines React." *New York Times. At War: Notes From the Front Lines,* blog (29 January 2013): http://atwar.blogs.nytimes.com/2013/01/29/women-in-combat-some-marines-react/. Accessed: 25 March 2016.

Brittain, Vera. *Testament of Youth: An Autobiographical Study of the Years of 1900–1925.* New York: Penguin Books, 1933.

Browder, Laura. *When Janey Comes Marching Home: Portraits of Women Combat Veterans.* Chapel Hill, NC: The University of North Carolina Press, 2010.

Brown, Hayes. "More Men Than Women Were Victims of Sexual Assault in Military, Report Finds." *Think Progress* (1 May 2014): http://thinkprogress.org/world/2014/05/01/3433055/dod-men-mst/. Accessed: 14 March 2016.

Browne, Kingsley. *Co-ed Combat: The New Evidence That Women Shouldn't Fight the Nation's Wars.* New York: Penguin, 2007.

Buck-Morss, Susan. *The Dialectics of Seeing: Walter Benjamin and the Arcades Project.* Cambridge, MA and London: The MIT Press, 1989.

Buck-Morss, Susan. *Hegel, Haiti, and Universal History.* Pittsburgh, PA: University of Pittsburgh Press, 2009.

Bumiller, Elisabeth and Shanker, Thom. "Pentagon Is Set to Lift Combat Ban for Women." *The New York Times* (23 January 2013): www.nytimes.com/2013/01/24/us/pentagon-says-it-is-lifting-ban-on-women-in-combat.html. Accessed: 24 January 2013.

Butler, Judith. *Antigone's Claim: Kinship Between Life & Death.* New York: Columbia University Press, 2000.

Butler, Judith and Athanasiou, Athena. *Dispossession: The Performative in the Political.* Cambridge, UK and Malden MA: Polity, 2013.

Butler, Judith. *Gender Trouble: Feminism and the Subversion of Identity.* New York and London: Routledge, 1990.

Butler, Judith. "Is Kinship Always Already Heterosexual?" In *Undoing Gender.* New York and London: Routledge, 2004. Pp. 102–130.

Butler, Judith. *Notes Toward a Performative Theory of Assembly.* Cambridge, MA and London: Harvard University Press, 2015.

Butler, Judith. *Parting Ways: Jewishness and the Critique of Zionism.* New York: Columbia University Press, 2012.

Butler, Judith. *Senses of the Subject.* New York: Fordham Press, 2015.

Callimachi, Rukmini. "ISIS and the Lonely Young American." *The New York Times* (27 June 2015): www.nytimes.com/2015/06/28/world/americas/isis-online-recruiting-american.html. Accessed: 12 December 2015.

Cather, Willa. *One of Ours.* Massachusetts [imprint]: Seven Treasures Publications, 2009.

Cavarero, Adriana. *Horrorism: Naming Contemporary Violence.* Trans. William McCuaig. New York: Columbia University Press, 2009.

Chamayou, Grégoire. *A Theory of the Drone.* Trans. Janet Lloyd. New York and London: The New Press, 2015.

Chanter, Tina. *Whose Antigone? The Tragic Marginalization of Slavery.* Albany, NY: State University of New York (SUNY) Press, 2011.

Chivers, C. J. "A Grueling Course for Training Marine Officers Will Open Its Doors to Women." *The New York Times* (8 July 2012): www.nytimes.com/2012/07/09/us/grueling-course-for-marine-officers-will-open-its-doors-to-women.html?pagewanted=all. Accessed: 9 July 2012.

174 Works Cited

Chivers, C. J. "Reassuring Hands: A U.S. Crew's Urgent Flight into the Afghan Desert." *The New York Times* (19 December 2010): www.nytimes.com/2010/12/19/world/asia/19delivery.html?pagewanted=all. Accessed: 3 January 2015.

Chow, Rey. "The Politics of Admittance: Female Sexual Agency, Miscegenation, and the Formation of Community in Frantz Fanon." In *Frantz Fanon: Critical Perspectives.* Ed. Anthony C. Alessandrini. New York and London: Routledge, 1999. Pp. 34–56.

Cixous, Hélène. *The Day I Wasn't There.* Trans. Beverley Bie Brahic. Evanston, IL: Northwestern University Press, 2006.

Cixous, Hélène. "The Laugh of the Medusa." In *Feminisms: An Anthology of Literary Theory and Criticism.* Eds. Robyn R. Warhol and Diane Price Herndle. New Brunswick, NJ: Rutgers University Press, 1993. Pp. 334–349.

Cixous, Hélène. "Letter to Zohra Drif." In *Volleys of Humanity: Essays 1972–2009.* Ed. Eric Prenowitz. Edinburgh: Edinburgh University Press, 2011. Pp. 106–114.

Cixous, Hélène. *L'heure de Clarice Lispector, précédé de Vivre l'orange (deuxième édition).* Paris: Des femmes, 1989.

Cixous, Hélène. "My Algeriance, in Other Words: To Depart Not to Arrive from Algeria." In *Stigmata: Escaping Texts.* Trans. Eric Prenowitz. New York and London: Routledge, 1998. Pp. 126–144.

Cixous, Hélène. "The Names of Oran." In *Algeria in Others' Languages.* Ed. Anne-Emmanuelle Berger. Ithaca, NY and London: Cornell University Press, 2002. Pp. 184–194. Cixous, Hélène. *Reading with Clarice Lispector.* Ed. and Trans. Verena Andermatt Conley. Minneapolis, MN: University of Minnesota Press, 1990.

Cixous, Hélène. *Reveries of the Wild Woman: Primal Scenes.* Trans. Beverley Bie Brahic. Evanston, IL: Northwestern University Press, 2006.

Cixous, Hélène. *So Close.* Trans. Peggy Kamuf. Cambridge, UK and Malden, MA: Polity, 2009.

Cixous, Hélène and Clément, Catherine. *The Newly Born Woman.* Trans. Betsy Wing. Minneapolis, MN and Oxford, UK: University of Minnesota Press, 1986.

Cocks, Joan. "On Commonality, Nationalism, and Violence: Hannah Arendt, Rosa Luxemburg, and Frantz Fanon." *Women in German Yearbook* 12 (1996): 39–51.

Cooke, Miriam. *Women and the War Story.* Berkeley, CA: University of California Press, 1996.

Corcoran, Neil. *Elizabeth Bowen: The Enforced Return.* Oxford, UK: Clarendon Press, 2004.

Cornum, Rhonda as told to Peter Copeland. *She Went to War: The Rhonda Cornum Story.* Novato, CA: Presidio Press, 1992.

Coulter, Chris. *Bush Wives and Girl Soldiers: Women's Lives Through War and Peace in Sierra Leone.* Ithaca, NY and London: Cornell University Press, 2009.

Creed, Barbara. *The Monstrous-Feminine: Film, Feminism, Psychoanalysis.* London and New York: Routledge, 1993.

Crow, Tracy. *Eyes Right: Confessions from a Woman Marine.* Lincoln and London: University of Nebraska Press, 2012.

Cunha, Euclides da. *Rebellion in the Backlands.* Trans. Samuel Putnam. Chicago and London: University of Chicago Press, 1944.

D'Amico, Francine. "Feminist Perspectives on Women Warriors." In *The Women and War Reader.* Eds. Lois Ann Lorentzen and Jennifer Turpin. New York and London: New York University Press, 1998. Pp. 119–125.

Das, Santanu. *Touch and Intimacy in First World War Literature.* Cambridge, UK and New York: Cambridge University Press, 2005.

Das, Veena. *Life and Words: Violence and the Descent into the Ordinary.* Berkeley, CA: University of California Press, 2007.

Works Cited **175**

Davis, Angela. "A Vocabulary for Feminist Praxis: On War and Radical Critique." In *Feminism and War: Confronting U.S. Imperialism*. Eds. Robin L. Riley, Chandra Talpade Mohanty, and Minnie Bruce Pratt. London and New York: Zed Books, 2008. Pp. 19–26.

De Landa, Manuel. *War in the Age of Intelligent Machines.* New York: Urzone, 1991.

Derrida, Jacques. "But Beyond . . . (Open Letter to Anne McClintock and Rob Nixon)." Trans. Peggy Kamuf. In *"Race," Writing, and Difference.* Ed. Henry Louis Gates, Jr. Chicago, IL and London: The University of Chicago Press, 1985, 1986. Pp. 354–369.

Derrida, Jacques. "Des Tours de Babel." Trans. Joseph F. Graham. In *Difference in Translation.* Ed. Joseph F. Graham. Ithaca, NY and London: Cornell University Press, 1985. Pp. 104–136.

Derrida, Jacques. "Force of Law: The 'Mystical Foundation of Authority.'" In *Deconstruction and the Possibility of Justice.* Eds. Drucilla Cornell, Michel Rosenfeld, and David Gray Carlson. New York and London: Routledge, 1992. Pp. 3–67.

Devi, Mahasweta. *Mother of 1084.* Salt Lake City, UT: Seagull Books, 1997.

Diana, Marta. *Mujeres guerrilleras: sus testimonios en la militancia de los sesenta.* Independencia, Argentina: Booket/Grupo Planeta, 1996.

Dietz, Mary G. *Turning Operations: Feminism, Arendt, and Politics.* New York and London: Routledge, 2002.

Digby, Tom. *Love & War: How Militarism Shapes Sexuality and Romance.* New York: Columbia University Press, 2014.

Dillon, Michael and Reid, Julian. *The Liberal Way of War: Killing to Make Life Live.* London and New York: Routledge, 2009.

Djébar, Assia. *Fantasia: An Algerian Cavalcade.* Trans. Dorothy S. Blair. Portsmouth, NH: Henemann, 1985.

Drones. Dir. Rick Rosenthal. Perf. Matt O'Leary, Eloise Mumford. Whitewater Films, 2013. Netflix.com.

Dubey, Madhu. "The 'True Lie' of the Nation: Fanon and Feminism." *Differences: A Journal of Feminist Cultural Studies* 10, 2 (1998): 1–29.

Duckworth, Tammy. "Foreword." In *Band of Sisters: American Women at War in Iraq.* Ed. Kirsten Holmstedt. Mechanicsburg, PA: Stackpole Books, 2007. Pp. vii–x.

Duramy, Benedetta Faedi. *Gender and Violence in Haiti: Women's Path From Victims to Agents.* New Brunswick, NJ and London: Rutgers University Press, 2014.

Dyer-Witheford, Nick. "Cyber-Negri: General Intellect and Immaterial Labor." In *The Philosophy of Antonio Negri: Resistance in Practice.* Eds. Timothy S. Murphy and Abdul-Karim Mustapha. London and Ann Arbor, MI: Pluto Press, 2005. Pp. 136–162.

Ehrenreich, Barbara. "Foreword: Feminism's Assumptions Upended." In *One of the Guys: Women as Aggressors and Torturers.* Ed. Tara McKelvey. Emeryville, CA: Seal Press, 2007. Pp. 1–5.

Eisenstein, Zillah. "Resexing Militarism for the Globe." In *Feminism and War: Confronting U.S. Imperialism.* Eds. Robin L. Riley, Chandra Talpade Mohanty, and Minnie Bruce Pratt. London and New York: Zed Books, 2008. Pp. 27–46.

Ellmann, Maud. *Elizabeth Bowen: The Shadow Across the Page.* Edinburgh, UK: Edinburgh University Press, 2003.

Elshtain, Jean Bethke. *Meditations on Modern Political Thought: Masculine/Feminine Themes from Luther to Arendt.* New York: Praeger, 1986.

Elshtain, Jean Bethke. *Women and War.* New York: Basic Books, 1987.

Enloe, Cynthia. *Maneuvers: The International Politics of Militarizing Women's Lives.* Berkeley, CA: University of California Press, 2000.

Enloe, Cynthia. "Women—The Reserve Army of Army Labor," *Review of Radical Political Economics* 12, 2 (Summer 1980): 42–52.

176 Works Cited

Fanon, Frantz. *A Dying Colonialism*. Trans. Haakon Chevalier. New York: Grove Press, 1965.

Finkel, David. *The Good Soldiers*. New York: Picador, 2009.

Fitz, Earl E. "The Passion of Logo (Centrism), or, the Deconstructionist Universe of Clarice Lispector." *Luso-Brazilian Review* XXV, 2 (1988): 33–44.

Fitz, Earl E. *Sexuality and Being in the Poststructuralist Universe of Clarice Lispector: The Différance of Desire*. Austin, TX: University of Texas Press, 2001.

Fraser, Nancy. *Unruly Practices: Power, Discourse and Gender in Contemporary Social Theory*. Minneapolis, MN: University of Minnesota Press, 1989.

Fugard, Athol with John Kani and Winston Ntshona. "The Island." In *Statements*. New York: Theatre Communications Group, 1986. Pp. 45–77.

Gambaro, Griselda. "Antígona Furiosa." In *Information for Foreigners*. Ed. and Trans. Marguerite Feitlowitz. Evanston, IL: Northwestern University Press, 1992. Pp. 133–159.

Garsten, Bryan. "The Elusiveness of Arendtian Judgment." In *Politics in Dark Times: Encounters with Hannah Arendt*. Eds. Seyla Benhabib with Roy T. Tsao and Peter J. Verovsek. Cambridge, UK and New York: Cambridge University Press, 2010. Pp. 316–341.

Gilbert, Sandra M. "Soldier's Heart: Literary Men, Literary Women, and the Great War." In *Behind the Lines: Gender and the Two World Wars*. Eds. Margaret Randolph Higonnet, Jane Jenson, Sonya Michel, and Margaret Collins Weitz. New Haven, CT and London: Yale University Press, 1987. Pp. 197–226.

Goldman, Nancy. "The Changing Role of Women in the Armed Forces." *American Journal of Sociology* 78, 4 (January 1973): 892–911.

Goldstein, Josuha S. *War and Gender: How Gender Shapes the War System and Vice Versa*. Cambridge, UK and New York: Cambridge University Press, 2001.

Goodell, Jess with John Hearn. *Shade It Black: Death and After in Iraq*. Havertown, PA: Casemate Publishers, 2011.

Goodman, Amy. "Lori Berenson After Being Held 20 Years in Peru: 'My Objectives Were to Achieve a More Just Society." *Democracy Now!* (4 January 2016): www.democracynow.org/2016/1/4/lori_berenson_after_being_held_20. Accessed: 5 January 2016.

Goodman, Robin Truth. *Gender Work: Feminism After Neoliberalism*. New York: Palgrave, 2013.

Goodman, Robin Truth. *Infertilities: Exploring Fictions of Barren Bodies*. Minneapolis, MN and London: University of Minnesota Press, 2001.

Goodman, Robin Truth. "Military Literati: Yasmina Khadra and the Veil." In *Policing Narratives and the State of Terror*. Albany, NY: SUNY Press, 2009. Pp. 121–144.

Grady, Denis. "Penis Transplants Being Planned to Help Wounded Troops." *New York Times* (6 December 2015): www.nytimes.com/2015/12/07/health/penis-transplants-being-planned-to-heal-troops-hidden-wounds.html. Accessed: 7 December 2015.

Grayzel, Susan R. *Women's Identities at War: Gender, Motherhood, and Politics in Britain and France During the First World War*. Chapel Hill and London: The University of North Carolina Press, 1999.

Greene, Carver. *An Unlawful Order*. Amazon Digital Services, LLC, 2011.

Gutmann, Stephanie. "Women in Combat: The Devil's in the Details." *National Review* (24 January 2013): www.nationalreview.com/corner/338699/women-combat-devils-details-stephanie-gutmann/. Accessed: 13 October 2014.

Habermas, Jürgen. "Hannah Arendt: On the Concept of Power." In *Philosophical-Political Profiles*. Trans. Frederick G. Lawrence. Cambridge, MA and London: The MIT Press, 1983. Pp. 171–187.

Hansen, Miriam. "Benjamin, Cinema and Experience: 'The Blue Flower in the Land of Technology.'" *New German Critique* 40 (Winter 1987): 179–224.

Works Cited **177**

Hanssen, Beatrice. *Critique of Violence: Between Poststructuralism and Critical Theory.* London and New York: Routledge, 2000.

Hardt, Michael and Negri, Antonio. *Commonwealth.* Cambridge, MA: Harvard University Press, 2009.

Hardt, Michael and Negri, Antonio. *Empire.* Cambridge, MA and London: Harvard University Press, 2000.

Hart, Lynda. *Fatal Women: Lesbian Sexuality and the Mark of Aggression.* Princeton, NJ: Princeton University Press, 1994.

Harvey, David. *A Brief History of Neoliberalism.* Oxford, UK and New York: Oxford University Press, 2005.

Hedrick, Tace. "Mother, Blessed Be You Among Cockroaches: Essentialism, Fecundity, and Death in Clarice Lispector." *Luso-Brazilian Review* 34, 2 (Winter 1997): 41–57.

Heidegger, Martin. "The Question Concerning Technology." In *The Question Concerning Technology and Other Essays.* Trans. William Lovitt. New York: Harper Torchbooks, 1977. Pp. 3–35.

Hemingway, Ernest. *A Farewell to Arms.* New York: Scribner, 1929.

Hepburn, Allan. "Trials and Errors: *The Heat of the Day* and Postwar Culpability." In *Intermodernism: Literary Culture in Mid-Twentieth Century Britain.* Ed. Kristin Bluemel. Edinburgh: Edinburgh University Press, 2011. Pp. 131–159.

Higonnet, Margaret R. and Higonnet, Patrice L.R. "The Double Helix." In *Behind the Lines: Gender and the Two World Wars.* Eds. Margaret Randolph Higonnet, Jane Jenson, Sonya Michel, and Margaret Collins Weitz. New Haven and London: Yale University Press, 1987. Pp. 31–47.

Hobbes, Thomas. *Leviathan.* Ed. Richard Tuck. Cambridge, UK and New York: Cambridge University Press, 1991.

Hoffman, Cara. *Be Safe I Love You.* New York: Simon & Schuster, 2014.

Holmes, Rachel. "Queer Comrades: Winnie Mandela and the Moffies." *Social Text* 52, 53 (Fall/Winter 1997): 161–180.

Holmstedt, Kirsten. *Band of Sisters: American Women at War in Iraq.* Michanicsburg, PA: Stackpole Books, 2007.

Holmstedt, Kirsten. *The Girls Come Marching Home: Stories of Women Warriors Returning from the War in Iraq.* Michanicsburg, PA: Stackpole Books, 2009.

Honig, Bonnie. *Antigone Interrupted.* Cambridge, UK and New York: Cambridge University Press, 2013.

Honig, Bonnie. "Toward an Agonistic Feminism: Hannah Arendt and the Politics of Identity." In *Feminist Interpretations of Hannah Arendt.* Ed. Bonnie Honig. University Park, PA: Pennsylvania State University Press, 1995. Pp. 135–166.

Horkheimer, Max, and Adorno, Theodor W. *Dialectic of Enlightenment.* Trans. John Cumming. New York: Continuum, 1991.

Inglesby, Elizabeth C. "'Expressive Objects': Elizabeth Bowen's Narrative Materializes." *Modern Fiction Studies* 53, 2 (Summer 2007): 306–333.

Irigaray, Luce. "The Eternal Irony of Community." In *Speculum of the Other Woman.* Trans. Gillian C. Gill. Ithaca, NY: Cornell University Press, 1985. Pp. 214–226.

Issacharoff, Avi. "The Palestinian and Israeli Media on Female Suicide Terrorists." In *Female Suicide Bombers: Dying for Equality?* Ed. Yoram Schweitzer. Tel Aviv: Jaffee Center for Strategic Studies, Tel Aviv University, 2006. Pp. 43–50.

Johnson, Penny and Kuttab, Eileen. "Where Have All the Women (and Men) Gone? Reflections on Gender and the Second Palestinian Intifada." *Feminist Review* 69 (Winter 2001): 21–43.

178 Works Cited

Joubert, Elsa. *Poppie Nongena: One Woman's Struggle Against Apartheid*. New York: Henry Holt and Company, 1980.

Kalinowski, Mariette. "A Victory for Women at War." *The New York Times* (4 December 2015): www.nytimes.com/2015/12/05/opinion/a-victory-for-women-at-war.html. Accessed: 7 December 2015.

Kamuf, Peggy. "Hélène Cixous: Writing for her Life." In *Literature and the Development of Feminist Theory*. Ed. Robin Truth Goodman. New York: Cambridge University Press, 2015. Pp. 128–139.

Kant, Immanuel. *Critique of the Power of Judgment*. Ed. Paul Guyer. Trans. Paul Guyer and Eric Matthews. Cambridge, UK and New York: Cambridge University Press, 2000.

Karpinksi, Janis, with Steven Strasser. *One Woman's Army: The Commanding General of Abu Ghraib Tells Her Story*. New York: Hyperion, 2005.

Khadra, Yasmina. *The Attack*. Trans. John Cullen. New York: Random House, 2005.

Kierkegaard, Søren. *Either/or, Volume I*. Trans. David F. Swenson and Lillian Marvin Swenson. Princeton, NJ: Princeton University Press, 1959.

Kilborn, Peter T. "Brazil's Economic 'Miracle' and Its Collapse." *The New York Times* (26 November 1983): www.nytimes.com/1983/11/26/business/brazil-s-economic-miracle-and-its-collapse.html?pagewanted=1. Accessed: 27 March 2016.

Kirkland, Sean D. "Tragic Time." In *The Returns of Antigone: Interdisciplinary Essays*. Eds. Tina Chanter and Sean D. Kirkland. Albany, NY: SUNY Press, 2014. Pp. 51–67.

Klay, Phil. *Redeployment*. New York: Penguin Press, 2014.

Klobucka, Anna. "Hélène Cixous and the Hour of Clarice Lispector." *SubStance* 23, 1 (1994): 41–62.

Kojève, Alexandre. *Introduction to the Reading of Hegel: Lectures on the Phenomenology of Spirit*. Ed. Allan Bloom. Trans. James H. Nichols, Jr. Ithaca, NY and London: Cornell University Press, 1969.

Koons, Jennifer. "Sexual Assault in the Military." *CQ Researcher* (9 August 2013): 693–716.

Kreilkamp, Vera. *The Anglo-Irish Novel and the Big House*. Syracuse, NY: Syracuse University Press, 1998.

Kroll, Renate. "Recuperación del yo por pérdida del sentido: sobre el principio estético en Clarice Lispector." *Revista de Letras* 44, 2 (July–December 2004): 13–29.

Krylova, Anna. *Soviet Women in Combat. A History of Violence on the Eastern Front*. Cambridge, UK and New York: Cambridge University Press, 2010.

Laclau, Ernesto. "Feudalism and Capitalism in Latin America." In *Promise of Development: Theories of Change in Latin America*. Eds. Peter F. Klarén and Thomas J. Bossert. Boulder, CO and London: Westview Press, 1986. Pp. 166–190.

Landes, Joan B. "*Novus Ordo Saeclorum*: Gender and Public Space in Arendt's Revolutionary France." In *Feminist Interpretations of Hannah Arendt*. Ed. Bonnie Honig. University Park, PA: Pennsylvania State University Press, 1995. Pp. 195–219.

Latif, Nadia. "'It Was Better During the War': Narratives of Everyday Violence in a Palestinian Refugee Camp." *Feminist Review* 101 (2012): 24–40.

Lazreg, Marnia. *The Eloquence of Silence: Algerian Women in Question*. New York and London: Routledge, 1994.

Lebanon. Dir. Samuel Maoz. Perf. Yoav Donat, Itay Tiran, Oshri Cohen, Michael Moshonov, Zohar Shtrauss. CTV International, 2009. DVD.

Lemmon, Gayle Tzemach. *Ashley's War: The Untold Story of a Team of Women Soldiers on the Special Ops Battlefield*. New York: Harper Collins Publishers, 2015.

Lispector, Clarice. *The Apple in the Dark*. Trans. Gregory Rabassa. Austin, TX: University of Texas Press, 1967.

Lispector, Clarice. *A Breath of Life*. Trans. Johnny Lorenz. New York: New Directions, 1978.

Lispector, Clarice. *The Foreign Legion*. Trans. Giovanni Pontiero. New York: New Directions, 1986.

Lispector, Clarice. *A hora de estrela*. Rio de Janeiro: Rocco, 1977.

Lispector, Clarice. *The Hour of the Star*. Trans. Benjamin Moser. New York: New Directions, 2011.

Lispector, Clarice. *Near to the Wild Heart*. Ed. Benjamin Moser. Trans. Alison Entrekin. New York: New Directions, 2012.

Lispector, Clarice. *The Passion According to G. H.* Trans. Ronald W. Sousa. Minneapolis, MN: University of Minnesota Press, 1988.

Luciak, Ilja A. *After the Revolution: Gender and Democracy in El Salvador, Nicaragua, and Guatemala*. Baltimore, MD and London: The Johns Hopkins University Press, 2001.

Maher, Ashley. "'Swastika Arms of Passage Leading to Nothing': Late Modernism and the 'New' Britain." *ELH* 80 (2013): 251–285.

Mahmood, Saba. "Religious Reason and Secular Affect: An Incommensurable Divide?" In *Is Critique Secular? Blasphemy, Injury, and Free Speech*. Eds. Talal Asad, Wendy Brown, Judith Butler, and Saba Mahmood. Berkeley, CA: University of California Press, 2009. Pp. 64–100.

Martel, James R. *Divine Violence: Walter Benjamin and the Eschatology of Sovereignty*. London and New York: Routledge, 2012.

Mattison, Laci. "Elizabeth Bowen's Things: Modernism and the Threat of Extinction in *The Little Girls*." *Twentieth-Century Literature* 61, 3 (September 2015): 393–413.

Mazurana, Dyan. "Women, Girls, and Non-State Armed Opposition Groups." In *Women & Wars*. Ed. Carol Cohn. Cambridge, UK and Malden, MA: Polity, 2013. Pp. 146–168.

McCafferty, Nell. *Peggy Deery: An Irish Family at War*. Berkeley, CA: Cleis Press, 1989.

McClintock, Anne. *Imperial Leather: Race, Gender and Sexuality in the Colonial Contest*. New York and London: Routledge, 1997.

McClintock, Anne and Nixon, Rob. "No Names Apart: The Separation of Word and History in Derrida's 'Le Dernier Mot du Racism.'" In *"Race," Writing, and Difference*. Ed. Henry Louis Gates, Jr. Chicago, IL and London: The University of Chicago Press, 1985, 1986. Pp. 339–353.

McCormack, W. J. *Dissolute Characters: Irish Literary History through Balzac, Sheridan, LeFanu, Yeats and Bowen*. Manchester, UK and New York: Manchester University Press, 1993.

Medeiros, Paulo de. "Clarice Lispector and the Question of the Nation." In *Closer to the Wild Heart: Essays on Clarice Lispector*. Eds. Cláudia Pazos Alonso and Claire Williams. Oxford, UK: European Humanities Research Center of the University of Oxford, 2002. Pp. 142–162.

Menninghaus, Winfried. "Walter Benjamin's Theory of Myth." In *On Walter Benjamin: Critical Essays and Recollections*. Ed. Gary Smith. Cambridge, MA and London: MIT Press, 1988. Pp. 294–325.

Miller, Brook. "The Impersonal Personal: Value, Voice, and Agency in Elizabeth Bowen's Literary and Social Criticism." *Modern Fiction Studies* 53, 2 (Summer 2007): 351–369.

Miller, Kristine A. "'Even a Shelter's Not Safe': The Blitz on Homes in Elizabeth Bowen's Wartime Writing." *Twentieth Century Literature* 45, 2 (Summer 1999): 138–158.

Miller, Steven. *War After Death: On Violence and Its Limits*. New York: Fordham University Press, 2014.

Mitchell, Brian. *Women in the Military: Flirting With Disaster*. Washington, DC: Regnery Publishing, 1998.

180 Works Cited

Moaveninov, Azadeh. "ISIS Wives and Enforcers in Syria Recount Collaboration, Anguish and Escape." *The New York Times* (21 November 2015): www.nytimes.com/2015/11/22/world/middleeast/isis-wives-and-enforcers-in-syria-recount-collaboration-anguish-and-escape.html. Accessed: 21 November 2015.

Moi, Toril. *What Is a Woman?* Oxford, UK and New York: Oxford University Press, 1999.

Mooney, Sinéad. "Unstable Compounds: Bowen's Beckettian Affinities." *Modern Fiction Studies* 53, 2 (Summer 2007): 238–256.

Moser, Benjamin. *Why This World: A Biography of Clarice Lispector.* Oxford, UK and New York: Oxford University Press, 2009.

Namorato, Luciana. "A tentação do silencio em 'Ela não sabe gritar' (ou 'A hora da estrela'), de Clarice Lispector." *Hispania* 94, 1 (March 2011): 50–62.

Negri, Antonio. *Insurgencies: Constituent Power and the Modern State.* Trans. Maurizia Boscagli. Minneapolis, MN and London: University of Minnesota Press, 1999, 2009.

Negri, Antonio. *Marx Beyond Marx: Lessons on the Grundrisse.* Trans. Harry Cleaver with Michael Ryan and Maurizio Viano. Ed. Jim Fleming. Brooklyn, NY: Autonomedia, 1991.

Norris, Margot. *Writing War in the Twentieth Century.* Charlottesville, VA and London: University Press of Virginia, 2000.

O'Brien, Tim. *The Things They Carried.* Boston and New York: Houghton Mifflin, 1990.

Ong, Aihwa. *Neoliberalism as Exception: Mutations in Citizenship and Sovereignty.* Durham, NC and London: Duke University Press, 2006.

Peach, Lucinda Joy. "Is Violence Male? The Law, Gender, and Violence." In *Frontline Feminisms: Women, War, and Resistance.* Eds. Marguerite R. Waller and Jennifer Rycenga. New York: Garland, 2000. Pp. 57–71.

Peixoto, Marta. *Passionate Fictions: Gender, Narrative, and Violence in Clarice Lispector.* Minneapolis and London: University of Minnesota Press, 1994.

Penrod, Lynn. "Algeriance, Exile, and Hélène Cixous." *College Literature* 30, 1 (Winter 2003): 135–145.

Penuin, Carlos. *Las guerrilleras: La cruenta historia de la mujer en el terrorismo. Somos* (2 December 1976): 10–17.

Pitkin, Hanna Fenichel. "Justice: On Relating Private and Public." *Political Theory* 9, 3 (August 1981): 327–352.

Pitre, Michael. *Fives and Twenty-Fives.* New York: Bloomsbury, 2014.

Pontiero, Giovanni. "Clarice Lispector and *the Hour of the Star.*" In *Feminist Readings on Spanish and Latin-American Literature.* Eds. L. P. Condé and S. M. Hart. Lewiston, Queenston and Lampeter: Edwin Mellen Press, 1991. Pp. 161–172.

Powers, Kevin. *The Yellow Birds.* New York and Boston, MA: Little, Brown and Company, 2012.

Puar, Jasbir I. *Terrorist Assemblage: Homonationalism in Queer Times.* Durham, NC and London: Duke University Press, 2007.

Rabassa, Gregory. "Introduction." In *The Apple in the Dark.* By Clarice Lispector. Trans. Gregory Rabassa. New York: Alfred A Knopf, 1967.

Rehms, Diane. "Calls for Women to Register for the Draft: How the Role of Women in the Military is Changing." *The Diane Rehms Show* (4 February 2016): https://thedianerehmshow.org/shows/2016-02-04/calls-for-women-to-register-for-the-draft-how-the-role-of-women-in-the-military-is-changing.

Remarque, Erich Maria. *All Quiet on the Western Front.* New York: Ballantine Books, 1929.

Remembering History. Produced by Peter Becker, Kim Hendrickson, Abeey Lustgarten, Alexandre Mabilon, Fumiko Takagi, Jonathan Turell, Perf. Henri Alleg, Zohra Drif-Bitat,

Works Cited **181**

Mohammed Harbi, Allstair Horne, Jacques Massu, Hugh Roberts, Yacef Saadi, Benjamin Sora, Roger Trinquier. Trans. Lynn Massey. Criterion Collection, 2004.

Riverbend. *Baghdad Burning: Girl Blog from Iraq.* New York: The Feminist Press of the City University of New York, 2005.

Rokem, Freddie. "Bertolt Brecht's Adaption of *Antigone.*" *Florida State University School of Theater, Tallahassee* (26 February 2016): Public Lecture.

Roy-Bhattacharya, Joydeep. *The Watch.* London and New York: Hogarth, 2012, 2013.

Sacks, Sam. "First-Person Shooters: What's Missing in Contemporary War Fiction." *Harper's* (August 2015): http://harpers.org/archive/2015/08/first-person-shooters-2/6/. Accessed: 23 July 2015.

Saltman, Erin Marie and Smith, Melanie. *'Till Martyrdom Do Us Part': Gender and the ISIS Phenomenon.* London: Institute for Strategic Dialogue, 2015.

Scarry, Elaine. *The Body in Pain: The Making and Unmaking of the World.* New York and Oxford, UK: Oxford University Press, 1985.

Schell, Jonathan. "In Search of a Miracle: Hannah Arendt and the Atomic Bomb." In *Politics in Dark Times: Encounters with Hannah Arendt.* Eds. Seyla Benhabib with Roy T. Tsao and Peter J. Verovsek. Cambridge, UK and New York: Cambridge University Press, 2010. Pp. 247–258.

Segal, Mady Wechsler. "Women in the Armed Forces." In *Women and the Use of Military Force.* Eds. Ruth H. Howes and Michael R. Stevenson. Boulder, CO and London: Lynne Rienner Publishers, 1993. Pp. 81–93.

Seitz, Barbara, Lobao, Linda, and Treadway, Ellen. "No Going Back: Women's Participation in the Nicaraguan Revolution and in Postrevolutionary Movements." In *Women and the Use of Military Force.* Eds. Ruth H. Howes and Michael R. Stevenson. Boulder, CO and London: Lynne Rienner Publishers, 1993. Pp. 167–183.

Shanker, Thom. "Marines Share Frank Views with Hagel on Women in Combat." *New York Times. At War: Notes from the Front Lines,* blog (19 July 2013): http://atwar.blogs.nytimes.com/2013/07/19/marines-share-frank-views-with-hagel-on-women-in-combat/. Accessed: 25 March 2016.

Shaw, George Bernard. *Saint Joan: A Chronicle Play in Six Scenes and an Epilogue.* Ed. Dan H. Laurence. New York: Penguin, 1924, 1930.

Sky, Emma. *The Unraveling: High Hopes and Missed Opportunities in Iraq.* New York: Public Affairs, 2015.

Sloan, Cynthia A. "The Social and Textual Implications of the Creation of a Male Narrating Subject in Clarice Lispector's *'A hora da estrela.'"* *Luso-Brazilian Review* 38, 1 (Summer 2001): 89–102.

Sophocles. "Antigone." In *Sophocles I.* Second Edition. Trans. David Grene. Eds. David Grene and Richmond Lattimore. Chicago, IL and London: University of Chicago Press, 1991. Pp. 161–212.

Sorel, Georges. *Reflections on Violence.* Ed. Jeremy Jennings. Cambridge, UK: Cambridge University Press, 1999.

Spargo, R. Clifton. "Toward a Theory of Apolitics." In *The Returns of Antigone: Interdisciplinary Essays.* Eds. Tina Chanter and Sean D. Kirkland. Albany, NY: SUNY Press, 2014. Pp. 241–259.

Spencer-Fleming, Julia. *One Was a Soldier.* New York: Minotaur Books, 2011.

Spivak, Gayatri Chakravorty. *Outside in the Teaching Machine.* New York and London: Routledge, 1993.

Spivak, Gayatri Chakravorty. "Terror: A Speech After 9–11." *Boundary 2* 31, 2 (Summer 2004): 81–111.

182 Works Cited

Stackdec, Liam. "Tashfeen Malik, Suspect in California Attack, Remains a Mystery to Relatives." *New York Times* (5 December 2015): www.nytimes.com/2015/12/06/world/asia/tashfeen-malik-suspect-in-california-attack-remains-mystery-to-relatives.html. Accessed: 8 December 2015.

Stealth. Dir. Rob Cohen. Perf. Josh Lucas, Jessica Biel, Jamie Foxx. Written by W. D. Richter. Columbia Pictures, 2005.

Steiner, George. *Antigones.* Oxford, UK: Oxford University Press, 1984.

Stout, Hilary and Harris, Elizabeth A. "Today's Girls Love Pink Bows as Playthings, But These Shoot." *The New York Times* (22 March 2014): www.nytimes.com/2014/03/23/business/todays-girls-love-pink-bows-as-playthings-but-these-shoot.html. Accessed: 24 March 2014.

Swofford, Anthony. *Jarhead: A Marine's Chronicle of the Gulf War and Other Battles.* New York: Scribner, 2003.

Tasker, Yvonne. *Soldiers' Stories: Military Women in Cinema and Television Since World War II.* Durham, NC and London: Duke University Press, 2011.

Taussig, Michael. *Mimesis and Alterity: A Particular History of the Senses.* New York and London: Routledge, 1993.

Taylor, Diana. *Disappearing Acts: Spectacles of Gender and Nationalism in Argentina's "Dirty War."* Durham, NC and London: Duke University Press, 1997.

Teekell, Anna. "Elizabeth Bowen and Language at War." *New Hibernia Review* 15, 3 (Autumn 2011): 61–79.

Thompson, Judith. *Palace of the End.* Toronto: Playwrights Canada Press, 2007.

Thorpe, Helen. *Soldier Girls: The Battles of Three Women at Home and at War.* New York: Scribner, 2014.

Tilghman, Andrew. "Report: Hazing Fuels Male-on-Male Sex Assault." *Military Times* (1 May 2015): www.militarytimes.com/story/military/crime/2015/05/01/sex-assaults-report/26649065/. Accessed: 25 March 2016.

Trumbo, Dalton. *Johnny Got His Gun.* New York: Bantam Books, 1939, 1959.

Tuten, Jeff M. "The Argument Against Female Combatants." In *Female Soldiers—Combatants or Noncombatants? Historical and Contemporary Perspectives.* Ed. Nancy Loring Goldman. Westport, CT and London: Greenwood Press, 1982. Pp. 237–265.

US Army TRADOC G2. "Female Suicide Bombers" (27 January 2011): https://info.publicintelligence.net/USArmy-FemaleSuicideBombers.pdf. Accessed: 12 October 2015.

Van Devanter, Lynda. *Home Before Morning: The Story of an Army Nurse in Vietnam.* Amherst, MA and Boston: University of Massachusetts Press, 1983, 2001.

Van Weyenberg, Astrid. "African Antigones: Pasts, Presents, Futures." In *The Returns of Antigone: Interdisciplinary Essays.* Eds. Tina Chanter and Sean D. Kirkland. Albany, NY: SUNY Press, 2014. Pp. 261–279.

Vargas Llosa, Mario. *La guerra del fin del mundo.* Barcelona: Editorial Seix Barral, 1987, 1991.

Viterna, Jocelyn. *Women in War: The Micro-Processes of Mobilization in El Salvador.* Oxford, UK and New York: Oxford University Press, 2013.

Weltman-Aron, Brigitte. "The Pedagogy of Colonial Algeria: Djebar, Cixous, Derrida." *Yale French Studies* 113 (2008): 132–146.

West, Rebecca. *The Return of the Soldier.* London: Virago Press, 1918.

Wharton, Edith. *Fighting France, From Dunkerque to Belfort.* CreateSpace Independent Publishing Platform, 2104; New York: Editora Griffo, 1915.

Wicomb, Zoë. *David's Story.* New York: The Feminist Press at the City University of New York, 2000.

Works Cited **183**

Williams, Kayla. *Plenty of Time When We Get Home: Love and Recovery in the Aftermath of War.* New York and London: W. W. Norton & Company, 2014.

Williams, Kayla with Michael E. Staub. *Love My Rifle More Than You: Young and Female in the U. S. Army.* New York and London: W. W. Norton & Company, 2005.

Willsher, Kim. "Islamic State Magazine Interviews Hayat Boumeddiene." *The Guardian* (12 February 2015): www.theguardian.com/world/2015/feb/12/islamic-state-magazine-interviews-hayat-boumeddiene. Accessed: 12 October 2015.

"Women in the Battlefield." Editorial. *New York Times* (24 January 2013): www.nytimes.com/2013/01/25/opinion/women-in-the-battlefield. Accessed: 25 January 2013

Woolf, Virginia. *Three Guineas.* San Diego, New York and London: Harcourt Brace & Company, 1938.

Woollacott, Angela. "Women Munitions Makers, War, and Citizenship." In *The Women and War Reader.* Eds. Lois Ann Lorentzen and Jennifer Turpin. New York and London: New York University Press, 1998. Pp. 126–131.

Wright, Stephen. *Meditations in Green.* New York: Vintage Contemporaries, 1983.

Yee, Jennifer. "The Colonial Outsider: 'Malgérie' in Hélène Cixous's Les reveries de la femme sauvage." *Tulsa Studies in Women's Literature* 20, 2 (Autumn 2001): 189–200.

Yoshino, Yuri. "'The Big House Novel' and Recent Irish Literary Criticism." *Journal of Irish Studies* 22 (2007): 48–54.

Young, Robert J. C. *Postcolonialism: An Historical Introduction.* Oxford, UK and Malden, MA: Blackwell, 2001.

Zabrouski, Monica A. and Kirschmann, Robert P. "The Ungendered Will and the Shavian Superman." *Shaw* 26 (2006): 79–99.

Zakaria, Rafia. "The Making of a Terrorist Bride." *Aljazeera America* (9 December 2015): http://america.aljazeera.com/opinions/2015/12/the-making-of-a-terrorist-bride.html. Accessed: 9 December 2015.

Zaremba, Michelle, with Christine Sima. *Wheels on Fire: My Year of Driving . . . and Surviving . . . in Iraq.* Ashland, OR: Hellgate Press, 2008.

Zerilli, Linda M. G. "The Arendtian Body." In *Feminist Interpretations of Hannah Arendt.* Ed. Bonnie Honig. University Park, PA: Pennsylvania State University Press, 1995. Pp. 167–193.

Zerilli, Linda M. G. "'We Feel Our Freedom': Imagination and Judgment in the Thought of Hannah Arendt." *Political Theory* 33, 2 (April 2005): 158–188.

Zizek, Slavoj. *Violence.* New York: Picador, 2008.

INDEX

Abdurakhmanova, Dzhennet 67
Abu Ghraib, feminist naiveté (death) 22
action, desire 34–5
Adorno, Theodor W. 7, 142
Afghanistan war, appearance 46
Agamben, Georgio 72
Alencar 149
alienation 48, 122–3
Aljazeera America (Zakaria) 68
allegiance, division 123
All Quiet on the Western Front 28–9,
    36 (Remarque); unemployment,
    expectation 47
Al-Qaeda, fundamentalist Islamic codes
    (prohibition) 114
Al Saffarh, Nehrjas 25, 50
Alvarez, L. 16
Americans, The (TV series) 9
Anderson, Chase (character) 30
Andreas, Carol 65–6
animal laborans 101, 104–5
An Nasiryah, militant kidnapping 17
Antigone 61; death 70; defiance 83;
    disconnection/banishment 76;
    femaleness 63–4; gender, impact 63;
    laws, voice 69–70; neoliberal stance
    62; physical/emotional pain 84;
    politicization 64–5; reconciliation, story
    63; suffering cries 72
Antigone 62, 69–73; analogy 65; movie 81;
    revisions 64
anti-Semitism, allegations 107

apocalyptic terrors, appearance 14
Arendt, Hannah 96–106, 168; violence,
    ascendance 109
Arendtian theory 105
Aristotle 102
armies: productivity rates 46; women,
    incorporation 7
armor, addition 42
armored security vehicles, expense 47
Armored security vehicles (ASVs),
    usage 47
Army Nurse Corps, organization 19
Army policy 43
Army Times (news site) 20
Asad, Talal 60–1, 68–9
Ashley's War (Lemmon) 22, 25, 167
*Asociación de Mujeres Nicaragüenas
    Luisa Amanda Espinoza* (AMNLAE)
    65–6
Athanasiou, Athena 72

Baader Meinhof Complex, The (movie) 10
Baghdad Burning (blog) 26
Bagnold, Enid 18, 29
Band of Sisters (Holmstedt) 25, 41–2, 166;
    bomb drop 45
banishment 75–6
"bare life" theory (Agamben) 72
Bartle, John (character) 41
Barton, Mary 38, 43
battlefield: features 37–8; structure
    4–5

186 Index

Battle of Algiers, The (movie) 10, 64
Battle of Britain 125
Battlestar Galactica (movie) 9; Cylons,
    characters 20
Bauer, Amy 51–2
Bauman, Zygmunt 28
beach-words 78
Belli, Gioconda 50
belonging, sense 128
Benedict, Helen 24–5, 29, 32, 42
Benhabib, Seyla 96, 106–7
Benjamin, Walter 96; divine violence 99,
    109; freedom, attribution 98; means-end
    logic rejection 97; mere life 105;
    mythical violence 103; mythic structure
    102; natural history 104; natural/positive
    law, division 101; origin, formulation
    103–4; redemptive catastrophe 105–6;
    violence/judgment, framings 99;
    "Work of Art in the Age of Mechanical
    Reproduction, The" 108
Be Safe I Love You (Hoffman) 24, 33
Biank, Tanya 25
"Big Brother" 31
Bigelow, Kathryn 9
big house 133–7
"Big House" literature, tradition 130
biological life cycles, women
    (immersion) 101
"Black Widow" 67
Blair, Jane 24, 27, 44–5
Bletchley Circle, The (TV series) 9
blitz, wreckage 123, 126
Bloch, Ernest 98–9, 107
Bloom, Mia 21, 61, 67
Blunt, Emily 10
body: bombs, change 60; exertions 46;
    function/impact 36–40; technology,
    merger 26
body-in-perpetual-motion 34–5
Borden, Mary 18, 38, 42–3; organic bodies,
    fixing 46
Born in the Flames (movie) 10
Boumeddiene, Hayat 67
Bourdieu, Pierre 8
Bowen, Elizabeth 121–5, 130–4, 168; story,
    adaptation 135–6
Bowen's Court (Bowen) 131–4; Irish
    insurgency, property claim 136–7; old
    order, cementing 135
Bowles, Jack (character) 110
Brady, Kate (character) 32
Brant, George 24, 28

Brasil, Assis 141
Brazil: military dictatorship, impact 143;
    nationalist history, military imagery 144;
    social realism 146
Brecht, Bertolt 62
Brennan, Thomas James 37, 167
Britain: future 136; war effort 124
Brittain, Vera 18
Brooks, Desma (character) 31, 46–8
Browder, Laura 39
Browne, Kingsley 11–12
Bumiller, Elisabeth 17
Butler, Judith 8, 23, 71–2, 101

Cage, Nicholas 9
Caprica (TV series) 9
care: conventions 28–34; distribution
    72–3; militarization 5–6
Cather, Willa 36
Cavarero, Adriana 49–52
Chamayou, Grégoire 109, 166
Chanter, Tina 63
character, voice-perspective (impact) 82
Charlie Hebdo offices (attack) 67
Chinese Communist Party 66
Chivers, C.J. 37, 51
Chow, Rey 129
Chun, John 167
citizens, actions 62–3
Cixous, Hélène 64, 77–8, 140; Algerian
    memoirs 73, 74–9; Lispector interest
    identification 145; non-recognition 73;
    work, reception 74–5
Cixousian label 145
Cixous, Jonas 76
Clay, Lauren (character) 33
Clinic d'Isly, Cixous travel 79
Clock Radio, slogans 157–8
Cohen, Rob 110
collective violence, forms 69
colonial alienation, impact 79
colonization, property (relationship) 131–3
Combat Endurance Test 37
combat, equalizer 21
combat, literature (usage) 24–8
combat, personification 144–5
commodity, violence 150
common economy, reproductive body
    (relationship) 48–52
conflict, space (change) 4
connectivity 52
conscience 107
consciousness, preservers/transmitters 67

Conselheiro, Antonio 146
constituent violence 153–4
continuity, ambiguity 156
conventions of care 28–34
Cooke, Miriam 3, 5
cooperative behavior 44
Corcoran, Neil 134
Cornum, Rhonda 24, 43
Coulter, Chris 66
counterterrorism teams, technology (reliance) 167
Courage Under Fire (movie) 9
creation narrative, repetition 157
creative economy, reproduction problem (relationship) 154–8
Creon 63–4, 70; representation 69–70; resolution 71; self-propelled administrative apparatus 81–2
crisis, social aspect 151–2
Critique of Judgment (Kant) 108–9
"Critique of Violence, A" (Benjamin) 96–7
Cromwell, Oliver 132
Cross, Jimmy (character) 37
Crow, Tracy 24
cultural devotions, private autonomy 62
Cultural Support Team (CST) 23
culture 9; referencing 11–12
Cylons, characters 20

da Cunha, Euclides 146; rebellion 147–8; report, impact 147
D'Amico, Francine 22
Dar al-Islam (newspaper) 67
Das, Santanu 18
database edits, workaday obsession 47
David's Story (Wicomb) 61
Davis, Angela 22
Day I Wasn't There, The (Cixous) 64, 75
death, organic processes (denial) 48–9
de Beauvoir, Simone 23, 100
decolonization 79; change 60; twentieth-century wars 122; violence 75, 78
decolonizing momentum, underpinning/ fueling 135–6
deconstruction 79, 89
Defense Department, consensus 21
De Landa, Manuel 44, 48–9, 53
de Medieros, Paulo 149
democratic militarization 109
developmental narrative 30
Derrida, Jacques 78, 93, 94, 116, 118
Devi, Mahasweta 50

Diana, Marta (informants) 66
Diane Rehms Show, The (radio program) 21
Diary Without Dates, A (Bagnold) 18, 29
Dick, Kirby 19, 39
Dietz, Mary 104–5
Digby, Tom 21
Dillon, Michael 5
disagreement, insinuation 63
dispossession: citizenship configuration 70; ideology, expression 60; occurrence 123–4; political/economic dispossession 62; presentation 63–4
Dispossession (Athanasiou) 72
Divergent (movie) 20
divine power 99
divine violence 99, 105; redemptive insertion 98
Djébar, Assia 62
"doctor of the poor" 153
Dollhouse (TV series) 9
domesticity, private sphere 103
Dorfman, Ariel 82
Drif, Zohra 64
drones 109–15; crosshairs 84; warfare, bodilessness 109
Drones (Rosenthal) 99, 109–12
Duckworth, Tammy 25, 41–2

economic blockade 28
economic insecurity 32–3
écriture algériance 73
écriture féminine 78
écriture (violence), impact 78
écriture (writing), impact 74
Edge of Tomorrow (movie) 9
Edukators, The (movie) 10
Ehrenreich, Barbara 22
Eichmann trial, Arendt coverage 106
Eisenstein, Zillah 22
Ellman, Maud 126, 134
Elshtain, Jean Bethke 2
emancipation, postcolonial politics 123
emotional lift, provision 31
emotional outbursts 82
Engels, Friedrich 101
England, Lyndie 25
Enloe, Cynthia 4, 22, 66
Entre Tiempo (TV series) 9
equipment repair, workaday obsession 47
equivalence, exchangeability (relationship) 144–5
exile 75–6

188 Index

Ex Machina (movie) 9
Extreme Deep Invader (EDI) 110
Eyes Right (Crow) 24, 39

fabrication, work 102
familial devotions, private autonomy 62
Farewell to Arms, A (Hemingway) 29, 39
Farook, Syed Rizwan 68
fate-imposed violence 97–8
female militant 60; framing 61
female neoliberal subjectivity, making 140
female sexuality, horror (equivalence) 12
female terrorists, increase 65
feminism: idea, influences 136–7; pacifism, relationship 2
feminist emancipation, technological rationality (limitations) 124
feminist naiveté, death 22
feminist political theory 60
feminization 151
Femmes de l'ombre, Les (movie) 9
Fergusson, Clare (character) 30
Fighting France, From Dunkerque to Belfort (Wharton) 26
Fire Birds: Wings of the Apache (movie) 9
Fives and Twenty-Fives (Pitre) 39
Flannigan, Bergan (character) 42, 44
flesh, seductions 11–12
Forbidden Zone, The (Borden) 18; unemployment, expectation 47
Foreign Legion, The (Lispector) 141
Forward Operating Base (FOB) 64, 80
freedom-crushing, attribution 98–9
"freedom fighter," transformation 60
Freud, Sigmund 1, 22
Frobenius, Nick (character) 81
Front de Libération Nationale (FLN) 79
Fuerzas Armadas Revolucionarias de Colombia–Ejercito del Pueblo (FARC) 65–6
fundamentalist Islamic codes, prohibition 114

Gannon, Ben (character) 110
gender 158–61; impact 16; militarization 109–10; politicization 100
gendered bodies, military understanding 4
genre, classification 27
G.I. Jane (movie) 9
Gilbert, Sandra 2
Girls Come Marching Home, The (Holmstedt) 25, 32, 46
gods, manifestation 97–8
Goldman, Nancy 19, 22

Goodell, Jess 24, 51–2
Goodman, Amy 66
Good Morning, Night (movie) 10
Gordimer, Nadine 50
Grady, Denise 1
Green, David 9
Greene, Carver 24
Grey, Dorian 36
Grounded (Brant) 24
guilt, retaliation 107
Gutmann, Stephanie 37

"habitat" 131
Hanssen, Beatrice 100
Harris, Elizabeth 20
Harvey, David 8, 136
Hathaway, Anne 25
Heat of the Day, The (Bowen) 121–36, 168; Britain replacement 129; feminism, idea (influences) 136–7; habitat 131; interior spaces 128–9
Hegel, Georg Wilhelm Friedrich 62, 70; *Antigone* interpretation 81; readings 73
Helton, Debbie (character) 31
Hemingway, Ernst 29
Henry VI, impact 132
Hepburn, Allan 125
hermeticism 141
heroic form, inheritance 144
Hershey, Lewis 39
Hesitation Kills (Blair) 24, 45; war, presentation 46
Higonnet, Margaret/Patrice 2
historical causality, tendencies 106
historical existence, interpretation 108
historicity, interpretation 97
Hobbes, Thomas 5, 34
Hoffman, Cara 24, 33–4
Holmstedt, Kirsten 25, 36, 42, 166; character description 46
Holocaust 96–7
Home Before Morning (Devanter) 24, 38; injury site 47; unemployment, expectation 47
Homeland (TV series) 9, 20
homo faber 101, 104–5
homosexuality, life cycle (identification) 24
Honig, Bonnie 61, 72, 100
Horkheimer, Max 7
hospital effectiveness, breakdown 33
Hour of the Star, The (Lispector) 140–3, 149–51; commodity, violence 150; exchange, balanced economy (impossibility) 145; feminist

interpretation 145; inequality, social importance 145; life, framing 160; narrative 155; national narrative framework 158; physical/conceptual impossibility 152–3; production shift 160; reproduction, crisis 144; reproduction, failures 154; resolutions, absence 146; self-reflection 154–5; social reproduction, crisis 150–1; violence, social importance 145; violence, symbolic problem 144–5; violence, women (relationship) 160–1
human action 105
human body, marginalization (increase) 43
Human Condition, The (Arendt) 101–4
human productivity, development (forces) 101
"humping" 46–7
Hunger Games (movie) 9
Hussein, Saddam 25, 29

"I," articulation 83
identity: formation, symbolic patterns 48; understanding 71–2
Idris, Wafa 68
Iliad, The (Homer) 25
"illegitimate, the" 76–7
Illuminations (Benjamin/Arendt) 96
image, term (Benjamin) 98
immanence 23
imperial state, condemnation (Bowen) 136
improvised explosive devices (IEDs) 16, 33, 47; attack 42, 44; truck damage 46
Indiana National Guard 31
indirect involvement 5
individuality, loss 49
individuated consciousnesses, impact 81
inhuman resolution 130
insurgencies, women (mass involvement) 65–6
intelligence picture 45
interior grief 61
"In Vietnam They Had Whores" 41
Invisible War, The (Dick) 19, 39
Iracema (Alencar) 149
Irigaray, Luce 70–1
Irish Civil War, outbreak 131
Irish insurgency, property claim 136–7
Irish Land Purchase 135
Irish neutrality, question 121–2
Islamic State (ISIS/ISIL) 68
Ismene-Masood 83–4

Jarhead (Swofford) 29, 37
Jassim, Naema (character) 32–3
jihad 21
job equalizer 27
Johnny Got His Gun (Trumbo) 37
Jones, Tommy Lee 9
judgment 107–9

Kahlil, Mahmoud (character) 99, 113–14
Kalinowski, Mariette 17
Kamuf, Peggy 74
Kandahar, Taliban arms manufacturer 23
Kant, Immanuel 108–9; reflective judgment 102
Karpinski, Janis 24
Kelway: Stella (character) 121–6; Robert (character) 121–6, 130–5; accusations (Stella) 136; exoneration 125
Kierkegaard, Soren 71–2
killers 121
killing machines, work (relationship) 40–8
kin, annihilation 84
kinship, representation 71
Kirkland, Sean 64
Klay, Phil 29, 40
Klobucka, Anna 145
Kojève, Alexandre 34–5, 48, 54
Kol Hazman (newspaper) 68
Korah, story (invocation) 105–6
Krylova, Anna 25
Kuwait City, Hussein invasion 29

Laclau, Ernesto 143
lamentation, feminist politics (critique) 61–2
Last September, The (Bowen) 134
"Laugh of the Medusa, The" 73–5
Lauro, Shirley 25
Lawson, Sue (character) 99, 110
League of Nations (international pacifist lecturing) 18
Lebanon (Maoz) 111–12
Lebanon's mise-en-scène 111–12
Legend of Rita, The (movie) 10
Lemmon, Gayle Tzemach 22, 25, 167
"Letters to Zohra Drif" (Cixous) 64, 75, 77
liberal contract theory 62–3
liberalism, consequence 79–80
liberal state, function 34
liberation movement 22
liberation war, women (mass involvement) 65–6
libidinal economies 145

190 Index

Life of the Mind, A (Arendt) 97, 103, 108
Lillie, Marcia (character) 46
Lioness (McLagan/Sommers) 19
Lispector, Clarice 140–3, 147, 151, 155,
　168; narrator, announcement 153;
　translator, observations 159
literary interest, surge 25
literature 6; antithesis 144; traditional
　trends 6–7; usage 24–8
Lobao, Linda 65
Lonely Soldier, The (Benedict) 25
Long March (Chinese Communist
　Party) 66
Love My Rifle More than You (Williams)
　24, 33
loyalty 83
Luisa Amanda Espinoza Association of
　Nicaraguan Women 65–6
Lynch, Jessica 17

Macabéa (character) 140–1; advertisement
　seduction 157–8; appearance/invention
　156–7; characterization 158; combat
　personification 144–5; heroic form,
　inheritance 144; insufficiencies
　147–8; life, framing 160; patheticness
　142–3; physical/performative
　inappropriateness 153
Maccabee, Judah 146
Mad Max: Fury Road (movie) 9
Maher, Ashley 127, 133
Mahmood, Saba 69
Major Barbara (Shaw) 24
"Make-Believe World of Sexual
　Integration" (Browne) 11
male language, authority 159
Malik, Tashfeen 67–8
Maneuvers (Enloe) 22
manhood/identity, erosion 1
manual laborer, self-identification 157
Maoz, Samuel 111–12
Marine Corps Times (news site) 20
Marines' Mortuary Affairs unit,
　chronicle 24
Marx, Karl 34, 108, 152
masculine body, physical strength 36
masculinity, attributes 13
Masood (character) 83
maternal retribution 98
Mathison, Carrie (CIA character) 20
Matrix series (movie) 9
McGrath, Amy "Krusty" 166
McLagan, Meg 19

"meaning-filled world" 104
mechanical drone warfare 96
mechanization, impact 43
Meditations in Green (Wright) 40–1; body,
　exertions 46
Medusa 73, 75
memory backflashes 82
mere life 100–6; formulation 105
"mere life," formulation 105
metaphysics, critique 145
metonymy, impact 79
militaristic escalation, excess 12
military apparatus, means-ends logic
　109–10
military narrative 146–9
military nation, impact 140
military technological innovation 44
Miller, Steven 36
mise-en-scène 112; Lebanon's *mise-en-scène*
　111–12
Mitchell, Brian 20
Moaveninov, Azadeh 68
modernism 133–7
modernist alienation, impact 142
modernist forms, postcolonial concerns
　(bridging) 126
Moi, Toril 168
Monroe, Marilyn 148
Montgomery, Polly (character) 35–6
Mooney, Sinéad 133
Morris, Francis (character) 124
Mother Courage (Brecht) 62
"Mother Courage" effect 50
Mother of 1084 (Devi) 50
Movimiento Revolucionario Túpac Amaru
　(MRTA) 66
Mr. and Mrs. Smith (movie) 9
Mugabe, Robert 66
Mumford, Eloise 99
Murphy, Ladonna (character) 41
"My Algeriance" (Cixous) 64, 75–7
My Son's Story (Gordimer) 50
mysterious region 152
mythic violence 97–8

Naema (character) 32–3
"Names of Oran, The" 64, 76, 78
Namorato, Luciana 144–5, 159
narrative divergences 82
natality 103–4
national belonging, social ideologies 60–1
national struggle, change 65–9
nation, revisionist allegory 149

natural history 104
"natural history" 104
Navy Rangers, call (answer) 23
Nazi bombings 126
Near to the Wild Heart (Lispector) 147
necro-ethics 109
Negri, Antonio 151–5; *Marx Beyond Marx: Lessons on the Grundrisse 152*–3
neoliberal depoliticization, effect 61
neoliberalism: crisis 79–80; goal 144
neoliberal state, impact 8
Newly Born Woman, The (Cixous) 73, 75
new power, creation 99
Niobe: arrogance 99; destiny 99; eternal repetition 103; legend 97; myth 105–6; predetermined rules 102; problems 98
Nizam (character) 80
non-conformity, insinuation 63
non-nationalized militant groups, affiliation 68
non-state violence 5
Norris, Margot 166
Not So Quiet . . . (Smith) 18

O'Brien, Tim 37–8; humping 46–7
Odyssey, The 28
One of Ours (Cather) 36
One Was a Soldier (Spencer-Fleming) 24
One Woman's Army (Karpinski) 24
On Revolution (Arendt) 99
Operation Desert Storm 19
opposed subjectivities, formation 152
Organization, The 68–9
origin, formulation (Benjamin) 103–4
Origin of German Tragic Drama, The 103–4
other, openness 145

pacifism, feminism (relationship) 2
Paintedcrow, Eli (character) 30
Palace of the End (Thompson) 25, 50
Panetta, Leon 16, 17, 21, 25; media coverage 20; women, combat (politics) 53
Pappas, Irene 81
Passion According to G.H., The (Lispector) 142–3, 148
"passporosity" 76
Patriot Front 66
Peggy Deery 50
Peixoto, Marta 145
"Penis Transplants Being Planned to Help Wounded Troops" (Grady) 1
Pentagon, consensus 21

Penuin, Carlos 66
peripheral vision 46
physical processes, control 49–50
physical/sexual weakness, treatment 39
Pickett, Abbie (character) 32
Piece of My Heart, A (Lauro) 25
Pitkin, Hanna 100, 102–3
Pitre, Michael 39
Plato, turning away 108
Plenty of Time When We Get Home (Williams) 24, 33
political community, possibility (introduction) 73–4
political connections, multiplicity 84–5
political power, organizational form 66
politics, marginalization 71
Pontecorvo, Gilles 64
Pontiero, Giovanni 159
Poppie Nongena (Joubert) 50
postcolonial concerns 126
postcolonial nations, complexity/hybridity 77
postcolonial politics 122–3
postcolonial rupture, resemblance 129
postmodernism 100
post-traumatic stress disorder (PTSD): control 24–5; experience 13; trigger 32
poverty, protest 159
Powder (Hoffman) 24
power: projection 111; violence, elision 103
Powers, Kevin 40
prescribed identification, barrier 84–5
prior "I," continuity (ambiguity) 156
privacy, importance 128–9
Private Benjamin (movie) 9
private life, women (immersion) 101
private sphere: disparagement 100; function 105; usage 104–5
property: colonization, relationship 131–3; liberalization, character (adoption) 123; moral prerogative 137; settlement 137
property-ownership 130
protection, distribution 72
psychological issues 61
Purcell, Henry (character) 110
pure means, correlation 108
pure thought 113
purpose, spontaneous sense 45

Rabassa, Gregory 141
racial exclusion, support 22–3
radical imagination 102

192 Index

radicalization, pathway 68
Rathbone, Irene 18
real estate: postcolonial legacy 121;
    violence, relationship 125–31
"Reassuring Hands" (Chivers) 51
Rebellion in the Backlands (da Cunha) 146
reconciliation, story 63
Red Crescent 68
Redeployment (Klay) 29, 40–1
Reed, Julian 5
reflective judgment (Kant) 102
Remarque, Erich Maria 29
reproduction: mechanisms, problems
    160; problem, creative economy
    (relationship) 154–8
reproductive body, common economy
    (relationship) 48–52
reproductive cycle, non-convergence
    152–3
reproductive function, technology
    capture 51
Reverie of the Wild Woman (Cixous) 64
Riverbend (author) 26
Rodrigo S.M. (character) 156–7, 159–60
Rokem, Freddie 62
romantic warrior, Brazilian tradition
    147–8
Roosevelt, Eleanor 20
Rosenthal, Rick 99
Roy-Bhattacharya, Joydeep 64

Sacks, Sam 17
sacred life 105
Saint Joan (Shaw) 24
Salinas, Estella (character) 26–7
Salomé, Jean-Paul 9
Salt (movie) 9
San Bernardino, shooting attack 67–8
Sandinistas (Nicaragua) 50
Sand Queen (Benedict) 24, 32, 48
Scarry, Elaine 35, 48
Scotus, Duns 103
Segal, Mady Wechsler 166
Seitz, Barbara 65
self-belonging 71
self-definition 128
self, establishment 72–3
"self-sacrificial acts" 60–1
semiotic body (Kristeva) 102
Sendero Luminoso 65–6
sentience, terms (replacement) 35
sertanejo 146–7
sex 133–7

sexism, cessation 21–2
Shade It Black (Goodell) 24, 51–2
Shanker, Thom 17
Sharia law, enforcement 68
Shaw, George Bernard 24
She Went to War (Cornum) 24
Shining Path, The (Sendero Luminoso) 65
shot-reverse-shot sequences,
    accomplishment 112
Sicario (movie) 9
678 (movie) 10
Sky, Emma 31
Sloan, Cynthia 141, 146, 159
Smith, Helen Zenna 18
social factory 149–54; advent 151
socially sanctioned gender, fit (problems) 3
social mechanism, "idle chatter" 106–7
social reform, military (impact) 3
social relations, preservers/transmitters 67
social reproduction, crisis 150–1
social structures 122–3
So Close (Cixous) 64, 75, 77–8
Soldier Girls (movie) 10–11
Soldier Girls (Thorpe) 25, 27, 29–31, 46–8;
    27, 29–31; Afghanistan war, appearance
    46; Desma (character) 46–8; injury site
    47; war, presentation 46
solitary consciousness 142
Sommers, Daria 19
Somos 66
Sophocles: differences 81; liberal reading
    69; play, allusions 81
Sorel, Georges 150–1; mysterious
    region 152
"Sorties" 75
sovereign authority, foundation
    (emptying) 83
sovereign crisis, formalistic devices 80–1
sovereign, exchange 71
sovereign power, impact 82
sovereignty, impact 80
Spargo, R. Clifton 63
spectatorship 107–9; pure means,
    correlation 108
Spencer-Fleming, Julia 24, 30
spies, impact 121
spiritualized materiality 128
Spivak, Gayatri 22, 77
spontaneous cooperative behavior 44
Stackdec, Liam 68
Starship Troopers (movie) 11–12;
    problem 14
Star Wars: The Force Awakens (movie) 9

Index

state combat roles, women (entry) 165–6
state politics, impact 5
state subversion, *écriture* (impact) 78
state violence 5
Stealth (movie) 110
Steiner, George 61–2, 70
Stillman, George (character) 30
Stout, Hilary 20
street-words 78
subjectivity 18; constructions 143
"suffering cries" 72
suicide bombers, increase 65
surplus value, expansion 153–4
surveillance state 127
survival vest, addition 42
Swofford, Anthony 29, 37
symbolic exchange, breakdown 79–80
symbolic resonance 122–3

Tamil Tigers 66
Tasker, Yvonne 10, 17
Taymor, Julie 25
technological rationality 8; impact 107–8
technological workplace, ascendance 49
technology: impact 42–3, 49–50;
    metaphor 43
Teekell, Anna 133
Terminator II/III (movies) 9
terror, impact 65–9
"terrorist," transformation 60
Testament of Youth (Brittain) 18
Thackeray, William 1
theater-words 78
Things They Carried, The (O'Brien)
    37, 40–1; body, exertion 46; enemy,
    confrontation 45; unemployment,
    expectation 47
"Thinking" 107–8
thinking, impact 106–7
Thompson, Judith 25
Thorpe, Helen 27, 29
Three Guineas (Woolf) 1
Tomb Raider (movie) 9
total militarization 107
toy makers, marketing 20
tragedy, impact 60
translation: barrier 84–5; impact 74
transnationalizing capitalism,
    intensification 61
Treadway, Ellen 65
Trumbo, Dalton 37
"turning away" 113
Tuten, Jeff M. 37

Undaunted (Biank) 25, 42
unemployment, expectation 47–8
University of Multan 67–8
Unlawful Order, An (Greene) 24, 30
Unmanned Combat Aerial Vehicle
    (UCAV) 110

"vaginality" 75
value 4; theory (Marx) 152
van Dam, Katelyn 21
Van Devanter, Lynda 24, 38, 43, 47;
    organic bodies, fixing 46
Vanity Fair (Thackeray) 1
Van Weyenberg, Astrid 64
Verhoeven, Paul 11
Veterans' Administration (VA)
    hospital 33
Vietnam War 13
Villeneuve, Denis 9
violence: characterization 147–8;
    constituent violence 153–4; critique
    96; military propensity 82; mythic
    violence 97–8; presence, foregrounding
    142–3; real estate, relationship 125–31;
    socialization 150; symbolic problem
    144–5; women, relationship 160–1
"violent appropriation" 72
visual confirmation, necessity 113–14
vitalism 128
Viterna, Jocelyn 67
voler (usage) 74

Wachowski, Lilly 9
Wade, Cara (character) 110
war: degendering 21–2; effects, flood
    33; literature 6; machine, disembodied
    control 51–2; men, primitive
    connection 13; novel, impact
    36–40; presentation 46; story, genre
    classification 27; violence, appearance
    129; women, inclusion 14; zone,
    resemblance 25
warfare, violence 125
war narrative: conventions 38; human body
    marginalization, increase 43; women,
    bodies (vulnerabilities) 39–40
"War on Terror": violence 52–3; women
    fighters, recruitment 65
warring body, obliteration (repercussions)
    48–9
warrior, impact 140, 146–7
"War Stories" 40
war story, women (presence) 16

194 Index

Watch, The (Roy-Bhattacharya) 64–5, 73, 79–85
Weather Underground (movie) 10
"We," intuition 107
Welfare Reforms (1996) 53
We That Were Young (Rathbone) 18
Wharton, Edith 26
Wheels on Fire (Zaremba) 24
Wicomb, Zoë 61
Widows (Dorfman) 82
Williams, Kayla 24, 33–4, 39
Wilmot, Michelle (character) 32
Wolin, Richard 107
"woman in combat" question 19
women: bodies, vulnerabilities 39–40; combatant body, technologization 50; combatant narratives 47; exclusion 3; fighter, adoption/embrace 7, 66; impact 140; mass involvement 65–6; military inclusion, opponents 167; military service entry 10; mobilization, relationship 2–3; moral superiority, feminist beliefs (criticism) 22; soldiers, narratives 29–30; state combat roles, entry (increase) 165–6; status, instability 100; values 4; work, transformation 19
women in combat: advocacy 167–8; developmental narrative 30; discussion 19; Panetta decision, politics 53; participation, arguments 17; restriction 16–17; war narrative, temporal framing 29; zone entry 7
"Women in the Battlefield" decision (Panetta) 21
Women in the Military (Mitchell) 20
Women's Armed Services Integration Act 16
Woolf, Virginia 1, 125
Woollacott, Angela 17
work: killing machines, relationship 40–8; mechanization 47–8
worker, impact 140
"Work of Art in the Age of Mechanical Reproduction, The" (Benjamin) 108
World According to G.H., The (Lispector) 149
world beyond appearances 106–7
"world-creating" 54
world, remaking 34–6
writer, impact 140

Yellow Birds, The (Powers) 40–1
Young, Sean 9

Zakaria, Rafia 68
Zaremba, Michelle 24, 28
Zehawi, Woleed (character) 114
Zerilli, Linda 101
Zero Dark Thirty (movie) 9
Zimbabwe National Liberation Army 66